GW01390029

The Teleology of the Modern Nation-State

ENCOUNTERS WITH ASIA

Victor H. Mair, Series Editor

A complete list of books in this series is available from the publisher.

The Teleology of the Modern Nation-State

Japan and China

EDITED BY JOSHUA A. FOGEL

PENN

University of Pennsylvania Press

Philadelphia

10   9   8   7   6   5   4   3   2   1

Published by
University of Pennsylvania Press
Philadelphia, Pennsylvania 19104-4011

Library of Congress Cataloging-in-Publication Data

The teleology of the modern nation-state : Japan and China / edited by Joshua A.
Fogel.
    p. cm. (Encounters with Asia)
    ISBN 0-8122-3820-6 (cloth : alk. paper)
    Includes bibliographical references and index.
    1. National state—Case studies. 2. Group identity—Japan—History. 3. Group
identity—China—History. 4. Politics and culture—Japan—History. 5. Regionalism—
Political aspects—China—History. 6. Japan—Politics and government. 7. China—
Politics and government. 8. China—History, Local—Historiography. I. Fogel, Joshua A.,
1950–. II. Series
JC311 .T43   2004
320.951—dc22   2004052641

Contents

Introduction: The Teleology of the Nation-State

It is a very common thing now-a-days to meet people who are going to "China," which can be reached by the Siberian railway in fourteen or fifteen days. This brings us at once to the question—What is meant by the term China?

—Herbert A. Giles (1911)

At the very end of May 1862, fifty-one Japanese—or, more correctly, men from many different domains of the land we now call Japan—set sail together with a British crew of eleven and a few merchants from Nagasaki to the port of Shanghai. This voyage was the first officially sanctioned mission to China in over three hundred years and only the second outside Japan since the loosening of the ban on travel several years earlier. It was also a trading mission, as the two countries still had no formal diplomatic ties. The fifty-one Japanese came from about fifteen different domains—in addition to several shogunal officials from Edo and a few Nagasaki officials responsible for trade. I have described this voyage elsewhere,[1] but I would like to stress something that transpired over the course of their travels in Shanghai.

While the overall purpose of the mission to Shanghai was to get a glimpse of the future in which Japan would perforce be engaging in international trade and to see what a trading port looked like, each of the Japanese of samurai status came with private agendas closely linked to their domains' needs. Thus, for example, Godai Tomoatsu (1836–85) shipped out as a sailor and actually purchased a battleship surreptitiously for the Satsuma domainal navy to be used in its future conflict against the central government. Takasugi Shinsaku (1839–67), perhaps the most famous of the passengers, burned with hatred for the shogunate and was looking at every turn for some means of bringing advantage to his domain of Chōshū.

As is well known, Shanghai in June and July is unusually hot and humid. Lord Oliphant (1829–88) described it three years earlier as "the most unhealthy [port] to which our ships are sent, the sickness and mortality being greater here than even on the west coast of Africa."[2] The year 1862 was no exception—it was unbearably muggy, and then of course there was no electricity and no running water. Poverty on a gigantic scale exacerbated in large part by the Taiping Rebellion (1851–65) had forced tens of thousands to seek shelter in the ill-equipped walled city of Shanghai. That year also witnessed a cholera epidemic that claimed many lives, including those of three of the Japanese while they were in port in Shanghai for six weeks.

Virtually all the Japanese travelers suffered from diarrhea on and off for much of the trip as well. This was generally believed to have been caused by the filthy water used to wash everything they ate. One voyager by the name of Hibino Teruhiro (1838–1912), a samurai from Takasu domain, only twenty-four years old at the time, found himself confined to his hotel room for much of the trip because of persistent dysentery.[3] The scene borders on the pathetic—Hibino was in a second-floor room, baking in the heat and humidity and yet insisting on wearing his Japanese garb including the two requisite swords all day long, and constantly having to jump up and run downstairs and outside to get to the outhouse. It was humiliating, needless to say, and he moans frequently about it in his diary.

One thing he laments of considerable interest is that, because of his illness, he is useless to his "country." He uses the word *kokka* (nation, state), which might seem a sure marker that we could point to someone thinking of the nation-state, and maybe for the first time in Japanese history. Traveling abroad, an experience denied virtually all Japanese for centuries, meeting Japanese from many different domains in a way that would have been extremely difficult within Japan, where even domestic travel was tightly controlled, seeing a victimized and chaotic China with which he sympathized—all of these might have been conducive to the emergent sense of something larger than the many small domains of his native land. In addition, he waxes exuberant describing parts of Japan seen from shipboard en route to China—even barren fishing islands which only a few fishermen had ever seen before—and he seems to identify with these spaces. Lateral domain-to-domain ties, which as Eiko Ikegami points out in her essay the Tokugawa state sought to cut off as much as possible, were actually forged, in many cases for the first time, during this trip.

While this might seem a reasonable and indeed logical avenue of analysis, the essays that follow by Luke Roberts and Mark Ravina demonstrate that even this apparent usage of a "modern" term is not what it might appear to be. And, we impose our much later sense of the nation-state back on its prehistory by interpreting *kokka* in this way. It can also simply mean a domain, synonymous in Japanese with *kuni* (state) and *han* (domain). So, was Hibino lamenting his inability to serve his country Japan or his miniscule domain of Takasu? A closer look at the source in question unfortunately does not clear up this puzzle. The term can be translated either way. In fact, the distinction may have been without meaning to Hibino.

Nonetheless, even if this is not the Ur-text for the Japanese nation-state in a political sense, we are beginning to find some of the ingredients for the emergence of that concept—travel abroad and seeing the international scene of trade and imperialism played out in the microcosm of Shanghai, contact with Japanese from other domains on board ships and overseas, contacts that would facilitate a movement to topple the Tokugawa regime and eventually attempt to build something bigger and stronger in the face of Western expansionism. The lesson Shanghai most forcefully brought home to the Japanese who saw it in 1862 was that, if you fail to prepare for the Western assault, you could end up just as chaotic and out of control of your fate as China.

Compare all this to the story of Takezaki Suenaga (b. 1246), a warrior from Kyushu who participated in the defenses against the Mongol invasions of Japan almost six hundred years earlier in 1274 and 1281 and who commissioned the painting of the famous Mongol Scroll (*Mōko shūrai ekotoba*), which has just been published in an English translation in 2001.[4] Foreign invasion and potential conquest might seem to provide an important ingredient for the emergence of national self-awareness. The scroll contains the narrative of Takezaki's journey to Kamakura, then the seat of the shogunal government, after the first Mongol invasion, in an effort to be rewarded for fighting in it. Along the way, Takezaki prays at various temples and shrines and meets many people, but he never once mentions "Japan." This would suggests that he had little or no consciousness that he had fought for his "country." Indeed, in his own mind, he may have seen himself as a mercenary. Clearly, much had changed by the mid-nineteenth century.

One other traveler on the 1862 voyage to China is worth mentioning in this context. A man by the name of Mine Kiyoshi traveled as an attendant to the trip's doctor. His account of the trip was only just published two or three years ago.[5] Mine was a samurai from Ōmura, a small domain that traditionally bore responsibility for protecting neighboring Nagasaki, the only Japanese port open to trade for the previous two centuries or more. He had studied astronomy, mathematics, and surveying techniques. Perhaps because he was a scientist, he was especially concerned with all the Japanese coming down with dysentery and the deaths from cholera. He points immediately to the filthy water, which must be treated before it can be consumed, and writes in his diary: "This is the gravest hardship for the men of our country (*wagakuni*) while resident" in Shanghai. Clearly, Mine is not thinking of Ōmura domain, nor is he thinking of "his country" in some vague, cultural sense. He is drawing a scientific conclusion. The heat of early summer in Shanghai, the foul water, and, as he put it, "the indescribable filth" of the city streets all worked together to produce a seriously deleterious environment which, he opines, must be attended to by "those who are in charge of the country" (meaning China), and the term he uses is *kokka*. While he does not employ the term to refer to the Japanese state, he does here interestingly for the Chinese state. He does this elsewhere as well, in a brush conversation—the traditional manner in which literate Chinese and Japanese (and Koreans, Vietnamese, and others in the larger Sinic sphere) communicated in written form, using literary Chinese, in the absence of a common spoken language—with a Chinese interlocutor, when he suggests that "the people who run this country (*kokka*) must store grain irrespective of whether there is order or disorder."

An even more poignant issue, already alluded to, that brought Japanese from different domains together in Shanghai and had them commiserating with one another was dying far from home. Aside from unfortunate fishermen who died as sea or abroad after being shipwrecked, dying overseas had not been a problem for the previous few centuries during which Japanese had not been allowed to travel beyond Japan's immediate waters. Not only did three Japanese die in Shanghai, but because of the heat their corpses had to be dealt with immediately. There was no surfeit of time to consider a variety of plans or how their cadavers might be transported back to Japan. They were eventually cremated and buried in a plot in the Pudong section of Shanghai, which no scholar has since been able to locate, but at the time the survivors were exceedingly anxious about their colleagues having died away from home. This seems to have transcended domainal differences, and it surely made every one of them reflect on his own mortality (especially, as he rushed to and from the outhouse).

In short, I might tentatively suggest that we have a small group of people who are mostly acting locally (that is for local, domainal interests back home) but thinking or at least beginning to think proto-nationally. Of course, we cannot fix a day on which the modern nation-states of China and Japan commenced; the process is not like that of a coronation or founding ceremony of a dynasty or shogunate. The political process probably took years and certain people, based on class and locale, probably acquired this sense before—even long before—others.

Let us move one decade later. Kume Kunitake (1839–1931), the great historian of a century ago, as a lad was charged with writing up the chronicle of the Iwakura Mission's travels through Europe and America, 1871–73—that massive text which has just appeared in a magnificent English translation.[6] In 1921, fifty years after the mission began in 1871, Kume recalled that it only dawned on him years later that some of the things he was witnessing in the West had no counterparts in East Asia. They had "society"—one of those things he pointed to a half century later—while we in Japan and China, he argued, only had a series of relationships but no genuine social ties. Whether this is true or not, Kume seems to have come to the realization of it much earlier than most Japanese.

Also, the sense of a larger political entity, something that transcended the small feudal domains—call it "Japan" or, as Eiko Ikegami puts it so elegantly, "a space called Japan"—probably emerged within different social groups at different times. In addition, something we could call "cultural Japan" also undoubtedly has a separate history which was related tangentially to the vector of its political career. That is, a cultural or literary conception of Japan was probably shared by certain sectors of the elite long before a political one emerged. This is strikingly so in the seventeenth and eighteenth centuries, but probably also in the latter half of the Heian period much earlier. Most though not all the essays in this volume focus on the idea of the nation-state—the political realm—but we should not forget that the cultural realm was not necessarily in complete synchronicity with it.

Can we point to a comparable event, the emergence of a semblence of the nation-state, in China? Perhaps, as Peter Perdue suggests in his essay, that event has yet to happen. As both he and Pamela Crossley argue in different ways, China did not come (if it did at all) to nationhood from feudalism but from transnational empire. China had long had certain features of the nation-state, such as standard weights and measures and standard currency across vast distances. Despite the structure of empire, how did individuals see themselves? When did "being Chinese" becoming a primary, or even secondary, mode of self-identification?

In Japan it was the Meiji state that created in top-down fashion the structures and infrastructures, mostly imported, of the nation-state—a standardized national education system, a national Diet, a national taxation system, train lines linking numerous localities, and countless other institutions. About a generation later, by the turn of the last century, we find Chinese going in large numbers to study in Japanese schools—to learn about the modern world through the recent experiences of their neighbor and former cultural kin. They were sponsored by the Qing dynasty in most instances, for it too planned to modernize itself into something resembling a nation-state.

Initially, these students organized themselves by the provinces from which they had come for a number of reasons: they were sent to Japan in this fashion by the late Qing government with a superintendent from each province overseeing them; they had difficult dialect differences to overcome; and the first generation of overseas Chinese students in Japan provided the necessary support structure for each other along provincial lines. Their first journals published in Japan—even the most radical ones—often bore the name of the region from which they hailed. Within a few years time, though, these regional groupings began to break down. This place called "China"—for the first time viewed from the outside—began to have a meaning for them, probably at least in part because the Japanese identified it as a unity, that is China as opposed to the continent of the Qing dynasty.

Every dynasty—Han or non-Han—throughout imperial Chinese history had worked desperately, if unconsciously, to erase any conceptual distinction between their dynastic regime and China the great land mass. Needless to say, no dynasty had plans for its eventual demise, as all planned to continue forever. Toward the end of the Qing dynasty, this distinction resurfaced for a number of reasons, and it was thrown into relief by living abroad, when China was that immense thing over there. Also, an awareness of the Japanese gaze played an important role, for the Japanese who ridiculed the Chinese male students for their bizarre hairstyle (the queue or pigtail) ridiculed them all equally as "Chinese." There was also the infamous Ōsaka Exhibition of 1903, coinciding with the high tide of Chinese study in Japan, in which Chinese women with bound feet were one of the exhibits of pre-civilized customs; the angry Chinese response in Japan transcended province-specific bounds.

It is highly significant that all the revolutionary groups of the late Qing—the Xing-Zhonghui in Guangdong, the Guangfuhui in Zhejiang and Jiangsu, and the Huaxinghui in Hunan and Hubei—were all regionally based, but the united group bringing them together, the Tongmenghui, was founded in Yokohama in 1905, and its leader, Sun Yat-sen (1866–1925), had not set foot in China for a decade at that point in time.

Although most scholars are fully aware of the fact that China and Japan were not modern nation-states until relatively late in their histories, we still blithely speak and write about Han-dynasty China or even Zhou China, as well as Muromachi Japan, let alone Jōmon Japan—without losing a second of sleep. And, virtually all historians refer without even a sense of irony to prehistoric China or Japan.

As a historian, literary scholar, or social scientist, one needs concepts to try to explain what one studies, concepts that assuredly were not used by people in the times and places of the past that one is studying. We must be extremely cautious, though, that concepts which almost always derive from our own arsenal of experience—such as religion, culture, art, government, authority, and the like—do not actually serve to distort the history we are examining. This issue afflicts many outside the East Asian studies fold. Surely, every Europeanist has read or knows the argument of Eugen Weber's pathbreaking study *Peasants into Frenchmen*,[7] and then goes on to speak of medieval France or fourteenth-century France.

As Luke Roberts and Peter Perdue make clear, in their respective essays on early modern Japan and China in this volume, this conflation of the national story on the local does great harm to the historical record. But, it does more as well. It serves the interests of the contemporary nation-state which is only too happy to invent its own "ancient" past and use it to continue to retain control over how the local stories may be told. This sort of anachronism is the handmaiden of the nation-state discourse, and its staying power is fierce.

The essays in this volume grew out of a conference held in February 2002, sponsored by the Andrew J. Mellon Foundation which funded for a number of years a program in East Asian studies at the School of Historical Studies, Institute for Advanced Study, in Princeton. At that time, there were, in addition to the eight presenters, eight discussants who helped immeasurably to bring out the strengths and weaknesses of each presentation: Paul Schalow, Joan Judge, Martin Collcutt, Susan Naquin, Gerald Figal, Ruth Rogaski, Lillian M. Li, and Michal Biran. To them, to the faculty and staff of the School of Historical Studies, and to the Institute's Director Phillip Griffiths, I wish to acknowledge my gratitude.

Part One
The Emergence of a "Japan" and a "China"

Chapter 1
The Emergence of Aesthetic Japan

Eiko Ikegami

The editor of this volume has posed a difficult question: When did "Japan" become Japan? The answer is obviously complicated, inasmuch as the identity of the geographical entity called Japan is complex, multi-dimensional, and fluid. The study of collective identities requires a brief ontological examination of identity formation. The identity of a person or collectivity—which I prefer to call a categorical identity—is internally complex, consisting of a loose network of meanings that are often in conflict with one another. Identity as such cannot be understood as a preconstituted structure, but only as a process of constant flux and alteration. Identities are therefore not only relationally but also path-dependently formulated. Yet, contradictory as it may seem, however fluid a given identity may be inherently, it always tends toward reification. In order for an identity to maintain its coherence over time, it is always seeking ways to construct stable structures for its self-identification. This form of essentialism seems to be almost inescapable for any identity dealing with itself as a subject. Thus, although Western academics generally consider essentialism a pejorative term as a specific intellectual methodology, the essentializing of categorical identities is an important issue that scholars cannot avoid.[1]

The study of the emergence of Japan, in particular with regard to its evolution into a modern nation-state, requires an examination of historical contingencies. I will select only one dimension of the process in order to explicate this complex question historically—namely, how did an aesthetic ideal become a core constituent of a sense of commonality among the Japanese people? I will examine a critical period in the genealogy of the rise of a Japanese aesthetic by focusing on the early modern era, the period of the Tokugawa shogunate. During the early modern period, social networks centered on the arts and poetry made room for private communicative spheres that allowed people to socialize outside long-standing feudal territorial and status boundaries. The remarkable rise of a commercial publishing industry further disseminated aesthetic knowledge that had been previously monopolized by exclusivist elites. I submit that this loosely integrated aesthetic image of a categorical identity of the space called Japan, brought people into a symbolic plane of commonality and made them aware of the presence of a set of Japanese "traditions" before the rise of the modern Japanese nation-state.

Contemporary Japanese, as well as outside observers, often associate Japan with distinctive aesthetic traditions in the arts and literature. Although such other aspects of Japanese tradition as political institutions, morals, and values were criticized and severely eroded in the process of westernization, an aesthetically defined image of Japan proved to be remarkably resilient both inside and outside the country as if it were a natural description of this society. Therefore, I focus my attention on an explication of the social mechanisms through which this supposed "naturalness" of an image of aesthetic traditionalism emerged.

The Politics of Naming in Ancient Japan

The emergence of Japan's aesthetic identity is a path-dependent phenomenon. Successive historical contingencies in the country's domestic and international politics played important roles in this process. As noted above, the identity of a person or collectivity is fluid and open to revision through interactions with others. This process of incorporating others into a given identity may operate through contacts with *actual* and/or *virtual* others. In premodern Japan, the most significant other was China;[2] Japan's identity formation in the premodern era was profoundly influenced by its experiences of actual sociopolitical and virtual cognitive interactions with imperial China.

Before launching into a discussion of the emergence of aesthetic Japan during the Tokugawa period (1600–1868) and the domestic factors involved in that emergence, let us examine the ancient origins of the term "Japan" itself. The derivation of the country's very name cannot be understood apart from the history of Japan's diplomatic contacts with her larger neighbor across the Sea of Japan. The various forms of "Japan" or "Zipangu" (Cipangu in the language of Marco Polo) in the different Western languages are said to be derived from the Chinese pronunciation of *Nippon koku*, which was then transcribed into the letters of the Roman alphabet. Although contemporary Japanese tend to think that "Japan has always been Japan," so to speak, the roots of this term *Nippon* or *Nihon* do not lie in native historical soil. On the contrary, the word is the product of intentional manipulation of political narratives produced by internal dynastic conflicts among Yamato rulers within the larger context of international relationships.

In the autumn of 702 C.E., the Japanese envoy to the Tang court landed on the Chinese coast near the mouth of the Yangzi River. To the local Chinese officials who met him at the river, the emissary declared that he represented "Nippon koku" (literally, "the country of Japan"). The officials who came to interview the Japanese visitors had never heard of this country.[3] After a series of questions, it turned out that the foreign envoy came from islands to the east that had been known for centuries as Wo, pronounced Wa or Yamato in Japanese. The Tang court, then ruled by the Empress Wu (648–705), received the Japanese emissary, Awata Mahito (d. 719). The court appreciated Awata Mahiko's cultured and gentlemanly manners, though the Chinese government was bewildered by the sudden change in name for this small country on the periphery of their empire. The land known as *Yamato* had been sending missions for centuries to China prior to this time and had established its identity as a semi-tributary kingdom. The Chinese officials even speculated that Nippon was originally a smaller country that had conquered Yamato. This eighth-century Chinese encounter with an ambassador from "Nippon" was the first time that the outside world officially recognized the existence of such an entity.[4]

Mahito had been sent on his mission in order to advertise the change in his country's name. This move was an important political gamble on the part of the rulers of Yamato. Prior to 702, the Japanese imperial court had been using the term Yamato to describe the sovereign and the territory under his rule for centuries. The emperor's court was located at that time in the area known as Yamato, but written with different characters, an area that includes the present Nara Prefecture. The Yamato court had just survived the Jinshin Turbulence of 672, a bloody civil war precipitated by two princes fighting over the imperial succession; and it was eager to stabilize its regime. The court consequently took deliberate political action to change the official name of the country once known as Yamato to a proud new name—Nippon—which allegedly referred to the place of the sun's rising. The name reflected the belief that the emperor was descended from the sun goddess, and it elevated the land's identity as a nation among nations as well as establishing the emperor as the supreme sovereign of the centralized state.

In the domestic political context, the *Taihō ritsuryō* (The Taihō Code, 701, modeled on the legal code of the Tang dynasty) also referred to the country as Nippon. Although specialists in the history of ancient Japan still debate the exact date that the term became the country's official name, most accept a date close to 689, the date of the Asuka Kiyomihara Code, which has unfortunately been lost. In addition, the use of Nippon to denote the country coincided with the emergence of the term *tennō*, or heavenly emperor, as the title of its sovereign. Thus, the use of Nippon as the official name of their realm was a major step in strengthening the power and authority of the Yamato rulers.[5]

As this brief review of the origin of the term Nippon indicates, there was nothing natural or inevitable about the origin of Japan; rather, the nation's emergence was a by-product of a deliberate political maneuver on the part of the Yamato rulers. In sum, the term Nippon was "originally the name of the Yamato dynasty" itself, as Yoshida Takashi has rightfully noted.[6] From this perspective, the name "Japan" was the equivalent of the names of such Chinese dynasties as Tang or Ming. In spite of this equivalence, however, it is curious that "Nippon" or "Nihon" has been consistently used as the name of the country for 1,300 years, in other words even after the demise of the regime who initiated it.[7] Most modern nation-states have names of comparatively recent origin; it would be highly unusual for a contemporary state to adopt the name of a premodern dynasty. As Amino Yoshihiko has noted, it is remarkable that even Japan's surrender in 1945, did not lead to proposals to change the name of the country—perhaps a question of this sort never even arose in the minds of the Japanese people.[8] Nevertheless, in spite of the fact that the word "Japan" entered history as the name of the Yamato dynasty, it began to denote an entity of the sort that Benedict Anderson has described as an "imagined community."

The apparent naturalness of the country's name cannot be understood without retracing the development of Japanese cultural self-images. Thus, the question of Japan's emergence as a nation with a clear sense of its own identity entails the investigation of cultural developments in which a large segment of the Japanese population began to accept certain cultural images and idioms related to what might be called "Japaneseness," or a Japanese cultural identity. I have chosen to focus on the aesthetic dimension of Japanese culture in this discussion. Although many traditional Japanese values and institutions have been challenged or opposed by home-grown as well as external critics, the characterization of Japan as a country with a keen appreciation of beauty is almost always assumed rather than questioned. From local good-will volunteers who receive foreign visitors to Kawabata Yasunari's (1899–1972) Nobel Prize lecture on "Japan, the Beautiful and Myself" (1968), contemporary Japanese draw on this image continually when they are required to introduce their country to outsiders.[9] On the other hand, the association of the realm of the beautiful and Japan is so much taken for granted that it can be put to use for commercial purposes. One recent magazine advertisement that exploited this well-established cognitive association (see Figure 1) conveys the flavor of the present situation. The advertisement featured two forms of "the beautiful" on two facing pages. On the left-hand page is a picture of a woman bowing slightly in an elegant but dignified manner accompanied by copy that read "Hito ga, utsukushi kuni" (As people, we form a beautiful country). The facing page has a picture of an automobile and Mt. Fuji with the words "utsukushii kuni no Merusedesu," which can be translated as "Mercedes fits the beautiful country."

The implicit message of this advertising copy is that one form of beauty—the art of *politesse*—represents the internal virtue of a person, and another form of beauty embodied in an automobile reflects the quality of a car. The advertisement was well received by the Japanese public.[10] It is not necessary, however, to read extensively in the literature of Japanese studies to develop a certain skepticism about these stereotypical images of aesthetic Japan—tea ceremony, *ikebana*, and all the rest—to detect an element of myth in such views. Nonetheless such images form a partial truth rather than a total distortion. More precisely, although there is clearly an aspect of "invented" tradition in the national political narratives, nonetheless the aesthetic ideal of Japan was rooted in the actual cultural practices of the Japanese people—to the degree that such descriptions of the Japanese aesthetic looked as if they were natural to the space called Japan.

Aesthetic Japan: Its Origin and the Tokugawa Version

This exploration of the historical process in which the realm of the beautiful played an important role in the public image of Japan provides us with a new perspective on Japan's emergence as a modern nation-state. Long before the rise of nationalism, Japan was ruled by Tokugawa shoguns who officially upheld a policy of strict status distinctions and territorial segmentation. These distinctions, however, were held together within a symbolic framework of commonality with regard to shared aesthetic idioms and images. The fact that a plane of commonality evolved primarily within the realm of the beautiful in Tokugawa society, which was otherwise decentralized and divided, holds some suggestive implications for the post-Tokugawa development of the modern Japanese nation-state. This development resulted from the close connection between the emperor's court and aesthetic interests or activities.

Beauty and power have always been closely related in Japanese history. This observation, unfortunately, sounds like a cliché from contemporary academic discourse regarding the arts and literature. Nevertheless, it is particularly relevant to Japanese cultural developments because control over the realm of beauty was a distinctive source of power in the ancient Japanese imperial system. This source of power resided not only in sociopolitical authority but also in cosmic ritual power. It was deeply rooted in the ontology of human erotic forces and animistic views of nature.[11] The public authority of the ancient imperial system was predi-

Figure 1. Japan the Beautiful. An advertisement based on Japan's reputation for beauty. On the left-hand page, a woman bowing, with the legend *Hito ga, utsukushi kuni* ("As people, we form a beautiful country"). On the facing page, an automobile and Mount Fuji with the words *utsukushii kuni no Merusedesu* ("Mercedes fits the beautiful country"). Daimler Chrysler, Japan Inc.

美しい国のメルセデス。E-CLASS　Mercedes-Benz

cated on the supremacy of this cosmic ritualism over those belonging to local clans and tribes. Poetry and the performing arts were understood to be infused by erotic and animistic energies (namely, by the same sources as the emperor's cosmic authority). Among the various cultural activities of the court, the compilation of the *chokusenshū*, or official anthologies of *waka* verse, was considered one of the emperor's most important undertakings. Beginning with the *Kokinshū* at the beginning of the tenth century, there were ultimately twenty-one anthologies commissioned by a succession of emperors. An excellent artistic performance, including the composition of poetry, was simultaneously perceived as an act of moving "heaven and earth (*ame tsuchi*) without using force" because it gave the gods pleasure.[12] The cultivated grace of *waka* poetry extended the aesthetic capacities of the native Japanese language to their fullest extent. In this context, performing artists were considered servants of the *kuji* (public affairs), because they enhanced the sovereign's authority within the ritual framework of his court.[13]

The close association of beauty and political power in the medieval period meant that Japan's distinctive aesthetic activities did not begin with the Tokugawa shogunate. Nor did the construction of Japanese cultural identities centering on aesthetic idioms and styles originate in the early modern period. For example, by the Heian era, the men and women of the emperor's court had already developed a complex self-understanding of "Japaneseness," centering on their aesthetic and poetic sensitivity that consciously distinguished itself from the classical Chinese style of literary culture. This development produced a gender-related dichotomy that represented the two states and their respective cultures: Japan symbolized the female, off-centered, and personal, while China stood for everything that was male, standard, and official.[14] The aesthetic sensibility cultivated at the Heian court, in particular its expression in *waka* poetry, exemplified this distinction. *Waka* poetry was written in the so-called "female hand," the *kana* phonetic letters that had been developed in Japan. The characteristic art forms of medieval Japan, such as Nō drama, linked poetry, and tea ceremony, reflected the prior development of a distinctive artistic tradition and sensibility at the imperial court. Although the emperor's court eventually lost its political power and centrality in medieval Japan, the cultural capital it accumulated was unmatched by those of other political forces. In sum, the institution of the *tennō* and aesthetic interests were closely related in the course of this earlier development.

Nonetheless, Japan of the Tokugawa period played a significant role in formulating the *popular* image and practice of aesthetic Japan. Prior to this period, cultural resources of outstanding merit were largely produced, patronized, and consumed by an elite circle of courtiers, priests, and higher-ranking samurai. The cultural practices that had originated in the vicinity of the ancient imperial court were exclusivist in nature. The transmission of aesthetic knowledge was protected by an institution called *sōden*, which referred to the private handing-down of higher-level artistic skills and teachings from teacher to student on a one-to-one basis. As a result, this body of cultural knowledge rarely functioned as an imagined linkage in the minds of the Japanese population at large. It was only during the seventeenth and eighteenth centuries that information about manners and the arts, derived originally from court culture, was reformulated for popular consumption. The rapid development of various information and communicative networks, including aesthetic associational networks and the rise of commercial publishing, accelerated this process. The production and consumption of new cultural practices in these communicative spheres were primarily governed by the laws of supply and demand in the marketplace rather than by traditional religious authorities or political elites.

For the first time in history, a large portion of the Japanese population began to assume the existence of objective cultural standards that should be met by those aspiring to gentility. The book trade of the Tokugawa period supported a growing sense of symbolic community among the Japanese through the objectification of a collective consciousness, the accelerated formation of communication networks, and material additions to the fund of common knowledge. The awakening of a sense of tradition in the public image was intimately related to the multiplication of private communities of discourse among ordinary citizens that centered on the sharing of artistic and literary pursuits. To be sure, this development does not imply the existence of an ideological consensus regarding the definition and contents of a Japanese collective identity. This field was a contested terrain that required, as Tetsuo Najita has described it, the "working out of a relationship between conflicting identities."[15] Nonetheless, there emerged a sense of symbolic "community" in Tokugawa Japan in terms of aesthetic participation. Long before the eruption of fervent nationalism in the late nineteenth century, Tokugawa Japan—though handicapped internally by a combination of a hierarchical status system and regional decentralization—was quietly forming symbolic planes of commonality that linked its people into imagined communities of discourse. The aesthetic image of Japan played a central role in this process of creating a sense of commonality.

On the other hand, the development of an aesthetic image of Japan during the Tokugawa period took place in a markedly different context from that of the post-Tokugawa construction of the modern nation-state. Japan's post-World War II emphasis on its role as a *bunka kokka*, or cultured nation, rather than a military power was another variation on the same theme. The formation of a nation-state is usually understood as a process of internal equalization of status among individual citizens. From this point of view, a territorial state becomes a nation-state only when it breaks down such older categories as birth, regional origin, or ethnicity and binds individuals directly to the state. Although Tokugawa Japan had become a politically integrated entity, its daimyo system and strict hierarchy of status distinctions meant that it hardly deserved the name of a nation-state. Furthermore, the shogunate was at bottom ambivalent about promoting any ideology that emphasized the unity of the country and its people, since the shoguns' official policy of rule by status enforced different roles and lifestyles on people according to their designated stations in society. What is noteworthy to us, however, is that in spite of the shoguns' divide-and-rule strategy, Tokugawa Japan began to develop common idioms of culture and language that were shared by politically partitioned people. In fact, much of this cultural development was orchestrated not by the state's agents, but by various market and social forces. In spite of these factors, however, the rise of the aesthetic image of Japan in Tokugawa Japan cannot be understood without articulating the institutional framework of the Tokugawa state. The state's role in the cultural sphere was important because of its ability to set up particular organizational-institutional frameworks for cultural developments.

This developmental pattern poses a methodological challenge for historians because the emergence of an aesthetic image of Japan during the Tokugawa period cannot be understood simply as the confluence of national political narratives. Under the highly integrated but deliberately compartmentalized Tokugawa state, it was the cultural *practices* of Tokugawa people, not articulated discourse about the definition of Japaneseness, which distinguished the Tokugawa phase of cultural development. To be sure, early modern intellectual historians have often focused on the role of political narratives in the Kokugaku (School of Native Learning) movement, which also contributed to the emergence of aesthetic images of Japan. It is not my intention to devalue the significance of such efforts. The Kokugaku scholars of the eighteenth and nineteenth centuries, most notably Motoori Norinaga (1730–1801), painted an idealized picture of the ancient Japanese aesthetic as expressed in the classical literature. Throughout his career, Norinaga sought the pure essence of *Yamato gokoro*, or authentic Japanese sensibility, as contrasted with *Kara gokoro*, or Chinese sensibility. Consequently, the work of Norinaga and his colleagues in looking for "true" Japaneseness in the Japanese classics gave additional publicity to the image of Japan as a country with a proud aesthetic heritage. Intellectual historians have been attracted to the Kokugaku movement because the group clearly had the potential to lay the symbolic foundations of a national identity before the rise of the nation-state. These scholars, however, did not single-handedly invent the image of an aesthetic Japan. Widespread enthusiasm for learning to compose poetry and the other arts, as well as the popularization of aesthetic knowledge through the commercial book trade, had already emerged during the first half of the Tokugawa period—much earlier than the peak of the Kokugaku movement. Although enthusiastic learners of arts and popular commercial publications did not involve themselves in intellectual arguments about the nature of Japan's aesthetic identity, they nonetheless popularized and naturalized an assumption that the space called Japan had a beautiful tradition of aesthetics.

The Tokugawa Network Revolution: New Channels of Communication

Cultural reformulation within a nation-state may be characterized by a process of constructing symbolic planes of commonality among the members of the state. A similar process of cultural transformation, however, can be observed when communicative networks suddenly expand in scale, density, and complexity. The resulting patterns of communication influence both the form and the content of the discourse conveyed through the networks. The kinds of cultural resources that are available at the time of network expansion will determine the range of content in the resulting cultural identities. In this way the extension of a society's communicative networks and the alteration of its cognitive maps are reciprocally influential.

Tokugawa Japan arrived at a critical moment of cultural history with the simultaneous developments of three kinds of social networks: (1) a phase of territorial state-making at the beginning of the seventeenth century involving the construction of decentralized and intentionally segregated, but yet well-integrated political networks; (2) the formation of nationwide trade routes and commodities markets together with the emergence of urban consumption centers; and (3) the development of infrastructures for communicational networks, including the rise of commercial publishing. These three conditions of possibility provided the socioeconomic backdrop for the vibrant informal spheres of civic culture that emerged within Tokugawa society. Within this environment, new sensibilities arose in the consciousness of individuals as well as in Tokugawa social life. Thus, although Tokugawa Japan had not yet become a modern state, the simultaneous expansions of communicative networks driven by the establishment of the shogunate, new markets, and the publishing industry helped to formulate a new cultural understanding of the space called Japan.

It was in this situation that what I would call the Japanese protomodern network revolution revitalized art and poetry circles as centers of communicative activity. These art and poetry circles had social functions similar to those of the cafés, salons, clubs, and reading circles of early modern Europe. The emergence of such centers of socialization and communication in Europe provided mechanisms of cultural diffusion that allowed the ideas of the Enlightenment to permeate the social fabric. By contrast, the fact that the Tokugawa centers of socialization were in essence aesthetic circles meant that what was diffused were aesthetic idioms stored within the various genres of art and poetry. To be sure, the emergence of new channels of communication and the subsequent diffusion of aesthetic knowledge in Tokugawa Japan were not linked to coherent centers of institutionalized intellectual movements. Rather, the initiatives for massive aesthetic enculturation came from largely profit-minded cultural entrepreneurs.

In fact, as will become evident in the discussion that follows, the popularization of aesthetic knowledge that characterized Tokugawa cultural developments was essentially market-driven. In the Tokugawa version of protomodernity, intricate networks of communication related to far-reaching economic changes facilitated the dissemination of knowledge beyond territorial and status boundaries. One is tempted to call the result a "national economy" even though it did not operate within the framework of a nation-state. To be sure, the development of extensive commercialization and a market economy by themselves might not have led to the diffusion of cultural knowledge across class boundaries if there had been no means of disseminating the information. As it happened, the rapid success of commercial publishing based on woodblock printing popularized cultural knowledge in the Tokugawa period according to the law of supply and demand.

On the other hand, the fact that aesthetic circles became centers of civilized socialization was closely connected with the idiosyncratic nature, trajectory, and structure of the Tokugawa neo-feudal state. Although historians generally pay more attention to the nineteenth century and the Meiji construction of Japanese cultural identities, the earlier transition from the medieval to the early modern state in many ways set forth the conditions of possibility for subsequent cultural development. The main governing strategy of the Tokugawa state can be described as *institutional segmentation* of its population through a decentralized, indirect control system. Institutional segmentation was critical to the stability of the system because the feudal authorities in medieval Japan had often been threatened by horizontal alliances of various people and groups known as *ikki*. Unlike the form of vassalage that eventually led to the formation of the Tokugawa state as the consolidation of the samurai's national hierarchies, the late medieval period was a golden age of *ikki* in which numerous horizontally structured alliances and mutual protection associations were formed among various kinds of people. The samurai authorities during the pre-Tokugawa period were confronted by the difficult problem of controlling contentious horizontal alliances. In response to this situation, the Tokugawa *bakuhan* (shogunate and feudal domains) state reinforced a hierarchical categorization by partitioning the population by regional, occupational, and status boundaries. This approach to social control became a central feature of the shogunate's government.[16]

For example, the Tokugawa shoguns repeatedly issued edicts prohibiting "the formation of *totō*" (parties) because they feared that private networks of horizontal alliances among individuals would lead eventually to collective action against their regime. The famous *Buke shohatto* (Regulations for the imperial court and aristocracy), the 1615 law representing the shogunate's basic regulation of military houses, clearly stated that the daimyo should discipline anyone who attempted to form a faction (*totō*).[17] A similar ordinance was promulgated among the shogunate's vassals. Additional edicts against the formation of political parties or groups were published in the outlying villages and towns of Japan throughout the Tokugawa period. In effect, the injunctions against *totō* became one of the best-known rules of the shogunate.[18] This prohibition made private aesthetic associations even more important for civic life during the Tokugawa period. Circles for sharing arts and literature were well accepted; they were safe ways to organize voluntary associations open to people from different social backgrounds. The result was the evolution of what I call a "civility without civil society" centered on aesthetic pursuits.

The Rise of Aesthetic Civility

By the end of the seventeenth century, the shogunate's construction of a decentralized yet integrated polity encouraged the development of a binary frame of reference among Tokugawa people. The shoguns' indirect system of social control led to the formation of localized publics; from villages to provinces governed by daimyo, these eccentric hubs of local politics became important centers of communicative activity. By the same token, the stable central government and the emergence of a national marketplace encouraged people to consider the world beyond their immediate localized networks of communication. The spread of reading further encouraged villagers in the outlying provinces as well as urban commoners to keep up with forms of social prestige and their associated bodies of cultural knowledge from sources outside their own communities. In particular, leading members of local communities, or *mura yakunin,* were eager to acquire the cultural polish of their aristocratic superiors, partly in order to upgrade their own social status. Beginning in the late seventeenth century, there is documentary evidence for a growing popular interest in learning *yūgei,* or "arts for pleasure," outside the court societies. A 1685 tourist guide to the city of Kyoto, called *Kyōhabutae,* lists the names of 241 "various masters" who earned their keep by giving instruction in different fields of learning, arts, and literature. The list includes the names of medical doctors and other scholars, but 130 of the 241 masters taught nothing but *yūgei.* A similar list found in the files of the Kyoto magistrate's office names 440 "various masters" (*shoshi*).[19]

By the late seventeenth and early eighteenth centuries, the organizational overhaul of Japanese society was complete, with an accompanying discipline centered on greater categorical stratification of the population. Every station in life now had a standardized image of proper deportment, covering every detail of language, gesture, manner, dress, and the degree and pattern of self-control. Whether the people in fact followed all these minute prescriptions to the letter is a different question, but the fact that a standard model of propriety was entering the popular imagination is beyond dispute.

The widespread enthusiasm for learning the arts was one of the most distinctive characteristics of the early modern civilizing process in Japan. Tokugawa people loved the world of the beautiful—they were not passive spectators of artistic performances, but active participants. This attitude of engagement stands in contrast to the relationship between patrons and producers of the arts in eighteenth-century Europe, in which sponsorship of the arts became a form of investment in status symbols. Tokugawa Japan developed its distinctive pattern of interest and participation in the arts because of the sheer size of its population of amateur art and poetry students. Many performing artists and poets were able to earn a decent living as teachers because people from all territorial, status, or occupational groupings were eager to pay for instruction in these arts. The widened base of economic support provided by teaching made Tokugawa artists and poets relatively independent of aristocratic patronage. Each artistic or poetic genre thus formed a shared universe comprised of sizable likeminded groups of people set apart from the outside world. The increasing autonomy of the artistic world became the basis of aesthetic publics in which the status distinctions that were operative in the political world were nullified.

In this context of intersecting aesthetic and economic concerns, amateur circles and professional schools related to the fine and performing arts gained new importance as a means of personal socialization. This process of socialization through aesthetic interests loosened up the rigid

hierarchical status system imposed by the shogunate and created opportunities for people to mingle with others from different status categories. The aesthetic circles and schools of the Tokugawa period were
the most vigorous forms of associational activities in a politically seg-
mented society. This widespread fascination with the arts at all levels of
society, however, resulted in a situation where persons with respectable
positions almost had to equip themselves with cultural information and
skills in order to socialize with others. Ihara Saikaku (1642–93), an as-
tute observer and one of the most celebrated writers of the time, described the Ōsaka merchants of his day:

In general, the Ōsaka rich are not descendants of old families that have pros-
pered for many generations. Most of them are the type of people who were formerly called "Kichizō" or "Sansuke," but now they strive to enrich themselves.
They have learned to socialize with people from "good" families while learning
poetry-making, playing *kemari* [a ball game], archery, the *koto* [lute], the flute,
drum music, the perfume game, or tea ceremony. By that time they have lost
their countrified accents.[20]

Saikaku captured the essential features of an upwardly mobile sub-
population at the epicenter of a developing market economy. In this
new economic climate, many young men from the more remote
provinces of Japan were working hard to establish themselves. For those
who were fortunate enough to attain a measure of success, the Tokugawa cultural circles served as finishing schools that turned entrepreneurs of humble origins into sophisticated urban businessmen.

The writers of the early Tokugawa period were aware of the attraction
of new money to old conventions. Nishikawa Joken (1648–1724), a contemporary observer, described the relationship among the country's
economic prosperity, the human desire for status, and the popularization of aristocratic manners in his *Chōnin bukuro* (The merchant's wis-
dom bag):

Now that the townspeople have piled up a lot of money, they proudly attempt to
raise their status by aping the manners of the aristocracy and the samurai. When
the rest of the people, whether educated or not, look at these newly refined city
folk, they are consumed with envy and push themselves to the limit in order to
imitate [their polite arts]. In this way, the behavior associated with the polite arts
has become the custom of the country as a whole.[21]

Joken's words convey the essential characteristic of the Tokugawa civilizing process. It was the more prosperous and reputable merchant families who attempted to emulate the cultural standards of the upper
classes and pioneered the process of mass enculturation. The circles that
usually accepted both samurai and non-samurai members resembled the

British gentlemen's clubs of a bygone era, in which socialization between members of the old aristocracy and the new business elite helped to create modern upper-class culture. In other words, the aesthetic means of socialization in Tokugawa Japan became an important mode of civility in this period. As long as artistic pursuits did not interfere with business matters, they were considered morally acceptable activities for members of the merchant class.

In the first half of the Tokugawa period, most participants in the amateur arts groups were male. Although many Japanese performing arts convey an impression of what the Western world stereotypes as "feminine," the early Tokugawa cultural circles were really more like "gentlemen's clubs." Male students in fact dominated even *ikebana*, the art of flower arrangement, which might appear to be a prototypically feminine activity, in this period (see Figure 2). It was only after the mid-eighteenth century that female students became conspicuous participants in these cultural groups. The gender gap was in part a reflection of Japanese women's social segregation during this period. More to the point, however, the fact that socially respectable and economically powerful men were eager to join the art circles indicated that the polite and performing arts were not simply accessories to their lifestyle.

The performing arts or verse composition in this period inevitably required students to learn not only the specific skills associated with the art form in question, but to gain some basic knowledge of older courtly aesthetic traditions. In this way an age of aesthetic popularization was at the same time an era of wide dissemination of knowledge previously reserved to the aristocracy. Tokugawa cultural popularization was fed and supported by a commercial publishing industry that made a large share of its profits from introductory guidebooks to the arts. All these cultural developments helped to form and perpetuate what might be labeled an aesthetic definition of civility, in the sense of Norbert Elias's (1897–1990) usage.

Many groups of amateur arts enthusiasts cut across status boundaries in this politically balkanized society. The *haikai* poetry circles are perhaps the most prominent example. During the eighteenth and nineteenth centuries, the social and cognitive networks associated with *haikai* poetry became so intricately interwoven with the fabric of Tokugawa society that we cannot understand any literary or artistic production in this period without some knowledge of the symbolic paradigms and actual social networks associated with *haikai*. Furthermore, the open and fluid networking styles of poetry circles were highly adaptable to the operation of commercial markets. With their remarkable ability to create private associations and make connections with the marketplace, *haikai*

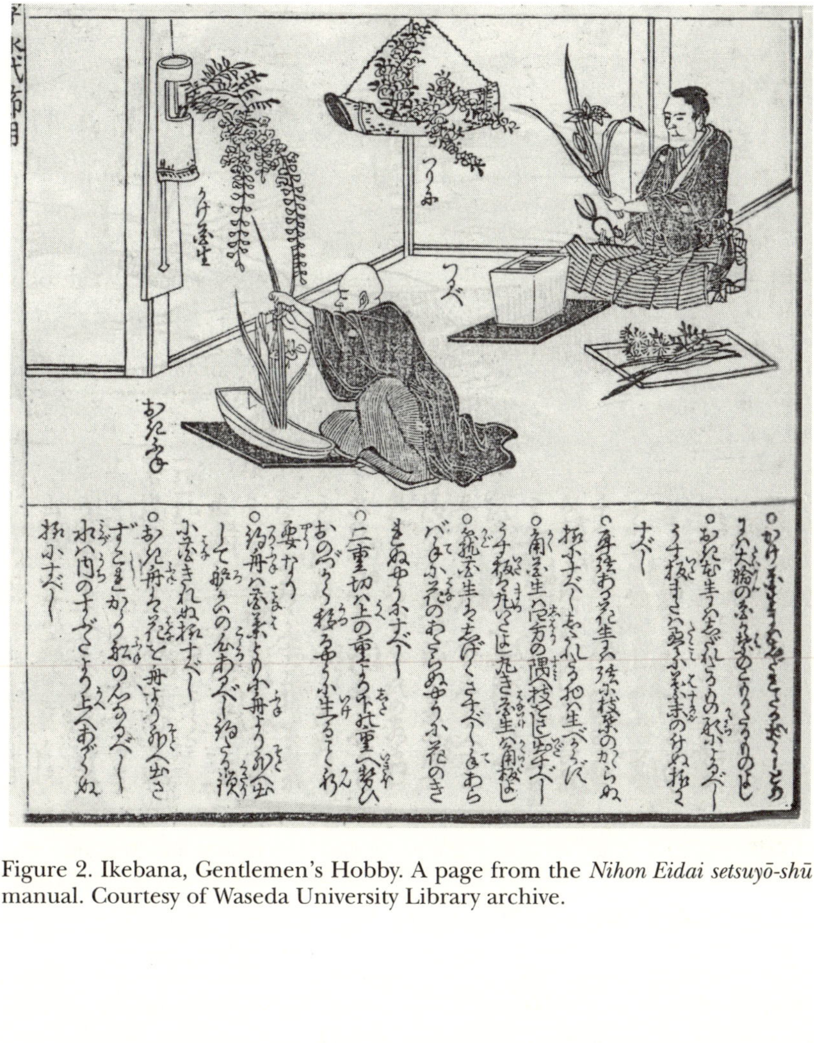

Figure 2. Ikebana, Gentlemen's Hobby. A page from the *Nihon Eidai setsuyō-shū* manual. Courtesy of Waseda University Library archive.

poetry networks epitomized the Tokugawa style of what I call aesthetic enclave publics. The *haikai* circles brought together persons from different regional, status, occupational, and gender categories within the temporary public worlds created by a common interest in this type of poetry.

Furthermore, learning how to compose *haikai* poetry was equivalent to receiving an inheritance—in this case, the vast cultural capital accumulated over centuries of the Japanese classical literary tradition. This cultural capital had become the personal endowment of a growing number of Tokugawa individuals. The social impact of the poetry circles was even more striking because they were always coupled with participants' incorporation into actual social networks, the endowment of so-called "social capital." A *haikai* poet in Tokugawa society never practiced his or her craft in isolation. Because the creation and appreciation of *haikai* required the presence of fellow citizens of the same symbolic universe, most amateur poets participated in local *haikai* circles that were usually connected to *haikai* masters with wider regional or national reputations. Through learning to compose and appreciate *haikai* poetry, men and women of humble backgrounds acquired their own forms of self-expression and extended their social networks. This accumulation of cultural and social capital in the supposedly inferior *watakushi* (private) realm allowed the *haikai* networks to contribute to a broad-based transformation of Tokugawa society.

At the beginning of the eighteenth century, there were at least 132 neighborhood poetry composition groups (*kumiren*) in the city of Edo alone.[22] There were also literary agents scattered throughout the city who actively connected these amateur poetry circles with professional master-poets. Most neighborhoods sponsored a *haikai* circle, and there was enough demand in the city to support several dozen professional poets specializing in different styles of popular *haikai*. The Edo master-poets were also able to run thriving monthly commercial poetry competitions. The networks formed by *haikai* poetry enthusiasts extended to the smaller towns and villages in every province of Japan, linking cultivated provincials to the master-poets in the larger urban centers.

We must note that in the hierarchically structured, status-oriented Tokugawa system, even the most privileged members suffered from a sense of confinement; the circumstances of noble birth circumscribed their opportunities for excitement and adventure as much as poverty or low status handicapped others. Although there were some minor mechanisms at work to incorporate some flexibility into this rigid status system, the Tokugawa regime never formally abandoned status distinctions as a structural element of the social order. In regard to formal appearance, status distinctions remained the basic organizing principle of

Tokugawa society for two and a half centuries. As a result, a person born into a specific station in life, whether high or low, had only a limited range of vocational possibilities to explore. Furthermore, each status ranking dictated one's lifestyle as well as the proper modes of relating to others. The formal code of civility that defined social relations between persons of different status alerted individuals to the need for continuous monitoring of their relative position on the social map.

By this point in time, Japanese society had also elaborated an idiosyncratic, full-blown distinction between the public and private spheres. In the reformulated hierarchy of publics under the shogunate, the realm of ōkōgi, or the "great public," was coextensive with the shogun's authority and dominated the hierarchy of lesser publics. Within this framework of the hierarchy of publics, no sphere was considered truly "private," as each level of involvement had its own assigned role and responsibility in the Tokugawa system of social control. Ironically, this distinctive characteristic of the Tokugawa state, which restructured the state-centered hierarchy of publicness, almost ended by redefining the private sphere in the area of aesthetic socialization, even though private life was regarded as inferior (watakushi) in comparison to the official hierarchy of publicness.

What were the attractions that made Tokugawa adults such eager students of aesthetic pursuits? There were, of course, some utilitarian reasons for joining aesthetic circles; a person might do so in order to extend the perimeter of his or her social networks. On the other hand, practical economic considerations do not fully explain the attraction of learning the performing arts. An elderly samurai in the early eighteenth century who had lived long enough to reflect on more than seven decades of history in his memoir, entitled *Mukashi mukashi monogatari* (Stories of olden days, ca. 1732), made frequent reference to the growing popularity among samurai of learning the popular performing arts:

When these men are able to sing *jōruri* songs well enough, they are given names with the suffix *tayū* [the customary ending of the artist names conferred on accomplished *jōruri* performers] by their teachers. The students feel honored by this treatment. Within the circle, they address each other only as "—*tayū*." Their samurai names are deemed appropriate only for official public matters. In their private life [*naishō*, or "hidden truth"], they use only their *tayū* names. How deplorable![23]

The old samurai lamented the situation in which his contemporaries of samurai status were delighted to be honored as entertainers in their private life. Although they were reared to devote their lives to public duties, they relegated their stuffy samurai names to dull official occasions. Their real enthusiasm was directed toward learning *jōruri*. The term *naishō* originated in a religious context; it is a Buddhist word implying a hidden or secret truth. A private life, with the added fillip of an enclave identity conferred by *tayū* names, became a hidden truth for the singing samurai; it was attractive enough to the younger men to induce them to discard their official names in favor of their *tayū* enclave identities. Only in using the *tayū* names were they able to socialize with one another as individuals without being hampered by the manners of socialization appropriate for their state-defined stations in life.

Artist names also served to create a new alternative reality in the realm of a particular art. With an artist name, a student could socialize with artistic peers and liberate himself (or herself) temporarily from the restrictions of the political status hierarchy. Although the students' official identities were widely known by members of the circle, referring to one another by their artist names underscored the fact that they inhabited a temporary community of enclave identities. A cultured person who participated in a number of different aesthetic groups might well have several artist or literary names. The use of artist names reflected the emergence of private social spaces in which the formal hierarchical norms of the Tokugawa state were irrelevant.[24]

Aesthetic pursuits became an important part of Japanese social life, not only among the elite, but also among urban and provincial commoners. From people of humble backgrounds to high-ranking samurai and daimyo, a society compartmentalized by feudal status boundaries was united on the aesthetic plane by love of beauty and aspirations toward higher culture. Although artistic interests did not ordinarily affect a person's social status, the sharing of similar standards and tastes made formal status boundaries less meaningful. Amateur circles, associations, and art schools thus became the basis of social networks that operated across regional and occupational groupings. In this way, the very nature of Japanese civility would carry with it a fundamental aesthetic component.

To be sure, this symbolic trespassing across official status boundaries was bidirectional. During the eighteenth century, the vital center of Tokugawa cultural activities moved from the ruling samurai class to the populations of the larger and more sophisticated cities. By this time, the cultural heritage of the medieval period had been assimilated, popularized, and translated into more contemporary cultural idioms. For example, commoners in the Tokugawa period had some knowledge of courtly *waka* poetry, the famous passages of Nō drama, and such classics of ancient and medieval literature as *The Tale of Genji* and *The Tale of Heike*. *Haikai*, popular styles of poetry-making, *kabuki* theater, and such popular illustrated stories as *gesaku* comic fiction—all these genres were associated primarily with the culture of urban commoners, and all assumed a certain basic knowledge of medieval literary themes. On the other hand, the samurai were also attracted to the liveliness and spontaneity of popular culture. Some lesser samurai even began to participate in *gesaku* and similar popular cultural productions.

Although the enclaves of aesthetic publics were not intended to threaten the authorities insofar as they were understood as private, or *watakushi*, loci for the temporary switching of fictional identities, the growing popularization of aesthetic networking practices began to blur the outlines of status-based categories. As the samurai and the urban commoners began to share similar cultural idioms and enthusiasm, they were implicitly contributing to the collapse of some parts of the rigid status system. From the side of the upwardly mobile, some rich commoners who aspired to greater cultural prestige took lessons in such "traditional" arts with medieval origins as the tea ceremony, Nō singing (*utai*), flower arrangement, and the composition of *waka* poetry. From the other direction, the samurai who should have been mastering the finer points of Nō music were attracted to *jōruri* and other performing arts that originated in popular commoner culture.

Popular Books and the Aesthetic Image of Japan

The rise of aesthetic circles in the Tokugawa period was closely connected to the emergence of a commercially viable publishing industry. Conversely, cultural entrepreneurs actively used print media to promote the arts and poetry. For example, the publication of anthologies of *haikai* poems, including pieces written by amateurs, was an integral part of the operation of *haikai* schools. Tokugawa aesthetic activities were, for the first time in Japanese history, mediated by printed resources. The significance of this development was that books had the ability to form centers of social interaction. In other words, books, pamphlets, and other printed matter served as mediators of "happenings" in the world. Book publishing was a constituent element of the Tokugawa communicative revolution, and its distinctive dynamics influenced the cultural style of Tokugawa proto-modernity.

The oldest Japanese publishing houses were established in Kyoto at the beginning of the seventeenth century, around the time that Tokugawa Ieyasu, the first shogun, was completing the country's pacification.[25] The following two centuries of development transformed the Japanese book trade into one of the most vigorous publishing cultures in the world at that time. The first Japanese trade catalogue, "The List of Books in Print," was published in 1666 and listed 2,589 books. By the time the 1670 catalogue appeared, this number had jumped to 3,866 titles; the 1685 list contained 5,934, and the 1692 list, 7,181 titles. Following this remarkable early growth, the eighteenth century saw the popular audience for books grow exponentially as publishers and traders cultivated new readership by introducing popular subjects in an appealing way. According to the city of Edo's official record for 1808, the capital alone had 656 commercial book-lending shops—a number nearly equaling the number of public baths.[26] Considering the Japanese fondness for bathing (a custom that had by this time become a part of the lifestyle even of the working population of Edo), it is reasonable to assume that renting books from such shops was also a commonplace activity.

In the Tokugawa book world, publishing was above all else a business. This characteristic meant that the supply-and-demand dynamic of a capitalist economy controlled the distribution and expansion of publishing. The themes of aesthetic civility, however, played a dominant role in the field of commercial publications. As the popularity of learning poetry and the performing arts increased, publishers began to find that introductory guides to these subjects were sure-fire money-makers. The popularity of "how-to" books and introductions to the arts indicates that the new Tokugawa readership was no mere collection of passive consumers but included active participants in cultural production. An excerpt from a conversation between two Tokugawa publishers illustrates the vitality of this rising industry:

[A publisher from Kyoto said:] "These days we have to put the heavy works on the back burner to keep the business in good shape. The stuff like *kōshokubon* ["Amorous Books"] and *chōhōki* [various kinds of manuals for gracious civilized life] is much more popular." A publisher from Ōsaka replied: "Oh, I couldn't agree with you more. Since *Kanai chōhōki* (Handbook for domestic life) hit the stands this kind of book has taken over the Ōsaka market."[27]

One can easily imagine this exchange occurring between two contemporary Japanese publishers, since romantic fiction and how-to books are still bestsellers in Japan and elsewhere. But in fact this conversational excerpt appeared in an essay called *Genroku taiheiki* (Peaceful chronicle of Genroku), published in 1702, when the long-lasting peace of the Tokugawa period had brought prosperity to a number of commercial ventures. Practical guidebooks for social life proved to be one of the most popular genres throughout the period. Of these various guidebooks, the *chōhōki* were especially popular during the Genroku period (1688–1702). *Chōhō* has a number of different meanings, among them "great treasure," "convenience," and "methods."[28] More than twenty different *chōhōki* came off the presses during the Genroku era, a period that witnessed the emergence of the lifestyle of urbanized commoners as a distinctive subculture in Tokugawa Japan. These manuals were also brimming with useful information, often accompanied by many illustrations, in response to people's desire for self-improvement and the acquisition of "upscale" knowledge. Through the information made available in commercial publications, therefore, Tokugawa readers were connected to a world of gracious manners that was, according to these books, uniquely associated with the entity called Japan.

In addition to the *chōhōki*, there were *setsuyōshū* (dictionaries, often encyclopedic); *shoreshū* (etiquette books); *kinmōzui* (illustrated encyclopedias written at the introductory level); *shoreishū* (guidebooks for formal manners); *shosatsushū* (guidebooks for personal and business correspondence); and *ōraimono* (collections of model letters that were used as elementary school texts). The selling point of the *chōhōki* and *setsuyōshū* was the provision of accessible forms of civilized knowledge. The *chōhōki* spanned a wide range of essential knowledge ranging from medical advice, such as information about childbirth and childrearing, to the formal titles of government officials and the idioms of court culture. Summaries of the polite arts and the components of formal letter-writing were standard entries in this genre. The *setsuyōshū*, by contrast, evolved from their original form as dictionaries in the sixteenth century into copiously illustrated tomes by the middle of the eighteenth. By then, no family that conducted written correspondence would have been without at least one copy of this type of *setsuyōshū*. The *setsuyōshū* were considered essential household items because they explained the meaning and pronunciation of Chinese ideograms—information widely considered the most difficult element of properly written Japanese. Although formal correspondence required the use of many Chinese characters, they were easily forgotten, especially those not frequently used. In addition, the combination of standard dictionary functions with convenient references to other branches of the polite arts, maps, and historical information made the *setsuyōshū* the most popular genre of Tokugawa handbooks of civilized knowledge.

The unpretentious pages of these guidebooks with their copious illustrations present us with a mosaic of the knowledge that these people considered valuable, as well as with a reflection of their enthusiasm for widening their mental horizons. Although these practical how-to books and manuals rarely impress us with their authors' intellectual force, given that they were intended to be little more than summary presentations of standard information, their tone of repetitive conventionalism proves my point precisely: it suggests the emergence of standardized accounts that represented the common cultural "database" of the literate population of Tokugawa Japan. Although various kinds of handbooks and manuals had different specialties and purposes, we can still identify two major recurrent topics in these books of civilized knowledge. The first concerns self-identification of position and orientation in time and space. The Tokugawa manuals are crammed full of introductory historical, geographical, and sociopolitical information. It is not an exaggeration to say that almost all the *setsuyōshū* open with either an eye-catching map or pictorial illustrations of famous cities and geographical landmarks.[29] The earlier published manuals sometimes included a rudimentary world map with illustrations of various actual and imagined countries (see Figure 3). The geographical information that was presented also tended to emphasize places and locations made famous by the *waka* poetry of the imperial court. The expression "Nihon" for Japan, such as "the three best landscapes in Nihon" (*Nihon sankei*) which often appeared in these manuals, is a typical example. On the other hand, Nihonbashi (the "Japan Bridge") in Edo was a frequently featured scene in these manuals as a famous starting point for major nation-wide roads. We should also note that the term Nihon (or Nippon) began to be used frequently in commercial publications during the Tokugawa period.[30] Although the term Nihon or Nippon had been used as the official name of the country for many centuries, the appearance of this term in commercial publishing coupled with the popularization of the geographical image of the space called Japan distinguished Tokugawa cultural development.

If the articles on geography reflected Tokugawa readers' need to orient themselves spatially, the historical articles helped them locate themselves in the dimension of time. For example, *Edo dai setsuyō kainaizō*, a typical voluminous encyclopedic *setsuyōshū* first published in the mid-eighteenth century, featured an article comparing famous historical figures of Japan and China, with well-drawn illustrations for each figure, in proper chronological order. This particular *setsuyōshū* also contains a long list of major historical events beginning with the legendary founding of Japan. Curiosity concerning one's position on the social and political ladders was directed to the articles on political offices or the names of provinces and their ruling daimyo. Many *chōhōki* and *setsuyōshū* provided lists of official titles for the imperial court in Kyoto as well as for the shogun's government.

The second category of information in these books may be called essential knowledge for gracious living. The introductory articles on various polite arts fit into this category. For example, *The Gentleman's Treasury* features a summary explanation of Chinese (*kanshi*) and Japanese (*waka*) styles of poetry. Some manuals of this type included lists of the most famous *waka* poets together with their portraits. The volume also includes an article on *utai* vocal music for Nō plays. The tea ceremony and the art of flower arrangement are topics that always appear in

Figure 3. World Map and People of Foreign Countries. Almost all the *setsuyōshū* (encyclopedic dictionary) open with eye-catching maps. This late seventeenth-century version features only a rudimentary world map and illustrations of people in actual and imagined countries outside Japan. It includes people of China, the Philippines, India, and Holland dressed in their own costumes as the Japanese imagined them. In addition, it features illustrations of imaginary lands such as a small people country and a tall people country. In later periods, maps in such publications became more and more accurate. From *Daii setsuyōshū*. Courtesy of Waseda University Library archive.

such works—including books intended for a male readership, as this specific title indicates. Articles on formal etiquette and manners also belong in this category.

Let us take as an example the *Tokai setsuyō hyakkatsū*, or "The City-Dweller's All-Purpose Dictionary," a typical encyclopedic dictionary published in 1801.[31] The volume begins with a two-page spread: a world map of rudimentary accuracy followed by a map of Japan with the names of all provinces spelled out. Unlike the mid-nineteenth-century handbooks that usually featured quite accurate maps of the world and Japan, the image of the world in this book was influenced by contact with Dutch traders—the only Westerners then privileged to trade with Japan. Holland was shown as much larger than Great Britain, and only Spain and Portugal are indicated as "Christian" in large letters.[32] Next to these maps was a bird's-eye view of the emperor's palace in Kyoto followed by colored pictures of famous landscapes—particularly religious shrines that many Japanese would have hoped to visit someday.

The dictionary also features articles on historical and legendary figures (see Figure 4), again accompanied by interesting illustrations; summaries of model letters; a concise description of the tea ceremony; an introduction to the art of flower arrangement; a writer's guide to the composition of *haiku* poetry; the names of all the daimyo houses and their family crests; the major positions in the shogun's government; an outline of imperial court rankings; and a calendar of annual events. The interested reader could also learn a wide variety of miscellaneous skills from the illustrations, including fortune telling and palmistry, the art of ceremonial gift wrapping, and the use of the abacus as a calculating machine. The dictionary proper, which comprises the main part of the book, explains the meaning and pronunciation of the difficult Chinese ideograms that were essential to formal letter-writing.

On page after page, a surprising variety of information was condensed into small multiple columns with lively illustrations. These entries would have induced their readers to think of their homeland as unsurpassed in beauty, filled with populous and prosperous cities, picturesque landscapes, sacred shrines and temples, and sites immortalized in literature or history. Furthermore, the guidebooks depicted the people of this land as cultured and gracious persons who had mastered the arts of politeness as well as aesthetic appreciation. A review of articles and books on formal etiquette and manners indicates that beauty played an important role as a control mechanism of body and mind in Japanese cultures. Tokugawa etiquette and manner books were usually rooted in the late medieval formulation of courtly manners, represented by the so-called Ogasawara School. The Ogasawara described their understanding of politeness in such terms as *rei* (Chinese *li*, the Confucian notion of

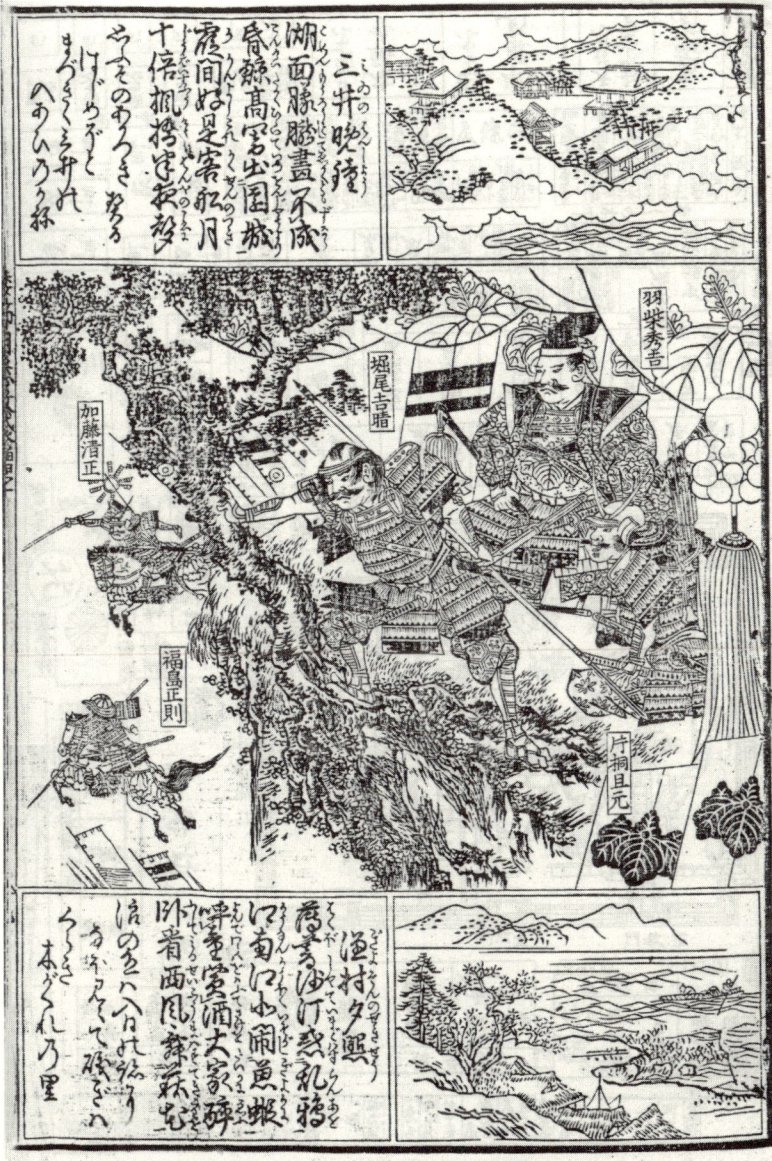

Figure 4. History as Civilized Knowledge. A scene of the commanding ruler Hideyoshi, the man who united Japan, and his two generals. Names and images of historical figures are popular features of Tokugawa manuals. In this page, the upper and lower columns feature famous landmarks in waka poetry. It is typical in Tokugawa manuals that different kinds of knowledge are packed into one page without logical connection. From *Yamato Setsuyōshū shikkai nō*. Courtesy of Waseda University Library archive.

propriety), or *shitsuke*, a native term for disciplined physical movements. Although the Ogasawara School used certain Confucian idioms, its formula differed from the classical Confucian understanding of propriety; it was closer to the tradition of Japanese court rituals and the performing arts. The School's rules of etiquette and manners were essentially those of the performing arts.

The indigenous term *shitsuke* conveyed the embodied characteristics of manners with beauty and precision. The ideogram for *shitsuke* is a symbolic representation of the Japanese ideal of the social body. It consists of two elements, the left part designating "body" and the right signifying "beauty." This particular ideogram was not imported from China, but was invented in Japan during the medieval period to denote good manners. Clearly, the Japanese people recognized that the Chinese character set lacked a suitable ideogram to describe their own conception of propriety. The character implies physical grace allied with habitual bodily discipline. In other words, the aim of *shitsuke-kata* was the embodiment of elegance and polish through physical training, a process that eventually led students to an integrated harmony of body and mind (see Figure 5). The concept of good manners reflected in the Japanese etiquette books is clearly quite different from its Chinese counterpart. The Japanese version located beauty in physical motion that included graceful gestures derived from the performing arts. In addition, the ideal of beauty in Japan had a deeper implication as the unfolding of inner goodness. For this reason training in the polite arts entailed not only the external discipline of the body but internal cultivation of soul and spirit as well.

To be sure, a stylized and elegant physical carriage was certainly appreciated in the courtly etiquette of Europe and elsewhere. But the strong influence of the performing arts in Japan meant that Japanese formal manners regarded beauty as a major implement of socialization. To give an example of formal table manners, Kaibara Ekken (1630–1714) recommended that well-bred people eating fish should eat only one side of their portion; the fish was then to be turned over in order not to display the eaten—therefore, messy—side to others at the table. Of course, we can speculate that only the rich who could afford this level of formality—such as the daimyo—would have practiced such a wasteful method of consumption. In eating round sweet dumplings, Ekken advised biting the same corner of the dumpling twice—because if one took only one bite, most likely the soft surface of the dough would retain the imprint of the teeth, which would "look ugly." His recommendations in such matters are noteworthy because they illustrate the importance of the criterion of beauty in governing Japanese formal manners.[33] Clearly, we should not assume that formal rules of good

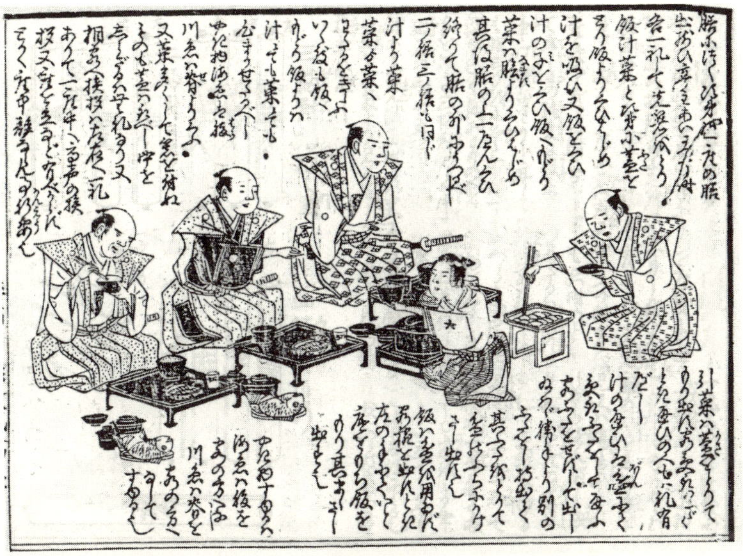

Figure 5. Elegant Manners. (1) Instruction on table manners and the method of serving food. The food was typically served on small, low individual tables with several small dishes. From *Yamato Setsuyoshu shikkai nō*. (2) The way of serving sake. "Holding the handle of the pot with your right hand, your four fingers should rest together on the underside of the handle with your thumb gently placed on the top. Your left thumb should lightly touch the cover, while the left-hand fingers hold the side." From *Onna shorei ayanishiki*. Courtesy of Waseda University Library archive.

manners, meticulously formulated for aesthetically pleasing social interactions, were always reflected in Tokugawa people's actual practices of
socialization. The point is that the dissemination of these formal rules of
socialization, through the texts of popular commercial handbooks, reminded the people of the existence of aesthetic standards that had originated in the courtly tradition.

The Emperor's Position and Its Consequences

The massive popular enculturation that took place in marketplaces
under the shogunate, had unexpected political consequences in light of
seventeenth-century state policy. At the beginning of the Tokugawa period, the shoguns attempted to distinguish between the emperor's court
as the realm of beauty and scholarship and the shogunate as the realm
of political and military power. In order to establish the shogunate as
ōkōgi, the supreme public authority, the emperor's position had to be
completely depoliticized. In order to achieve this end, the first Tokugawa shogun adopted the unusual tactic of compiling a comprehensive
set of rules for the Kyoto court. The *Buke shohatto* (Regulations for the
imperial court and aristocracy) of 1615 stipulated that the emperor and
his court should be devotees of various arts (*shogeinō*), in particular,
learning (*gogakumon*). Learning, in this context, meant the learning of
traditional court rituals and ceremonies. The emperor was expected to
be the master of ceremonial traditions, which included courtly polite
arts. This devotion was to be their special service to the state, comparable to the samurai's provision of military service to the shoguns. This
policy had significant implications for the Tokugawa cultivation of
beauty. In contrast to the ancient court, in which the emperor's relationship to the beautiful was linked to the ritual source of his political
power, emperors under the Tokugawa regime had to be confined within
that realm in order to render them politically harmless. Under this policy, however, the shogunate generously underwrote the cultural activities
of the emperor Gomizuno-o (1596–1680), which re-established Kyoto as
the center of Japan's aesthetic tradition.

The depoliticization of the emperor's court through restricting it to
the pursuit of beauty, however, had an unexpected side effect that became apparent only later on. The emperor held an exceptional position
within the framework of the Tokugawa feudal status system. The status
hierarchy in Tokugawa Japan had a twofold structure. The first and
more obvious hierarchy placed the shogun at the top of the status pyra-
mid, while the second, less evident hierarchy was headed by the emperor. Although the shoguns were not opposed to artistic pursuits and
were in fact eager to enhance their own cultural standards as the mili-

tary rulers, they had no interest in supplanting the emperor as the *arbiter elegantiarum*.[34] The Tokugawa status system derived a certain depth of perspective from a combination of these two foci: the actual and political hierarchy headed by the shogun, and the virtual and cultural hierarchy headed by the emperor. Even when the emperor was all but powerless politically, he never lost his high position in the esteem of the people because of his implicit dominion over the virtual realm. In fact, in the middle of the Tokugawa period, when the *pax Tokugawa* looked as if it would last forever, the shogun's authority seemed to require no legitimation by the emperor. Yet, in the popular mind, the emperor never completely lost his symbolic power precisely because his court and the image of traditional courtly aesthetic traditions came to be more closely intertwined. Anyone in Tokugawa society who claimed to be aesthetically refined would recognize the courtly aesthetic, poetry, and polite arts as the ultimate standard of high culture. Thus, the more widely the civilizing process of Tokugawa Japan was disseminated, the more entrenched the cultural position of the imperial court became in the imagination of the Japanese people.

As the standardized images and idioms of "beautiful Japan" were inscribed in the mind of cultured Tokugawa people, the position of the emperor was never lost in their collective memory. Thus, as more individuals eagerly sought higher levels of cultural refinement through enjoyment of the arts and poetry, the central role of the imperial court in maintaining Japanese aesthetic traditions became self-evident. This situation facilitated, at least in part, the sudden revival of imperial symbolism in the late nineteenth century, as the center of national unity when the Tokugawa shogunate's inability to respond to the forces of Western imperialism became clear.

Tokugawa Proto-Modernity and the Modern Nation-State

My analysis so far has concentrated on explicating the location of communicative activities and channels in the social life of the Tokugawa Japanese. The spheres of aesthetic socialization were considered private, informal, and voluntary compared to the public, formal, and obligatory nature of communicative spheres within the framework of the *bakuhan* state. Although the government officially relegated communicative spheres devoted to aesthetic pursuits to the inferior domain of the private or *watakushi*, they were nonetheless more active, open, and attractive loci for socialization. The popular images of Japan as a land dedicated to beauty were cultural, emergent properties that were manifested in these spheres of communication.[35] Since aesthetic socialization brought together people who were otherwise divided and confined by the Tokugawa policy of institutional status divisions, it also connected people with the common culture of Japan. Although Tokugawa people were separated from one another in terms of their social roles, lifestyles, and fashions, they nonetheless began to share the same cultural idioms, aesthetic activities, and images of Japanese tradition. The aesthetic image of Japan became a central component of the country's self-identity well before the rise of the modern Japanese nation-state.

The experience of a sense of commonality formed through shared aesthetic experiences paved the way for the next phase of Japanese cultural developments in the process of constructing a modern nation-state. It is important to note that the appearance of images of Japan as a country defined by aesthetic excellence was not the result of political initiatives on the part of rulers, but was rather the product of market forces. Although the Tokugawa state's idiosyncratic structure and policies did leave their mark on the course of cultural developments, it was primarily the cultural entrepreneurs of this period who created a variety of new channels of communication and cultural diffusion. The identification of Japan with beauty was promoted and internalized through these new centers and media of communication. The Tokugawa popularization of aesthetic knowledge was primarily driven by market forces rather than top-down enforcement of an ideology.

In addition, the participatory nature of popular artistic activities was a distinctive feature of the Tokugawa civilizing process. People voluntarily networked with one another through the arts. In these networks, they actively participated in sharing, performing, and creating arts. Tokugawa people enjoyed their culture's traditional arts as active performers and participants in their own right; they did not attend cultural events as admirers or patrons of professional artists and musicians. Even though a student was motivated to learn an art only for the purpose of socialization, immersing oneself in the rules, aesthetic standards, and spiritual disposition required by an art through actual performance or production represented a much deeper level of enculturation than simply being a passive spectator of "real" artists. In this context, learning the skills of poetry composition or any other of the performing arts represented a process of embodiment of aesthetic knowledge.

As a consequence of these two distinctive features of the Tokugawa aesthetic popularizing process—its market-driven and participatory characteristics—the notion of a Japanese aesthetic tradition came to feel much more "natural" to the people living under the Tokugawa regime. Thus, Japan reentered the world of global politics in the mid-nineteenth century with a relatively coherent view of its own cultural tradition. Its encounter with the hegemonic power of the Western nations required Japan to reconstruct its ethnic cultural identity in the global political theater, as well as fashion a notion of citizenship and national cultural identity within the framework of its new political constitution. Preexisting images of Japan as an aesthetic nation were quickly exploited in order to shape Japanese cultural identities for the global context as well as domestic needs.

The rise of a new model of civility and the proliferation of social interactional spheres centering on poetry and performing arts during the Tokugawa period lead us to conclude that, prior to Japan's intensive period of Westernization following the Meiji Restoration in 1868, Tokugawa Japan was moving toward its own version of "protomodernity" or "modernity before modernization" in the dimension of cultures of socialization. The Tokugawa culture of socialization had an unmistakably modern flavor in its own way even though the shogunate's political system was premodern. The aesthetic networks of this period were not primordial communal or kinship ties but constructed through the voluntary participation of individuals who joined these circles for private satisfaction. This distinctive pattern of socialization leads to the insight that Japan took an alternative path to modernity that had little in common with the Western model. The form and content of Tokugawa protomodernity were very different from those of Western modernity, whose ideological foundations were laid by Enlightenment rationalism and the methodologies of modern science. The Western form of modernity—linked to the emergence of the image of a "modern" person as an isolated autonomous self—is a unique historical constellation that happened to become the most influential model because of the cumulative advantages conferred by scientific and technological knowledge and the West's domination of global politics. In contrast, Tokugawa protomodernity emphasized a culture of socialization centered on aesthetic practices associated with the performing arts and poetry—a culture that employed intuitive and tacit modes of communication rather than rigorous discursive logic. If we focus only on the reflexive and rational quality of modern life, we cannot grasp the distinctive protomodern quality of Tokugawa social life.

My usage of the term "protomodernity" is influenced by the concept of *proto-industrialization*, used to describe the first phase of European industrialization. Since the 1970s, economic historians have generally used proto-industrialization with reference to "the type of industry—the traditionally organized, principally rural handicrafts—[that] barely fits the image one has of a modernizing economy," in the words of Franklin Mendels.[36] *Industrial revolution* better describes the subsequent second phase of modern machine-based industrialization. Although the phrase "industrial revolution" conveys an image of abrupt discontinuity, the introduction of the factory system in the nineteenth century built upon the earlier proto-industrialization of the European countryside. The evolution of cottage industries in rural Europe not only helped to expand trading and commodities networks but also brought numerous significant changes in "a life experience faced by ordinary people."[37] Following the introduction of the phrase "proto-industrialization" in the European historical literature, Japanese economic historians began to apply it to eighteenth-century Japan.[38] They maintained that the Tokugawa shogunate experienced a similar process of rural industrialization, although tillage rather than herding was the basis of the cottage industries of rural Japan. In the eighteenth century, these industries included the manufacture of cotton and silk textiles, production of dyestuffs and indigenous ceramics, and the brewing of sake.

The phenomena associated with so-called modernization in non-Western societies did not appear suddenly at the beginning of Westernization and globalization. Many non-Western societies had developed indigenous processes of modernization before their incorporation into a world system under the hegemony of the Western imperial powers. Although these various forms of protomodern development were interrupted or profoundly altered during their societies' forced incorporation into the global system, nonetheless these earlier patterns affected the trajectory and timing of the second stage of their modernization. Japan has undergone rapid changes following the Meiji Restoration of 1868. In particular, the fact that the process of nation-building under the Meiji regime was based on the Western model of modern nation-states with strong armies and centralized bureaucracies increased the penetration of central government control into local communities and regional cultural practices. The process of modernization that Natsume Sōseki (1867–1916) called "internally motivated" in his 1911 lecture on "The Civilization of Modern-Day Japan," namely the civilization that developed "naturally from within, as a flower opens"[39] during the Tokugawa period, "was sidetracked." Sōseki observed that Japan had been "painfully" compelled by the external forces of Westernization to take a different and less congenial route to modernity.

Let us not, however, overlook a critical point. Westernization and modernization cannot be described simply as a transition from the "naturalness" of *Gemeinschaft* to the "artificiality" of *Gesellschaft* as such. The Japanese themselves became highly self-conscious about externally coercive forms of civilization because they had already developed a cultural identity predicated on their perceived "traditional" and "natural" civilization and their ways of life. In fact, the culture of Tokugawa Japan was the product of what the historian Ōishi Shinzaburō (b. 1923) has called "the most deliberately and politically created society in Japanese history."[40] It was precisely because Tokugawa Japan had already drawn a clear cognitive map of its own culture—not simply as a "natural" given, but as a construct articulated through such "artificial" means of communication as commercial publications, that such Meiji Japanese as Sōseki could become remarkably self-critical and reflective regarding their "externally forced" pattern of "civilizing."

The construction of Japan as a modern nation-state and the development of industrialization within this new political framework were thus facilitated by the presence of a cognitive framework among post-Tokugawa Japanese people that presupposed the existence of a natural sense of *Gemeinschaft* in Tokugawa Japan. Historians and social scientists have often probed the reasons for the swiftness of Japan's emergence as a modern nation during the Meiji period through the use of imperial symbolism, when the emperor had been virtually deprived of actual political power for centuries. Behind the political accomplishments of the Meiji government, however, there had been a less visible but nonetheless distinguished cultural achievement that allowed Meiji Japanese to regard their cultural identity as a given. This "taken-for-grantedness" allowed the leaders of the Meiji period to explore various options for mobilizing the loyalty of Japanese citizens for the long-term effort of nation-building. The tradition of an aesthetic Japan inherited from the Tokugawa period was not the sole, but certainly an important, dimension of creating an image of Japan that connected the people to their own past in a distinctive way.

Chapter 2

The North(west)ern Peoples and the Recurrent Origins of the "Chinese" State

VICTOR MAIR

Historical, archeological, folkloric, literary, and other types of evidence show clearly that the peoples of the Yellow River Valley (namely, the East Asian Heartland [hereafter, EAH]) have been interacting closely with the peoples to their north, northwest, and west since before the establishment of the first states in the territory of what is now known as China and continuing up to the present time. The frequency, intensity, and duration of this contact are so great that the question of north(west)ern involvement in Chinese state-formation naturally arises. A pattern of the repeated establishment of dominant political entities by (or through the agency of) north(west)ern peoples emerges.[1] In an effort to measure the extent to which north(west)ern peoples were responsible for the foundation and perpetuation of states in the EAH, the ethnic and regional affiliations of ruling houses for the past three thousand and more years are compiled and briefly analyzed. The results of this investigation reveal not only that the north(west)ern peoples were extraordinarily active in the organization of states in the EAH, but that it was these same peoples who were nearly always responsible for the recurrent creation of an Extended East Asian Heartland (EEAH)—when EAH-based governments incorporated large tracts of land south of the Yangzi River, southwest to the Himalayas, west as far as the Pamirs, and north as far as the Altai Mountains, Lake Baikal, and the Amur River. This overwhelming political predominance is all the more remarkable in light of the relatively much lower population densities of the largely pastoral and nomadic north(west)erners vis-à-vis the sedentary Sinitic peoples, and in view of their presumptive lack of civilization.

Preliminaries

Dimidium facti qui coepit habet [He who has begun his task has done half of it].

—Horace, Epistulae, *I.ii.40*

Because I wish to raise a number of fundamental issues concerning the formation, evolution, and conceptualization of "the Chinese state," it is necessary to begin with the definition of basic terms that will be used in this discussion.[2] Furthermore, since the topics addressed are rather sensitive in nature and the conclusions reached may be viewed by some as radical, it is essential that the usages employed be as rigorous and objective as possible. *Faute de mieux,* I shall refer to the main object of our discussion as "China," with the proviso that this usage is a convenient stopgap. Normally, I shall avoid the use of so-called scare quotes, but wish to emphasize that reference to China is merely a temporary expedient, one that this essay ultimately attempts to circumvent. The difficulties surrounding the application of this name to precontemporary political entities have already been recognized and will be further elaborated in the course of the following remarks.[3] Suggestions will also be made for suitable alternatives.

A group of key players in this drama (the origins and development of the Chinese state) are the often overlooked and frequently marginalized "north(west)ern peoples." By "north(west)ern peoples" is meant not only the "non-Chinese" (non-Sinitic) groups living immediately north of the Great Wall, but also those to the northwest and west, since there were no fixed boundaries between them.[4] Furthermore, the north(west)ern peoples were distinguished by a constantly shifting complex of confederations, alliances, and identities, making it nearly impossible to carve up the steppes that they inhabited into neat, discrete parcels of land and nameable groups of occupants.

The gradient of the steppes was such that, before the beginning of the Common Era, the migration of peoples and the transfer of culture generally flowed from west to east, including fairly freely through China all the way to the far south.[5] After the beginning of the Common Era, however, the gradient of the steppes gradually tipped in the other direction and started to flow primarily (but not wholly) from east to west.[6] The causes of this monumental tilt are both subtle and profound; their investigation and explication would require monographic treatment.

The parameters of the present, more limited inquiry are determined by the words "teleology" and "nation-state." The former implies that the object of our study (China) is the outcome of a coherent and essentially uninterrupted evolution from a germinal core, while the latter stipulates that the political body we are examining has—since the era of that supposed germinal core—been autonomous and that it has been inhabited predominantly by a people sharing a common culture, history, and language. The fact that we are focusing on the teleology of the *modern* Chinese nation-state does not preclude our pursuing its origins to a distant past when the nuclear germ of the present entity is presumed to have come into being. *For the purposes of this exercise,* we reject the possibility that the modern Chinese nation-state may have arisen through random, dysteleological processes. This is not to assert, however, that there may in actuality be no controlling, guiding purpose that has resulted in today's China. Indeed, the current configuration of the Chinese state may be no more than the sum of its proximate causes (Confucian ethics, Marxist programs, Christian missionary ideals, Islamic networks, Buddhist reform movements, secret societies, and the like).

It is not merely an assumption that the modern Chinese nation-state possesses a teleological raison d'être. During the past century alone, the explanations proffered for why, after all, there is a China have varied from traditional myths and legends, to modern ideological justifications, to universalizing doctrines, to various combinations thereof. Consequently, there are actually multiple teleologies available to choose from when attempting to explicate how the Chinese nation-state came into being, why it has persisted, and what its destiny is. It should be noted that the teleological narrative of the nation shifts, whether subtly or dramatically, depending upon the predispositions of the political and intellectual powers-that-be.

My purpose in this particular endeavor is slightly different. Instead of trying to determine the precise content of the current (or any previous) teleology of China, I shall intentionally adopt an antiteleological approach. That is to say, I accept the fact that various teleological explanations for the existence of the Chinese state have been put forward, but do not feel obliged to recognize any of them as historically accurate or logically convincing without proof. My antiteleology consists of skeptically scrutinizing the fundamental premises of conventional explanations for the presumed perpetuity of the Chinese nation-state, then starting over from scratch to see it if is possible to discern an alternative rationale that is in conformity with historical reality.

In carrying out this etic (externally analytical and descriptive) operation, several straightforward questions may serve as guideposts. The primary question posed here is simply the following: what are the ultimate origins of the modern Chinese nation-state? Secondarily, we may ask: when did "China" initially come into existence? Has "China" continually existed since the time of its first appearance? If so, what may we identify as the uninterrupted quintessence of the Chinese polity? If not, what were the processes whereby the Chinese state periodically was able to reconstitute itself (assuming that it did)? Among the tertiary questions to be posed are these: at any given moment in history, and in the aggregate of all successive moments in history, has there only been a single, legitimate ruling authority within the territory of what is now China since the founding of the first state there (the Shang or, in the opinion of some, the Xia)? Is it accurate to refer to premodern dynasties as "China?" If so, what are the continuities and commonalities that sanction such a usage?[7] If not, what are the discontinuities that forbid such an application of the name?

Teleological processes can persist only so long as the entity to which they pertain survives. In searching for the origins of the modern Chinese nation-state, we must determine how far back in time the entity we now refer to as "China" may be traced. Was there a rupture in the teleological development of the Chinese nation-state with each change of dynasty? Was there something that transcended the changes of dynasties, a nucleus of the nation-state that neither disintegrated nor was ineradicably altered with the collapse of each old dynasty and the establishment of each new dynasty?[8]

Obviously, it would be impossible to provide exhaustive answers to all of these questions in such compact compass. Instead, the aim of this chapter is, above all, to assemble as much relevant data as possible in hopes that they might suggest further avenues of research leading to eventual solutions to the complex issues at hand.

Initial pursuit of pertinent evidence enables us to present the following hypothesis: the histories of the Chinese state and of the north(west)ern peoples are so intimately interwoven that, were it not for the north(west)ern peoples, there would be no China.

Myth, Scripture, and Archaeology

One may as well preach a respectable mythology as anything else.
—*Mary Augusta Ward*, Robert Elsmere, *chap. 5*

As outlined above, the modern Chinese nation-state possesses multiple teleological raisons d'être. An example of a traditional explanation may be found in attempts to trace the nation-state back through time to its earliest putative political and cultural founders. This is justification by mythology. Except for the most naïve, however, few would any longer be willing to invoke mythology as a credible argument for the supposed millennial depth and continuity of the Chinese nation-state. The work of Gu Jiegang (1893–1980) and his associates in the *Gu shi bian* (Verifying ancient history) project demonstrated that the foundational myths of China were invariably late (and often grossly anachronistic) constructs dating to the Warring States period or the Han.

Another example of a traditional justification for the hoary antiquity of the modern Chinese nation-state was resort to historical, philosophical, ceremonial, and literary texts purporting to date from the Zhou dynasty, Spring and Autumn period, Warring States period, and Han dynasty. As all such texts are subjected to intense critical scrutiny, however, it becomes increasingly clear that they themselves tend to be fraught with contradictions and that many of them are demonstrably the products of centuries-long accretional and redactional processes. The most spirited challenge to taking every word of Han and earlier texts at face value has been mounted by E. Bruce Brooks and A. Taeko Brooks, but they view their own research as essentially following the path of the *Gu shi bian* School and the evidential learning (*kaozheng xue*) of Qing scholars who themselves had been inspired by critical methodologies brought to China by Jesuit missionaries and other Westerners.[9]

Now that texts can no longer be relied on as sacrosanct gospel to validate the view that the modern Chinese nation-state has multimillennial depth, proponents of that claim have enthusiastically turned to another tool, namely, archeology. Archeology has the distinct advantage of employing scientific techniques to investigate the past. Unfortunately, it has recently become obvious that—whether draped with the trappings of science or not—archeology is also subject to manipulation and misinterpretation. Nowhere is this clearer than in the enormous international flap and furor over the attempt of the Chinese government to match the antiquity of Egypt and Mesopotamia with its costly Sandai Project. This started out as a massive effort to combine the three approaches mentioned above (mythology, textual studies, and archeology) to substantiate the Xia Dynasty and to come up with precise dates for the Shang and Western Zhou. The result has been little more than an avalanche of acrimonious accusations and recriminations.[10]

The failure of advocates for a particular teleological purpose to use mythological, textual, and archeological sources critically does not mean that such materials cannot yield fruitful information when appropriately handled. Take textual sources for example. Yu Taishan, the prominent historian, has written a series of studies dealing with the relationship of the EAH to "the Western Regions" (Xiyu, meaning Eastern Central Asia and beyond) in ancient times. His most recent work, entitled *Gu zu xin kao* (A new examination of ancient peoples)—translated into English as *A Hypothesis About the Source of the Sai Tribes*—relies solely on written materials (including oracle bone inscriptions), inasmuch as

Yu's method requires that he adamantly eschew archeological, genetic, and linguistic evidence as being outside the purview of the historian in the strictest sense.[11] Yu's sources are mostly Chinese, but he also refers to Greek and Latin writers. His meticulous readings permit him to show the intricate intertwining of the pastoral-nomadic steppe peoples and the settled peoples in the Yellow River Valley during the second and first millennia B.C.E.

Even myth, which is often dismissed as fiction, half-truth, or worse, may be of value to the historian when skeptically scrutinized and methodically analyzed.[12] For instance, the Han fantasies concerning the Yellow Emperor (Huang Di) are capable of being reassessed as containing a kernel of truth about a stock-breeding ruler having intimate affinities with the chariot-riding peoples of the steppe. Likewise, his *Doppelgänger*, Chiyou (god of weapons who had seventy-two [N.B.] brothers), reflects the close association of the northern peoples with the development of metallurgy in East Asia[13] and with the mysterious roots and unusual characteristics of the Miao (Hmong) people, whose legends claim that they long ago came from somewhere in the northwest and whose physical appearance until the last century would seem to bear them out.[14]

Mythic accounts, textual materials, and excavated data can be fruitfully consulted for the purposes of understanding antiquity, but only when subjected to the most severe evaluation. Their true value and meaning are distorted when they are used to justify a preconceived political or ideological purpose.

What Is in a Name? Nihon/Nip(p)on/Japan Versus Qin/China

When names are not correct, then what one says will not make sense.
—*Confucius*, Analects, *13.3*

The teleologies of the modern Chinese nation-state and the modern Japanese nation-state are quite different in many respects. Not the least of these is that the very notion of a "Japan" is premised on an autonym which is redolent of the aspirations of its people ("Root of the Sun"). By contrast, "China" began as the autonym of a small state in the northwest hinterland approximately three millennia ago and was applied to the EAH around 2,250 years ago, but then became an exonym after the fall of the Qin dynasty in 207 B.C.E., less than two decades after unifying the empire.[15] The Japanese have referred to their state as "Japan" since the accession of Emperor Kōtoku in 645 and the engineering of the Taika reforms in that year. By contrast, until the twentieth century neither the predecessors of the modern Chinese state nor the ancestors of the contemporary Chinese people have had a consistent name that lasted beyond the fall of a given dynasty.

Although the formal title of Republican China was Zhonghua minguo (lit., Republic of the Central [Cultural] Florescence) and the full, formal title of the People's Republic of China is Zhonghua renmin gongheguo (lit., People's Republic of the Central [Cultural] Florescence), both have been commonly known as simply Zhongguo (Central State)—by way of abbreviation—taking the first and last syllables of their full names. From time to time, grandiloquent patriots and misinformed Sinophiles (or Sinophobes, their alter egos) assert that the name Zhongguo implies that China is the centermost state in the world. This, however, is to misinterpret a term that—until the twentieth century—never referred to a specific state occupying the whole of the EAH, much less to the EEAH.[16] Rather, before modern times, Zhongguo served as a vague reference to the Central Plains, the capital, or the imperial court. Had Zhongguo referred to a particular political entity associated with the EAH or the EEAH, the Buddhists would hardly have been so bold or obtuse as to use the same term as a direct translation of the Sanskrit word *Madhyadeśa*, signifying the central portion of the Indus Valley.

The term *huaxia* ("florescent [and] grand") is likewise sometimes invoked as proof of the millennial continuity of the Chinese state. While it has long been employed as an amorphous reference to the Central Plains and the people who lived there, throughout history *huaxia* has never been used as the name of an actual state in the EAH. Rather, it seems to be a conjunct form of two favorite epithets for the people(s) and culture(s) of the EAH. Although the first of its components has—in recent times—been employed in the full, formal names of the two states that have occupied the EAH and EEAH from 1911 to 1949 and from 1949 to the present (see above), *hua* by itself has never served as the title of a major political entity in the EAH. Xia, on the other hand, was allegedly the name of a shadowy dynasty that preceded the Shang, but virtually nothing about it is securely known, certainly nothing that can meet the test of a critical historian.[17]

The epithets *hua* and *xia* as viable state names are further complicated, if not entirely compromised, by the fact that both of them—already reputedly from the time of the Spring and Autumn period (722–481)—occur in parallel collocations that are emphatically plural: *zhuxia* and *zhuhua*, "the various grand [ones]" and "the various florescent [ones]," it being unclear precisely what is being described (peoples? cultures? fiefdoms?). It would seem that the grammatical plurality of *zhuxia* and *zhuhua* rules out the possibility that either *hua* or *xia*, at least from the time of the Warring States (481–221) on, could have been designations for a single, predominant political force in the EAH.

Perhaps more than any other designation, that of "Han" has become preeminently identified with the modern Chinese nation-state: the majority ethnic group is called *Hanzu*, the Sinitic group of languages is denominated as *Hanyu*, the script consists of *Hanzi*, the sinicization of other peoples is styled *Hanhua*, and so forth. Furthermore, Han was a favorite title for ephemeral dynastic pretenders during the Sixteen Kingdoms (317–420) and the Five Dynasties (907–60) periods which, ironically, were more often than not themselves non-Sinitic. Still, the name Han has not been chosen as an official designation of the republic that now occupies the EAH and EEAH.

The overlapping proliferation of terms that apply to the people and the polities of the EAH (Hua, Xia, Han, Tang, Zhongguo, and so forth) by itself would seem to indicate that none of them possesses exclusive legitimacy as the designation of a perduring sovereign state. Rather, all of these terms would seem to function as intermittent titles or epithets for a wide variety of groups that have aspired to political control in the EAH and EEAH.

This excursus on the names of the most recent nation-states located in the EAH indicates that, whether for political or ideological reasons, they have chosen not to employ one of the old dynastic titles, but have instead selected nontraditional titles consisting mostly of calques (*minguo* "republic," *renmin* "people's," *gongheguo* "republic") and the early medieval expression *zhonghua* ("central florescence") which originally signified the culture and people of the Central Plains. While the previous three terms are completely unprecedented in East Asia, the last term is admittedly of considerable vintage and composed of two elements that hearken back to still earlier times. Yet neither of these elements by itself (and certainly not the two together) had ever been used as the formal name of a state that succeeded in dominating the EAH or the EEAH before the twentieth century. In terms of nomenclature, then, during the twentieth and twenty-first centuries, there has been a complete rupture with the past that echoes the cataclysmic institutional and cultural break with tradition that occurred between 1911 and 1919.

If we examine the entire record of the succession of states that have occupied the EAH throughout history, we find that each dynasty—upon coming to power—designated itself by a name that emphasized its difference from the preceding dynasty.[18] Again and again, founders stressed imperial discontinuity rather than continuity. When we look for reiterative patterns, however, the most salient is the initiative taken by north(west)ern peoples in establishing states in the EAH.

Data

> *The rise of Tuoba Gui [371–409, founder of the Northern Wei] led to the hardening of the North-South partition, which in turn led to the eventual absorption of the South by the North. Alas, from the Sui era onward, 60 to 70 percent of those who were prominent in their times have been descendants of the Tuoba [and other Xianbei and Xiongnu groups]!*
>
> —Hu Sanxing (1230–1302), commentary to Sima Guang (1019–86), Zizhi tongjian *(A comprehensive mirror for aid in government), scroll 108*

Perhaps the best way to get a general idea of the degree to which the north(west)ern peoples were responsible for state-formation in the EAH and EEAH is simply to list each of the ruling houses, their ethnic affiliations, and regional affinities, together with the total extent of the states that they founded (see table).

A few words of qualification are in order, however. First of all, it is not always possible to pinpoint the exact ethnicity of a ruling group. The precise origins of a ruler and his closest associates may simply not be known, or they may reflect a more or less complex confederation of clans and tribes. Usually, though, one of these (that of the ruler himself) will be the dominant force in the establishment of a dynasty. The question of ethnicity is further complicated by the fact that many individuals who were key figures in the founding of a given dynasty (both politically and militarily) may have been north(west)erners who took Sinitic surnames themselves, whose recent or distant ancestors from the north(west) may have taken Sinitic surnames, or whose maternal line of descent may have been purely north(west)ern, and so forth. For all these reasons, the ethnic affiliations of the founders listed in the following table undoubtedly appear to be far more Sinitic than they actually were.[19]

Second, the regional affinities of a ruling house may be just as complicated as its ethnic identity. For example, a dynastic founder may have moved to or even been born in Shaanxi but be the descendant of a people who for centuries lived in Mongolia. The regional affinities specified here normally refer to the location of the ruler's ancestral homeland, but occasionally may signify his main power base when that is deemed to be the overwhelmingly more operative element in his gaining the throne. Third, the boundaries of premodern states in East Asia are difficult to map with exactitude. The central authority nearly always claimed more territory than it actually controlled. Furthermore, the borders of states constantly fluctuated as a consequence of local rebellions, incursions, and occupations by neighboring peoples and competing states, and sheer lapses in administrative capability. For the purposes of this study, the maximum extent of a given dynasty is determined by the establishment of functional local magistracies and military districts or regions that were actually garrisoned. Areas that were only under nominal or temporary control are excluded.

Finally, this is a tentative, initial attempt to view the entire sweep of Chinese history in what may be thought of as the terms of political science. It is inevitable that the level of accuracy and documentation will be improved upon in future reassessments of the available material. For all of these reasons, the data presented here yield only a rough approximation of the dynamics between the north(west)ern peoples and the states of the EAH. Still, they are enough to see clearly that the role of the north(west)ern peoples, far from being one of mere peripherality, lurking furtively in the wings to await the opportunity to "trade and raid," ironically moves right into the spotlight of center stage.

Gaps in the chronology may appear during brief interregnums or when the state is so hopelessly fragmented that no central locus of power can be discerned. Consideration of the alleged Xia dynasty is omitted here due to lack of historical evidence for its existence.[20] Because of their insignificance in terms of the overall dynamics of central-state formation, a number of very small splinter-states that appeared for a few years at the end of one dynasty and before consolidation at the beginning of a new dynasty (such as during the Sui-Tang and Yuan-Ming transitions) are not listed. Similarly, numerous rebels who arose in various districts and prefectures from time to time but had no lasting impact beyond their own locales have not been entered in this list, even though they may have declared the establishment of a dynasty of sorts—such as Huang Chao's Great Qi Dynasty (878–84) or the 1120–21 rebellion of the Manichean Fang La, which, though tumultuous and instrumental in weakening the Northern Song, was distant from the affairs of the central government and had no direct effect upon the realignment of domination of the EAH). Countless other tiny, ephemeral contestants for power of various ethnicities that appeared sporadically in different regions of what is now China are also omitted because they were not important factors in politics relating to the EAH or EEAH. Names of modern provinces are given strictly to indicate location. They are listed in order of declining centrality for each dynasty. The primary sources of the data given here are the dynastic histories, historical atlases, and modern historical scholarship.[21]

Both the late Shang and the Western Zhou used characters for writing, albeit in extremely circumscribed and largely formulaic circumstances (oracle bone inscriptions and bronze inscriptions). It is difficult to tell from the extant records precisely what the spoken languages of the Shang and the Zhou were like, and historical linguists disagree over whether they belonged to the same language group:

> We still cannot flatly assert . . . that the spoken languages of the Shang and Zhou peoples were the same or even that they were both forms of Sinitic. What we know is that the chancellery languages of Shang and Zhou were both forms of Sinitic. We do not know in either case what portion of the population as a whole spoke Sinitic. There may have been small Sinitic-speaking aristocracies ruling over non-Sinitic subject populations; or . . . the Shang rulers could have been originally non-Sinitic speakers who had adopted the language of their . . . subjects.[22]

It is worth noting in this context that it was no less than the "Second Sage" of Confucianism, Mencius (371–289 B.C.E.), who declared that King Wen, the revered nominal founder of the Zhou Dynasty, was "a man of the Western Yi" (barbarians) (4B.1).[23] As for the ethnic affinities of the Shang rulers, Han Kangxin and He Chuankun have pointed out that no physical anthropological studies have been done on any human remains from the royal graves at Yinxu, and that this remains a primary desideratum for research on the origins of the Shang.[24] The physical anthropological studies of human remains from Yinxu have by and large been carried out on specimens recovered from sacrificial pits. The individuals whose bodies were interred in such circumstances were most likely either members of the subject population or prisoners of war.

Ruling house	Ethnic affiliations	Regional affiliations	Total extent
*Shang (1570–1045)	unknown, but with steppe associations	north-northwest (Henan, Shanxi, Shaanxi)	NC, N, E
*Zhou (Western) (1045–771)	unknown, but with steppe associations	north-northwest (Shaanxi, Shanxi)	NC, N, NE, E, SC, SE
Spring and Autumn (770–476)	various	various (nine major states, approximately 140 minor states)	NC, N, NE, E, SC, SE
Warring States (475–221)	various	various (seven major states)	NC, N, NE, E, SC, SE
*Qin (221–207)	Sinitic with likely central Eurasian heritage	northwest (Shaanxi)	NC, N, NE, E, SC, SE, SW, S, FS

*Western Han (206 BCE–8 CE)	Sinitic with likely central Eurasian heritage	east (but the name "Han"derives from a river that rises in the northwest [Shaanxi])	NC, N, NE, NW, E, SW, SC, SE, WSW, S, FSWS, FS
Xin (9–24)	Sinitic	north-central(?)	NC, N, NE, NW, E, SW, SC, SE, WSW, S, FSWS, FS
*Eastern Han (25–220)	Sinitic with likely central Eurasian heritage	north-central	NC, N, NW, NE, FNE, E, SW, SC, SE, WSW, S, SWS, FS
Three Kingdoms (220–65)			
Wei (220–65)	Sinitic	east	NC, NE, E
Shu (221–63)	Sinitic (unusual physiognomy)	northeast	SW, WSW
Wu (222–80)	Sinitic	southeast	SC, SE, S, SES, FS, FSE
*Western Jin (265–316)	Sinitic	east	NC (small part), E (part), SC, SE, S, SES, SWS, FS, FSE
Chouchi (296–317)	Di •Yang (originally surnamed Linghu)	northwest	NW
Sixteen Kingdoms (plus Dai, Ran Wei, and Western Yan) (304–439)			
Han, Former Zhao (304–29)	Xiongnu (Hun) •Liu	northwest	NC, E
Cheng Han (304–47)	Ba Di / Bin •Li	southwest	SW, WSW
Former Liang (317–76)	Sinitic	north	NW
Later Zhao (319–51)	Jie •Shi	north	NC, N, NE, E
Dai, Later Wei (338–76)	Tabgatch (Särbi)	north	NC, N
Ran Wei (350–52)	Sinitic	east	E
Former Yan (337–70)	Xianbei (Särbi) Proto-Mongolian	northeast	E, NE
Former Qin (350–94)	Di	north	NC, N, NW, E, SW
Later Qin (384–417)	Qiang •Yao	northwest	NW, NC, SC (part)

Later Yan (384–407)	Xianbei (Särbi)	northeast	N and NC (parts toward east only), NE
Western Yan (384–94)	Xianbei (Särbi)	northeast	N and NC (parts toward east only), NE
Western Qin (385–431)	Xianbei (Särbi)	northwest	NC (western part only)
Later Liang (386–403)	Di •Lü	northwest	W (eastern part only)
Southern Liang (397–414)	Xianbei (Särbi)	northwest	W (eastern part only)
Southern Yan (398–410)	Xianbei (Särbi)	northeast	E
Western Liang (400–21)	Sinitic	northwest	NW
Xia (407–31)	Xiongnu (Hun) •Liu (changed to Helian Bobo)	north	NC, N
Northern Yan (407–36)	Sinitic	northeast	NE
Northern Liang (397–439)	Sinitic founder; Xiongnu (Hun) chancellor for four years then ruler	southeast northwest	NW
Eastern Jin (317–420)	Sinitic	north-central	SC, SE, S, SES, FS, FSE, WSW, SWS

Northern and
Southern Dynasties
(420–589)

Northern Dynasties

Northern Wei (386–534)	Xianbei (Särbi)	north	NC, N, NW, NE, E (part)
Gaochang (460–640)	Tabgatch and various Turkic groups in later stages •Qu	Turfan (Eastern Central Asia)	FFNW
Rouran (464–520)	Asin Abar Tabgatch ancestors	far north	FN, NWN, FNWN, FFNW
Eastern Wei (534–50)	Xianbei (Särbi) ·	north	NE, E
Western Wei (535–57)	Xianbei (Särbi)	north	NC, N, NW
Northern Qi (550–77)	Xianbei (Särbi)	north	NE, E

Northern Zhou (557–81)	Xianbei (Särbi) (or Särbized Sinitic)	north	NC, N, NW, SW, WSW
Southern Dynasties			
Song (420–79)	Sinitic	northeast	SC, E (part), SE, SW, WSW, S, SES, FS, FSE
Qi (479–502)	Sinitic	southeast	SC, SE, SW, WSW, S, SES, FS, FSE
Liang (502–57)	Sinitic	southeast	SC, SE, SW, WSW, S, SES, FS, FSE
Chen (557–89)	Sinitic	southeast	SE, S, SES, FS, FSE
*Sui (581–618)	father most likely Xianbei (Särbi) or Särbized Sinitic of the Yuwen clan; mother Särbi •Yang	north-central and northeast	NC, N (eastern part only), NW, NE, W, SW, SC, SE, WSW, S, SES, FS, FSE
*Tang (618–907)	father most likely Xianbei (Särbi) or Särbized Sinitic; mother Särbi •Li	north-central	NC, N (eastern part only), NW, NE, W, SW, SC, SE, WSW, S, SES, FS, FSE
Zhou (690–704)	Xianbei (Särbi) •Wu (actually Helan)	northwest (Gansu)	NC, N (eastern part only), NW, NE, W, SW, SC, SE, WSW, S, SES, FS, FSE
Bohai (698–925)	Mohe (Tungusic or perhaps [less likely] Amuric) •Li	northeast (Manchuria)	NE, FNE
Nanzhao (748–84) (878–937)	Tibeto-Burman •Zan	far southwest (Yunnan)	SWS
Yan (756–63)	Turko-Sogdian •An (from Parthian name Arsacid)	northeast (Manchuria)	NE
Tubo (Tibet) (815–38)	Tibetan	far southwest (Tibet)	FSW, FFSW, FFW, FW

Five Dynasties and Ten Kingdoms (907–79)

Wu (902–37)	Sinitic	southeast	E (southern part only), SC, S
Later Liang (907–23)	Sinitic	east	NC, NE, E, SC
Wu Yue (907–78)	Sinitic	southeast	SE
Later Tang (923–36)	Shatuo (West Turk) •Li	north-central	NC, N, NE, SC (eastern part only), E
Later Jin (936–46)	Shatuo (West Turk) •Shi	north-central (?)	NC, N, NE, SC (eastern part only), E
Later Han (947–50)	Shatuo (West Turk) •Liu	north-central	NC, N, NE, SC (eastern part only), E
Later Zhou (951–60)	Sinitic	north-central	NC (eastern part only), N, NE, SC (eastern part only), E
Southern Tang (937–75)	Sinitic	southeast	E (southern part only), SC, S
Chu (927–51)	Sinitic	south-central	SC, S
Min (909–45)	Sinitic	southeast	FSE
Southern Han (917–71)	Sinitic	far south	FS
Former Shu (907–25)	Sinitic	south-central	SW, WSW
Later Shu (934–65)	Sinitic	southwest	SW, WSW
Jingnan (Nanping) (924–63)	Sinitic	north-central	SC (southwest quadrant only)
Northern Han (951–79)	Shatuo (West Turk) •Liu	north-central	NC (eastern part only)
Qidan (907–15)	Khitan	northeast	NE
Yutian (912–40)	Khotanese •Li	Khotan (Eastern Central Asia)	FFNW
Eastern Dan (926–36)	Khitan	northeast	NE
Liao (916–1125)	Khitan	northeast	N (northern part only), E, FNE, FN, NWN, FNWN, FFNWN

Dali (938–1254)	Bai(zi) (Tibeto- Burman or Mon- Khmer or Tai) •Duan	far southwest	WSW, FWSW SWS
*Northern Song (960–1127)	Sinitic	northeast	NC, E, SW (eastern part only), SC, SE, WSW (eastern part only), S, SES, FS, FSE
Western Xia (1032–1227)	Tangut •Li, Zhao	northwest	N, NW
Jin (1115–1234)	Jurchen (Tungusic)	northeast	FNE, NE, E, NC
Qi (1130–37)	Sinitic (swearing allegiance to the Jurchens)	north-central	NC
Western Liao (1124–1216)	Khitan	northeast	FFNWN, FFNW, FFW, FW, FNW
Southern Song (1127–1279)	Sinitic	northeast / southeast	SW (eastern part only), SC, SE, S, SES, FS, FSE
Mongolia (1206–71)	Mongol	far north	FN, NWN
*Yuan (1271–1388)	Mongol	north and far north Only the lands of the Empire of the Great Khan. The Mongols' other empires that stretched all the way across Asia and into Russia are not included here.	N, FN, FNE, NWN, NW, NE, FNW, FW, W, NC, E, FFW, FFSW, FSW, SW, SC, SE, WSW, S, SES, SWS, FS, FSE
*Ming (1368–1644)	Sinitic	east	NC, NE, E, NW, SW, SC, SE, WSW, S, SES, SWS, FS, FSE
Later Jin (1616–43)	Manchu (Tungusic)	northeast	NE, FNE
*Qing (1644–1911)	Manchu (Tungusic)	northeast The Manchus pushed the boundaries of the EEAH farther than any other dynasty in history.	NE, FNE, E, N, NC, FN, SC, SE, NWN, FNWN, FFNWN, NW, FNW,

		The Republic of China and the People's Republic of China have lost some of the territories acquired by the Manchus, but have managed to hold on to most of them.	FFNW, W, FW, FFW, FFSW, FSW, SW, WSW, S, SES, FS, FSE, SWS
Southern Ming (1644–62)	Sinitic	far southeast	S, SE, FSE, FS, SW, FSW, FFSW
Taiping Tianguo (1851–64)	Sinitic	far south	SC, SE

————End of the Qin (i.e., **Chin**ese) Imperial Tradition————

*Republic (1911–49)	Sinitic	far south	FFNWN, FN, FNE, FFNW, FNW, NW, N, NE, FFW, FW, W, NC, E, FFSW, FSW, SW, SC, SE, WSW, S, SES, SWS, FS, FSE
*People's Republic (1949–)	Sinitic	south	FFNWN, FN, FNE, FFNW, FNW, NW, N, NE, FFW, FW, W, NC, E, FFSW, FSW, SW, SC, SE, WSW, S, SES, SWS, FS, FSE

---

* unifying dynasty
• founder surname (to show that Sinitic surnames do not always indicate Sinitic ethnicity)
At different times, the Southern Ming regime had capitals in Nanjing (Jiangsu), Shaoxing (Zhejiang), Fuzhou (Fujian), Zhaoqing (Guangdong), Wuzhou (Guangxi), Kunming (Yunnan), and Burma.

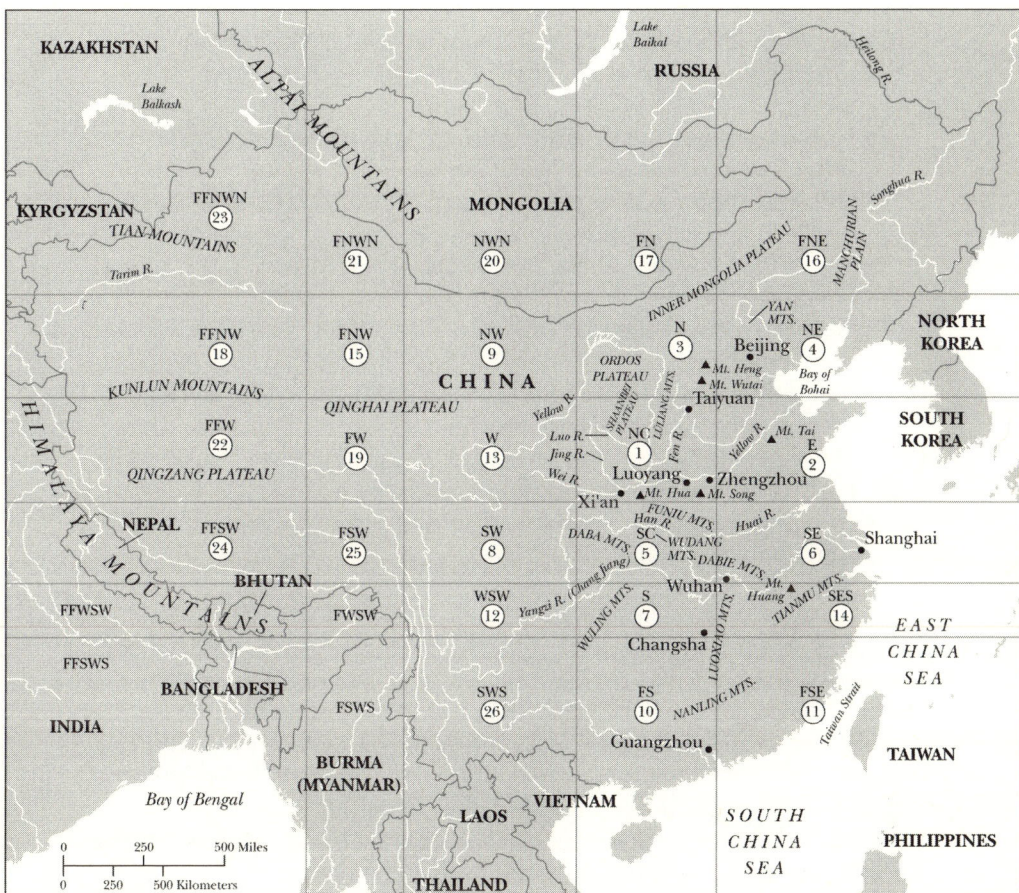

KAZAKHSTAN

Lake Baikal

Lake Balkash

RUSSIA

ALTAI MOUNTAINS

Heilong R.

KYRGYZSTAN

TIAN MOUNTAINS

FFNWN
(23)

MONGOLIA

Songhua R.

Tarim R.

FNWN
(21)

NWN
(20)

FN
(17)

INNER MONGOLIA PLATEAU

FNE
(16)

MANCHURIAN PLAIN

FFNW
(18)

FNW
(15)

NW
(9)

C H I N A

YAN MTS.

N
(3)

Beijing

NE
(4)

NORTH KOREA

ORDOS PLATEAU

LÜLIANG MTS.

▲ Mt. Heng
▲ Mt. Wutai

Taiyuan

Bay of Bohai

KUNLUN MOUNTAINS

QINGHAI PLATEAU

Yellow R.

SHANXI PLATEAU

NC
(14)

SOUTH KOREA

FFW
(22)

FW
(19)

W
(13)

Luo R.
Jing R.

Fen R.

Yellow R.

▲ Mt. Tai

E
(2)

QINGZANG PLATEAU

Wei R.

Luoyang

Zhengzhou

Xi'an

▲ Mt. Hua ▲ Mt. Song

HIMALAYA MOUNTAINS

NEPAL

FFSW
(24)

FSW
(25)

SW
(8)

DABA MTS.

Han R.

FUNIU MTS.

SC
(5)

WUDANG MTS.

DABIE MTS.

Huai R.

SE
(6)

Shanghai

BHUTAN

WULING MTS.

Yangzi R. (Chang Jiang)

Mt. Huang ▲

TIANMU MTS.

SES
(14)

FFWSW

FWSW

WSW
(12)

S
(7)

Wuhan

LUOXIAO MTS.

E A S T
C H I N A
S E A

FFSWS

Changsha

BANGLADESH

FSWS

SWS
(26)

FS
(10)

NANLING MTS.

FSE
(11)

INDIA

Bay of Bengal

Guangzhou

BURMA (MYANMAR)

LAOS

VIETNAM

Taiwan Strait

TAIWAN

0   250   500 Miles

0   250   500 Kilometers

THAILAND

S O U T H
C H I N A
S E A

PHILIPPINES

Map 1.

N = North, S = South, E = East, W = West, C = Central. In addition to these basic directions which may be combined in various ways, "F" signifies "far," hence FN means "far north." Two "F"'s signify greater distance from the core of the heartland, thus FFNW implies a region very far to the northwest.

The sectors of the map are numbered according to the approximate sequence when they became attached to the EAH for the first time. Many of them later detached themselves, and they may have become attached and detached several times in history. The four sectors at the bottom left have never become part of the EAH empire, hence they are not numbered.

Intermezzo

Midway through our investigation, we may present the following summary findings drawn from the above data:

- Most of the unifying dynasties in the EAH were founded by peoples with clear north(west)ern associations.
- Dynasties occupying more than half of the EAH were predominantly linked to north(west)ern peoples.
- The largest expansions of the EEAH occurred under the rule of non-Sinitic peoples.
- Sinitic dynasties following expansive non-Sinitic dynasties invariably lost territories.
- The dynasties having the greatest longevity tended to be ruled by groups with north(west)ern associations.
- Many of the Sinitic dynasties had extremely close ties to their north(west)ern neighbors.
- More dynasties were established in and around the north-central zone than elsewhere.

What overall pattern, if any, has emerged from the data assembled here? The north(west)ern peoples are frequently portrayed as constantly threatening the stability and very existence of the states in the EAH. I would like to suggest that, quite the opposite, it was the north(west)ern peoples who were responsible for the creation of the first states in the EAH. It was also they who, more often than not, were responsible for the building of vast empires in the EEAH.

Given that the north(west)ern peoples played such a vital role in the formation of EAH polities, in the following sections we shall attempt to determine more precisely: who these alien dynasts were; how they acquired and maintained power in the EAH; and what their fate was.

Modus Operandi: Keep Moving and Keep Ruling

> *Having neither cities nor forts, and carrying their dwellings with them wherever they go; accustomed, moreover, one and all of them, to shoot from horseback; and living not by husbandry but on their cattle, their waggons the only houses that they possess, how can they fail of being unconquerable, and unassailable even?*

—*Herodotus*, The Persian Wars, *IV.46*

There is intriguing evidence that the Shang—even in the late period of its rule—was not yet a fully settled state with a fixed capital in a single location.

The king displayed his power by frequent travel, hunting, and inspecting along the pathways of his realm. . . . The *peripatetic nature of the king's role* can be judged from the large number of hunt-plus-place-name divinations that constitute a significant proportion of the total corpus of oracle-bone inscriptions. . . . These divinations remind us that the journeys were not without peril, . . . and that the king's power and safety were frequently exposed to the dangers, political and spiritual, of travel through potentially unfriendly hinterlands.[25]

This is highly reminiscent of the modus operandi of the Scythian kings and other warrior-chieftains of the steppes during the long period from the first millennium B.C.E. through the second millennium C.E.

The itinerant quality of the Shang capital was a theme well known even to the Eastern Han poet and scientist, Zhang Heng (78–139), who wrote near the end of his lengthy "Xi jing fu" (Western metropolis rhapsody):

How can one compare this transfer [from Chang'an] to Luoyang with the Yin
    [i.e., Shang] who were always moving their capital?
In the former period there were eight and in the later period five.
They dwelled at Xiang, were flooded out at Geng.
They never permanently occupied the same land.
Pangeng made a declaration:
He led the people by making them suffer.[26]

The translation (emphasis and explanations mine) is by David Knechtges, who provides the following notes:

These lines allude to the numerous transfers of the capital undertaken by the Shang Dynasty rulers. According to the *Shi ji* [Records of the Scribe-Historian, by Sima Qian, 145–c. 90 B.C.E.], the capital was moved eight times before the Shang founder, Tang, settled in Bo. Identifying the names of all these capitals involves a certain amount of speculation. . . . The *Shi ji* also reports that after Tang officially founded the dynasty until the reign of Pangeng, the Shang capital was moved five more times. Tang moved from Southern Bo to Western Bo. The Emperor Zhongding moved to Ao. Hedanjia occupied Xiang. Zuyi moved to Geng. Pangeng established the Shang capital at Western Bo (which is where Tang seems to have transferred it several stages earlier) . . . .
    Before Pangeng transferred his capital to Western Bo, he made a long speech to his people in which he declared the reasons why a move was necessary. The "Pangeng" chapter in the *Shu jing* (Classic of Documents) purports to be a record of this speech. The line "they never permanently occupied the same land" is derived from a similar line in the "Pangeng" chapter. The people were unwilling to leave their home and Pangeng had to cajole them into following him. Hence, the reference to "leading them by making them suffer."[27]

Let us hear Pangeng speak for himself, at least insofar as he is represented in the *Shang shu*.[28] It does not matter that the textual history of the *Shang shu* is highly vexed and that the version of this particular document which it contains may well date to a thousand or more years after the time of its alleged pronouncement. What matters is that, from the second century B.C.E. on, there was a tradition that the Shang dynasty frequently moved its capital, and that this tradition is corroborated by evidence from the oracle bone inscriptions:

Pan'geng wished to move to Yin, but the people would not go to dwell there. He therefore appealed to all the discontented, and made the following protestations.

He said, "Our king came and fixed on this settlement. He did so from a deep concern for our people, and not because he would have them all die, where they cannot now help each other to preserve their lives. I have examined the matter by divination and obtained the reply: 'This is no place for us.' When the former kings had any business, they reverently obeyed the commands of Heaven. In a case like this especially *they did not indulge a constant repose—they did not abide ever in the same city.* Up to this time, the capital has been in five regions. If we do not now follow the practice of the ancients, we shall be refusing to acknowledge that Heaven is making an end of our mandate here. How little can it be said of us that we are following the meritorious course of the former kings! As from the stump of a felled tree there are sprouts and shoots, Heaven will perpetuate its decree in our favor in this new city. The great possession of the former kings will be continued and renewed. Tranquillity will be secured to the four quarters [of the domain]."

Whether Pangeng and the other Shang rulers were moving greater or lesser distances is moot (archeologists and historians are still uncertain of exactly where the places named in the various documents were located). What matters is that the available evidence indicates a strong desire on the part of the Shang rulers to keep changing the site of the capital on a regular basis.

Normally, it goes against the grain of steppe peoples to establish a permanent city for their government headquarters. The Scythians, for example, bragged about having no capital except the burial place of their ancestors. When, in 1220, Chinggis Khan (1167–1227) established his capital at Karakorum on the upper Orhon Gol (river) in north-central Mongolia, he was undoubtedly planning to use it as a base of operations for his invasion of the EAH. Once that was successfully completed, the capital was moved to Khanbaliq (Beijing) by Khubilai Khan (1214–94) in 1267. Most of the later khanates were associated with capitals as well: the Golden Horde established one at Sarai on the lower Volga within a generation after they consolidated themselves in power over the sedentary kingdoms in the region. They probably did this to facilitate the gathering of tribute. Sarai, it is said, "sprung up around one of Batu's usual camps,"[29] and existed from 1253 to 1395, when it was destroyed by Timur (Tamerlane < Modern Turkish Timurlenk < Persian Tîmûr-i Lang ["Timur the Lame"]; cf. Turkic Aqsaq Temür ["Timur the Lame"], 1336–1405). The latter, a Turkicized Mongol of the Barlas tribe who was both an exceptionally ruthless and enormously successful conqueror, never took up a permanent abode.

He personally led his almost constantly campaigning forces, enduring extremes of desert heat and lacerating cold. When not campaigning he moved with his army according to season and grazing facilities. His court traveled with him, including his household of one or more of his nine wives and concubines. He strove to make his capital, Samarkand, the most splendid city in Asia, but when he visited it he stayed only a few days and then moved back to the pavilions of his encampment in the plains beyond the city.[30]

In 1404, Timur made vast preparations for an expedition against China. He set out at the end of December, but succumbed to illness at Otrar on the Syr-darya west of Chimkent, where he had assembled a huge army. Tamerlane died in February 1405, at the age of sixty-nine. Had he lived another year or two, he would undoubtedly have reestablished Turko-Mongol Islamic rule over the EAH, and the history of the world would have been very different indeed.

There was no reason for nomads to have a permanent capital unless they became overlords of a nearby farming kingdom and had no other efficient way to gather tribute. Capitals were useful to establish a place for negotiations and for meeting ambassadors, but only when the nomadic group was so prosperous that it required such a place in order to extract maximum benefits. Given the cost of grain transport in Shang times, it would probably have been cheaper for the king and his court to go to the grain, rather than have the grain come to the king and his court. Some grain inflow would have been needed to feed the labor force in the bronze casting and other workshops, which would not have been nearly so movable as the king and his court.

The Mongols and the Manchus maintained the symbolism and the actuality of the royal hunt,[31] including camping in tents, long after they were installed on the throne of China. They and their advisers seem to have realized that the ability to organize and carry out such large-scale operations of armed men, ranging over tremendous expanses of territory, was both a source of strength and an assertion of their dynamic power to control.[32]

Equally as remarkable as the mobile quality of the Shang court[33] was the nature of the Shang polity:

If, as the inscriptions suggest, the state was in origin an *alliance of independent groups* whose tutelary spirits were incorporated into the genealogy and ritual structure of the court as their leaders joined the Shang *federation* . . . , then the king in his travels would have moved through a landscape pregnant with symbolic meaning, sacrificing to the local spirits, giving and receiving power at each holy place, and thus renewing the religious and kin ties (fictive or not) that bound the state together. And the king, as he traveled, would have been a force for cultural as well as political unification, impressing the local populations with his language, his writing system, his sumptuary displays, his weaponry, his tastes, and his beliefs.[34]

Except for the mention of writing, this description could just as well be applied to the Scythian and other steppe rulers. And even the specific nature of Shang writing, which had as its sole verifiable purpose the recording of divination on animal bones (primarily bovine scapulae), resonates with the tremendous attention given to divination by the steppe peoples.[35] It is no accident that herding peoples would notice (and interpret) the patterns of cracks in animal bones thrown on their campfires. Nothing could be more natural than for pastoralists to have developed scapulimancy. Conversely, nothing could be less likely than for settled agriculturalists (namely, non-herders) to have done so. Equally worthy of note is the fact that the Scythians and other Iranian groups, as well as their Indo-European kin, the early Celts and Germans, were deeply devoted to divination with bundles of sticks, which immediately calls to mind the achilleomancy of the Zhou people.[36]

From the above survey, it would appear that the first historically attestable EAH dynasty, the Shang, possessed remarkable congruities with peoples of the steppes.[37] As hard evidence of the north(west)ern background of Shang royalty, we may mention the famous "bow-shaped object," one of the most enigmatic artifacts in all of EAH archeology. It has clear linkages to the north(west)ern peoples, stretching all the way to the Minusinsk Basin. The structure of the device itself, as well as its position in burials and on anthropomorphic stelae, indicate that it was most likely a reins holder that would be strapped around the charioteer's waist, freeing up his hands so that he could wield a weapon and still maintain limited control over his team of horses. Six of these devices were found in Fu Hao's tomb alone, three with horsehead terminals. In fact, so much military equipment was found in her tomb that some scholars have suspected "she" was actually a "he." But Fu Hao was really a woman, and there are oracle bone inscriptions that can be used to prove it. She was a consort of the Shang king Wu Ding. (It should be noted that women, including queens, were often warriors among early steppe peoples.) Her tomb is relatively small, but it is the sole unlooted Shang tomb ever discovered and hence gives an overwhelming impression of tremendous wealth. One can only imagine what treasures must once have been placed in the tombs of the Shang kings themselves. Many of the items found in Fu Hao's tomb, such as distinctively-shaped bronze knives, indicate strong ties to the north(west). Buried with Fu Hao were over 3,500 pounds of bronze utensils, the *sine qua non* of aristocratic greatness during the Shang and Zhou periods. There were also approximately 7,000 cowries, another sign of tremendous wealth indicating long-distance trade.[38] Equally impressive were the 755 jades, the largest such assemblage ever unearthed. Chinese archeologists have remarked that much, if not all, of the jade in Fu Hao's tomb must have come from Eastern Central Asia.[39]

Fu Hao's tomb did not include a chariot burial, but the deposition of six reins holders alongside her body was surely meant to evoke this technologically advanced form of transport. Many of the Shang and Zhou royal tombs did include sumptuous chariot burials, and often involved the sacrifice of sizable numbers of horses, a clear sign of steppe affiliations. So intimately linked was the chariot with images (and actualities) of supreme authority in Shang times that the word *yù* for "drive (a chariot)" also came to signify royal control and ultimately could be applied to anything associated with an emperor (e.g., *yùbǐ* ["the emperor's brush/handwriting"]).[40] Thus the idea of *yù* is aptly rendered in Latin as *auriga* ("charioteer").

Chariots in Shang China employed the same basic technologies (namely, heat-bending, gluing, and joining) as used in the West and also showed striking similarities in details of construction and related horse-gear: nave, nave hoop, axle sleeve, axle block, linch pin, pole-end block, pole saddle, curved yoke, yoke saddle, cheekpiece, bits, whip stock, D-shaped floors of plaited leather, and the like.[41] The chariot in the EAH and the chariot in western Eurasia during the late Bronze Age were two manifestations of the same complex invention, just as were the automobile in China and the West during the twentieth century. The technology in either case is so complicated in details both large and small that it is impossible that these vehicular inventions could have arisen independently and spontaneously in China and in the West. The chronological sequence of archeological finds makes certain that the path of transmission was across the steppes from the west to the east.[42]

Physical Realia: Full Beards and Long Noses—Tropes of the Imperial Visage

> *One may say that the beard of the* hu *(person from the [north]west) is red, but one may also speak of there being a red-bearded* hu.
> —*Zen* kōan

Just as the Shang occupies an extremely important place at the beginning of the evolution of states in the EAH, so does the Han stand at a crucial position in the development of the imperial and bureaucratic traditions of empires in the EEAH. Indeed, the majority group in China still call themselves *Hanren* ("Han people") and, as we have seen, their language[s] *Hanyu* ("Han language[s]"). Given the foundational importance of the Han dynasty for the mainstream ethno-political tradition of succeeding periods, it is worth noting of its founder, Gaozu (247–195, r. 206–195), that he "had a prominent nose (*long zhun*) and a dragon-like face [or forehead], with beautiful hair on his chin and cheeks. On his left thigh were seventy-two black moles." This striking passage occurs both in the *Shi ji* and in the *Han shu* (History of the Han).[43]

Inasmuch as China's first two respected historians, Sima Qian and Ban Gu (32–92), both matter-of-factly observed that Gaozu possessed a long nose and full beard, and since they were both writing not long after the time of Gaozu, we have little reason to doubt that the founding emperor of the Han dynasty actually possessed these distinctive physical features. Moreover, Wang Chong (27–90?) quoted this passage about Gaozu in his chapter on "Anthroposcopy" or "Physiognomy."[44] Although Wang Chong was the most rational and skeptical of early EAH thinkers, he believed that external physical features actually did reveal much about an individual's character and talents.

It is highly unlikely that Gaozu could have had these distinctive physical features unless he had the blood of the steppe peoples running in his veins. When anyone is described in Sinitic texts as having a great deal of facial hair, it is virtually certain that there must have been persons from the far northwest or west among his ancestors.

We should not feel obliged to take literally the number of moles Gaozu is said to have borne on his left thigh. Nonetheless, the number alleged is worth noting for another reason: 72 is an auspicious zodiacal (base-12) number throughout Eurasia. Mathematically, 72 is one-fifth of 360 (the number of degrees in a circle and roughly the number of days in a year). The ancients also recognized that the vernal point advances by one degree of the zodiac every 72 years. From these mathematical and calendrical usages, the number 72 came to be applied to all manner of auspicious phenomena: the standard number of drillings in the plastrons of turtles used for divination (according to Zhuang Zi [355?-275]), the number of villainous rulers (*Zhuang Zi*, chapter 14), the number of noble houses of antiquity who performed the Feng sacrifice at Mt. Tai and the Shen sacrifice at Liangfu (both numinous sites in Shandong),[45] the life-span of Confucius, the number of Confucius's disciples (variant 70), the number of disciples Jesus sent out into the world (one for each name of Yahweh) to preach the gospel in the 72 languages of the world, the length of years Lao Zi remained in his mother's womb (variant 81), the number of Daoist immortals, the number of companions who accompanied the Yellow Emperor's apotheosis, the height of the mythical emperor Yao in inches and the number of years that he ruled, the number of scholars it took to translate the Old Testament into Greek in the time of the Egyptian king Ptolemy II (variant 70, hence *Septuāgintā*, "of the seventy"), the number of bells on the priest's breastplate according to Christian exegetes of Exodus 28.17–21, the number of Adam's children (36 pairs of twins), the number of diseases mentioned by Mohammed, the number of companions who died of thirst together with Imam Hussein (626–80), a favorite number in the *Arabian Nights*, the number of different transformational powers of the monkey-king in the famous sixteenth-century Chinese novel titled *Xiyou ji* (Journey to the West), the number of hero-bandits in another Chinese novel from about the same time entitled *Shuihu zhuan* (Water margin), the number of Turkic heroes (variant 70), the number of divisions in the rebel army of Li Zicheng (1605–45) at the end of the Ming Dynasty, the number of baleful stars in Daoist religion, the number of blessed lands in Daoist religion, the number of heavenly lords in Daoist religion, the number of auspicious physical characteristics of a "perfected" (*zhen*) adept in Daoist religion, the number of devas (heavenly beings) according to Buddhist teachings, the age at which the Buddha preached the *Lotus Sutra*, the types of proper deportment observed by a Buddhist novice, the number of auspicious syllables uttered by Brahmā to save the world, the number of bishops among the Manichean Cathars, the number of fake tombs constructed by the military dictator Cao Cao (155–220) to prevent his real tomb from being looted, the number of Saddam Hussein's palaces (to prevent the discovery of his location), the number of guilds in the city of Ghent according to the Treaty of Gavre (July 24, 1453), the traditional number of guilds or occupations (*hang*) in China, the number of five-day periods (*hou*) in a year, and (rather astonishingly) the number of martyrs of the 1911 Revolution that brought an end to more than two millennia of imperial rule in the EAH. The list could be extended indefinitely; its spatial and temporal randomness conveys the degree to which seventy-twoness resonates throughout Eurasia and joins it into an integral sphere of cultural interaction. Thus, the number of moles alleged to be on Gaozu's left thigh actually reveals that the EAH was very much a part of the Eurasian ecumene.[46]

Gaozu was not the only Han ruler who sported a bushy beard and prominent proboscis. According to his biography in the *History of the Later Han* by Fan Ye (398–445), Guangwudi (6 B.C.E.–57 C.E., r. 25–57), an orphan who was raised by his uncle and the founder of the Eastern or Later Han Dynasty, was unusually tall for his time (he was just under 5 feet 8 inches in height) and "had a beautiful beard and eyebrows, a large mouth, and a prominent nose (*long zhun*)."[47]

Because both Gaozu and Guangwudi were said to have *long zhun*, it behooves us to say a few words about what exactly this unusual term signifies. Alone, *long* (pronounced *loong*) means "lofty, eminent." As this attribute pertains to noses, it indicates that they are "high," that is, "long." The next term, *zhun*, is more difficult to deal with. Basically it means "instrument for determining levelness" and, by extension, "a rule, standard." It is also used in expressions that have to do with accuracy and straightness (such as *zhunsheng* ["a carpenter's marking or plumb line"]). Its application to nasal shapes must derive from this connotation. Thus, to say that somebody had a *long zhun* probably meant that his or her nose was both big and straight. Gaozu was so closely identified with his big, straight nose that in later literature he came to be known as Long Zhun ("Big Nose") or Long Zhun Gong ("Long Nose Lord").

It could hardly be a coincidence that the founders of both Han dynasties are described as having full beards and large noses. When we read in Sima Zhen's eighth-century *Suoyin* commentary to the *Records of the Scribe-Historian* that their predecessor, the First Emperor of the Qin (259–210, r. 247–210), himself had "wasp's eyes and a long nose" (*chang zhun*), this would seem to confirm the suspicions of those who hold that the ancestors of the Qin were themselves non-Sinitic north(west)erners or closely intermarried with them.[48] Fortunately, we can look forward to the excavation of his massive tumulus outside Xi'an for confirmation from his remains.

Whatever the exact physical appearance the First Emperor of Qin may have been, there can be no doubt that facial hair was an important attribute among Qin males generally. According to Qin law, having the beard shaved off was one of the most common forms of punishment. A special term (*nai*) was used to designate this type of punishment, and it frequently occurred in the expression *nai wei li chen* ("to have the beard shaved off and to be made a bond servant").[49] More serious crimes called for various types of corporal mutilation. In other words, shaving off the beard was tantamount to physical deformation of the normal male body.[50] The Qin laws cited here were preserved in a large collection of statutes and legal manuals that was discovered in 1975 near the town of Shuihudi in Hubei Province. These manuscripts date to the mid-third century B.C.E. and are the oldest legal texts ever discovered in China. Of course, a beard that is shaved off can always grow back, but it takes a certain amount of time for that to happen, especially where a full beard is concerned. Thus, the shame that derived from an adult male's being forced to go beardless even for a period of a month or two must have been quite serious. Still more serious was to have one's beard and eyebrows completely pulled out. Not only would this have been extremely painful in and of itself, chances are that someone subjected to this punishment would never again have a full complement of facial hair. In any event, it is clear from the Qin laws that the majority of the male population must have sported beards and, furthermore, that the absence of a beard was a sign of extreme unrespectability. Also pertinent is a passage from the biography of Lü Buwei (d. 238 B.C.E.) in the *Records of the Scribe-Historian* where the lover of the Queen Dowager, Lao Ai, is made to have his beard plucked out as part of a sham castration so that he could continue his affair with her in private.[51]

Worth Dying For: Shades of Tsar Nicholas II (1868–1918)

> *If you want to understand a matter, it's like standing in front of an old mirror; when a* hu *[person from the (north)west] comes before it, then a* hu *appears in it, but when a* han *[person from the East Asian Heartland] comes before it, then a* han *appears in it.*
>
> —Chuan deng lu *(Record of the transmission of the lamp)*, 18

Having a long nose and possessing abundant facial hair were a mixed blessing in the EAH. On the one hand, when the times were propitious they could make you emperor. On the other hand, at the wrong moment they were enough to get you killed. When, in the middle of the fourth century C.E., Ran Min made himself lord of Zhao in northern Henan, which had formerly been ruled by Xiongnu (Hunnish) Jie, he ordered the extermination of all Jie.[52] In and around the city of Ye, more than two hundred thousand were slain.[53] But how could the forces of Ran Min tell for sure who were Jie and who not? Simple: kill everyone with "high noses and heavy beards (*gao bi duo xu*)."[54] In other words, they slaughtered everyone who had the physical characteristics of the First Emperor of Qin, the founding emperor of the Western Han, and the founding emperor of the Eastern Han.

Such calculated murders of individuals with long noses and abundant facial hair were not uncommon in the history of the EAH. They reflect a swaying balance of power along a shifting cline across which competing ethnic groups faced each other.

This is in complete contrast to the Taliban, who required men to wear full beards and would punish (or even kill) those who were unwilling or unable to do so. This rabidly pro-beard attitude was by no means the invention of the Taliban, for many Central Asian peoples during the past two millennia and more required all adult males to sport a face full of whiskers. This was both a sign of manliness and warriorlike qualities and a marker of ethnic identity.[55] Unfortunately, no matter how badly one may wish to grow a full beard, if one is not genetically programmed in that direction, it will not happen. The noble warrior at Pazyryk in the Altai who was entombed sometime around 300–250 wearing a false beard must have been prey to such a dilemma.[56]

Among the Jews, Turks, Persians and many other peoples, the beard has long been a sign of manly dignity, and to cut it off willfully is a deadly insult. Muslims swore by the beard of the Prophet and to swear by one's beard was an assurance of good faith. To pluck or touch a man's beard was an extreme affront, hence "to beard" is to oppose boldly or impertinently.[57]

Until about the Han period, the Yellow River Valley was a zone where people with beards and long noses were noticeable but not discriminated against. On the contrary, having such physical characteristics would appear to have been advantageous for those who had aspirations to rule. Spatially, the farther north and west one went, the greater the number of individuals having these attributes there were. Conversely, the farther south and east one went, the fewer the number of individuals with beards and long noses were to be found. Temporally, from the end of the Han onward, the number of bearded, long-nosed individuals in the EAH dramatically declined, until—by the Tang and Song periods—such physical features were clear indicators of derivation from the Western Regions. The *huzi* ("foreigner from the West") was equated with the *huzi* ("bearded person"). Originally the two words were written identically, but later (Yuan or after) radical 190 (*biao*, "hair on the head") was added to the *hu* syllable of the latter term to distinguish it from the former.[58]

In the arena of contact between the EAH and the steppes, full beards, prominent noses, and deepset eyes were manifestly markers of ethnic identity. (To avoid making the matter unnecessarily complicated, the question of light eye, skin, and hair color—although relevant—will not be taken into account here.) These were not typical features of persons of East Asian and Southeast Asian descent. Whenever we encounter such physical characteristics (full, heavy beard, large nose, and deepset, round eyes lacking an epicanthal fold) among individuals from East Asia and Southeast Asia, it is likely that they possess—to greater or lesser degrees—genetic affinity with peoples to the west. This is especially the case with individuals possessing full, curly beards or all three of these traits.

Individuals with these physical characteristics would have seemed quite outlandish to those from communities where they were totally absent. Indeed, the sudden appearance of persons with *hu* traits in secluded villages of the EEAH, where they have never been encountered before, can still cause a tremendous commotion today.[59] More than anything, it was the beards of the Hu that most fascinated Sinitic commentators. These were thick, curly, and seeming—to EAH observers—to turn upward above the cheeks (this characteristic is stressed in some Tang pottery figurines and exaggerated to the point of caricature in many later paintings and drawings), not straight and wispy strands hanging down only from the sides of the mouth and the bottom of the chin.

Sinitic authors were obsessed with the unusual physical appearance of the north(west)ern peoples. Among the characteristics they repeatedly singled out were the following: deepset, round eyes (sometimes described as blue, green, blue-green, or hazel); high (that is, long), straight noses; long, flowing locks of hair (often described as red, yellow, or light brown); full, thick, curly beards and abundant bodily hair; and tall stature and pronounced musculature (namely, having a strong, powerful build). These physical traits of people impinging upon the EAH from the north(west) caught the attention of Sinitic observers from the Han through the Tang and on to the end of the imperial historical period. The Sinitic observers tend to state that "all" (*jie, jun*, etc.) the people of such-and-such a place possess these characteristics.[60] Furthermore, the abundant historical and anecdotal records describing the physical appearance of the north(west)ern peoples have now been corroborated by the investigations of physical anthropologists studying the human remains of Bronze Age, Iron Age, and the historical period from areas to the northwest and west of the EAH.[61] Finally, this complex of traits is exceedingly complicated and highly marked. The presence of even one of these traits is easily noticed, but it is particularly significant that they usually occur together, not singly.

Since such comments by a wide variety of Sinitic authors pertaining to the physical features of peoples of the north(west) (particularly those of the so-called Western Regions [Xiyu]) are numerous and consistent over a period of more than a thousand years (Han-Tang and beyond), one cannot lightly dismiss them as idle or meaningless. Sinitic observers felt that there were significant physical characteristics that distinguished the peoples to the north(west) from themselves and used the blanket appellation "Hu" to refer to such peoples. Wang Guowei (1877–1927) provides evidence which shows that the physical appearance of the Western Hu was strikingly different from that of other peoples, and that the main difference lay in their deepset eyes, long noses, and abundant facial hair (particularly the first and the last of these three traits). So distinctive were these features thought to be of the Hu, Wang Guowei goes on to say, that—ever since the Sui and the Tang periods—even those individuals who were not really Hu (that is, had not really come from the northwest) but possessed such physical features were also called Hu. It is clear that many Hu persons (whether actually from the northwest or not) were mixed among the inhabitants of the EAH and that they were easily distinguished from the rest of the population by their full beards, long noses, and deepset eyes. Wang Guowei cites sources from the Six Dynasties and Tang which show that such individuals were called *hu* or *huzi*. Through the Six Dynasties, *huzi* referred to bearded individuals of northwestern extraction, but by the Tang even EAHers who had full beards (and long noses or deepset eyes) were being called *huzi*. Thus, these physical features, which during the Six Dynasties—and particularly during the Han and before—were clearly identified by EAH writers with persons of northwestern extraction, from Tang and later times (including colloquially right up to the present day) could also apply to individuals from anywhere in the EAH or the EEAH who possessed similar features. In other words, even though such distinctive physical features from the northwest had—over the course of two thousand and more years—gradually and partially been absorbed by a portion of the indigenous population of the EAH and the EEAH, they were still associated with an alien (non-EAH, northwestern, "barbarian") heritage.

Many heroes in Sinitic literature were noted for their full beards and large stature, and later writers would sometimes jokingly call them "Hu." In *Sanguo zhi yanyi* (Romance of the Three Kingdoms), Zhang Fei is said to be "eight *chi*" (about 6'4" according to Three Kingdoms era measurements) and graced with a bushy "tiger's beard." At "nine *chi*" (7'1" by Three Kingdoms' standards), Guan Yu is even taller and described as having a beautiful, long beard. In *Shuihu zhuan*, Li Kui is modeled upon Zhang Fei, and Lin Chong, another hero in the same novel, is also patterned after him.

Even as late as the Jin period (265–420), descendants of the Xiongnu (Huns) were often reported as having similar features (deepset and round eyes, long noses, and full beards). After the Han period, the strength of the Xiongnu faded and they were replaced by the Xianbei (Särbi) as the leading power in the north(west). Although these physical features were less pronounced among the Särbi than they were among those of other north(west)ern groups who had preceded them, the Särbi were still basically *hu* people and referred to as such by the inhabitants of the EAH, over whom they established a succession of dynasties.

Middle Age Maneuvers

> *The Tang dynasty originated from the Barbarians.*
> —Zhu Xi (1130–1200), Zhu Zi yulei *(Classified conversations of Master Zhu), scroll 136*

The early medieval period (from the latter part of the Eastern Han to the Sui dynasty), when the EAH appears to have been hopelessly divided and even chaotic (Three Kingdoms, Sixteen Kingdoms, Northern and Southern Dynasties), was a vital prelude to the formation of the modern Chinese nation-state. However, it was precisely during this period that fundamental cultural (literary, artistic, religious, intellectual, linguistic), political, institutional, and economic patterns and practices were established that were prevalent in the EAH and EEAH right up to the end of the imperial system in the early twentieth century. The jockeying for power among a series of non-Sinitic rulers in the north(west)—culminating in reunification by the Sui and Tang who were closely related to the north(west)ern peoples—may be seen as an extended effort to put Humpty Dumpty back together again after he had crashed at the end of the Eastern Han. The notion of *wu hu luan hua* ("the Five Barbarians disrupting the Florescent [Land]") needs to be rethought. In many respects, it bears resemblance to that other best-known time of division, the Warring States period, which was the most vibrant period in Chinese intellectual history. As we have seen above, the Shang period—when the first historically verifiable state was established in the EAH—seems to have witnessed a constant series of campaigns by a still semi-nomadic power against regional forces (the various *fang*). One and a half millennia later, similar conflicts were still occurring in the same arena. The north-central zone is both the birthplace of EAH civilization and the place where the most wars have been fought for control over the EAH. This is the contested core of East Asia.

Scholars universally recognize that there has been a monumental and prolonged series of interactions between the settled peoples of the EAH and their north(west)ern neighbors. There is, however, sharp disagreement over how to interpret the nature of the relationship between these two large groups. The prevailing view is that of Sinicization, according to which the civilized inhabitants of the EAH assimilate the uncouth invaders from the north.[62] In its most extreme and virulent form, the doctrine of Sinicization holds that the peoples of the EAH absorbed the north(west)ern peoples and their cultures so thoroughly that they essentially annihilated them.

Since it was the north(west)erners who were the generally predominant political and military force in the EAH arena of conflict from at least the middle of the second millennium B.C.E. to the end of the second millennium C.E., such a simplistic, sinocentric outlook is patently false. There can be no doubt whatsoever that the north(west)erners, who repeatedly imposed their political and military will on the EAH, had an enormous social and cultural impact on their subjects. At the same time as they were establishing the first and many later polities in the EAH, the north(west)erners brought basic technologies and fundamental concepts with them. Even the question of the emergence and evolution of Sinitic languages needs to be reexamined carefully and thoroughly for evidence of fundamental influences from the north(west).[63]

Iranian and other Indo-European peoples were moving across Asia already by the third millennium B.C.E. There is good evidence for the presence of Iranian magi at the Western Zhou court, and it is likely that they were active during the Shang period as well.[64] Iranian peoples continued to play a major role in Eurasian history during the second half of the first millennium B.C.E. with the Scythians / Saka / Sai (*$s\partial k$) ranging all the way from the Crimea across the steppes and down to the south of what is now China.[65] The linguistic identity of the Xiongnu (Huns) and the Särbi is contested, but during the second half of the first millennium C.E., Proto-Turks and Turks began to make their presence felt, and during the second millennium C.E., other Altaic peoples—notably the Tungus and the Mongols—became the dominant players impinging upon China from the north.

The notion of an interaction sphere between the north(west)ern peoples and the inhabitants of the Yellow River Valley has been a common theme in analyses of East Asian history. Among the many scholars who have made important contributions to the debate on this subject are Owen Lattimore, Yü Ying-shih, Claudius C. Müller, Helwig Schmidt-Glintzer, Klaus Tietze, S. A. M. Adshead, Thomas Barfield, Sechin Jagchid and Van Jay Symons, Jenny F. So and Emma C. Bunker, and Nicola Di Cosmo.[66] While they have stressed different aspects of the relationships between the peoples of the EAH and their north(west)ern neighbors (no one doubts that trade, cultural exchange, intermarriage, and various forms of diplomatic dealing took place among them), a basic assumption respected by all is that the autochtonous denizens of the EAH were the superior organizing and governing force in the region. Perhaps it is time to question this model and to posit the unthinkable: that it was the north(west)erners and their heirs who, after migrating south, were responsible for most of the major polities in the EAH. The ability of non-Sinitic peoples to conquer and control all or part of the EAH and EEAH for long periods of time is a demonstrable fact of history. The dominance of the north(west)erners in East Asia was certainly not due to superior numbers, for they were always but a tiny minority compared to the settled, subject population.[67] What is necessary is a thorough examination of the dynamics of power within the confederations of the north(west)erners themselves and a careful analysis of the mechanisms whereby these principles of control were imposed upon the inhabitants of the EAH.

Omphalic Ordos: The Ever-Shifting Center of Power

> The Yellow River [is the source of] countless disasters; only its Great Bend [brings] blessings.
>
> —popular saying

In his magisterial study entitled *Felt Tents and Pavilions*, Peter Alford Andrews has documented the Eurasian nomadic tradition of the princely tent as locus of authority.[68] To comprehend the apparent contradiction between the maintenance of a central power and the innate nomadic urge to wander, we may focus on the *ordo/ordu* and the like as symbol of the portability of government. This was the guarded residence of the *qan/qaghan* where he normally resided.

The *ordo* is mentioned already several times in Han sources (the chapters on the Xiongnu [Huns] in the *Shi ji* and *Han shu*) in the transcription *outuo* (the individual characters used to write the word mean "earthenware bowl" and "shed"). The earliest Chinese commentators describe the *outuo*, probably partly mistakenly and under the semantic influence or interference of the characters used to transcribe the word, as earthen houses or subterranean caves. A bit closer to the mark is the somewhat later explanation that the *outuo* were frontier observation posts or border patrols. The impression one gains from reading all of the Han references to *outuo*, however, is that they were well-organized garrisons. Indeed, they seem to have been armed camps "of considerable size and great political significance" that functioned as the center of the Xiongnu state.[69] Eventually the word was adopted into other Central Asian and Inner Asian languages (Turkic, Khitan, Mongolian, and so forth). Persian appears to have adopted the word from Turkic, and from Persian it passed to Urdu.[70] Indeed, the word Urdu is but a variant of *ordo* and means quite literally "the language of the camp." By another channel, *ordu* reached English, via Northwest Turkic *ordï* ("residence, court") and Polish *horda*, as "horde." This has come to mean "crowd, swarm" in general, but originally applied specifically to large groups of Asiatic nomads.

Such an important concept as *ordo* merits special study. While this essay is not the place to embark upon a thorough philological investigation of the word, several aspects of its evolution may be noted. First of all, *-rd-* is an unusual combination of sounds in Turkic languages.[71] This suggests that *ordo* was borrowed into Turkic from some other language group. Although imperfectly represented in its Sinitic transcription as *outuo*, the *ordo* was already a characteristic feature of the Xiongnu *modus vivendi* during Han times, long before there is any clear and direct evidence for Turkic languages. Turkic and Xiongnu are thus unlikely to have been genetically related. There are other reasons (archeological, cultural, and historical) for doubting the frequent claim that the Xiongnu were Proto-Turks. While it would take us too far afield to discuss the probable cultural affiliations of the early Xiongnu, we may perhaps gain a general idea of the linguistic milieu in which they operated from the considerations presented in this section.

There is an old Turkic word *karşi:* meaning "(royal) palace" that, in all probability, was borrowed—like many other terms for key social, political, and cultural concepts—from Tocharian. In this case, we may note that Tocharian B *kerciye*[72] has the same meaning as Turkic *karşi:*. The latter term drops out of use early in Turkic and seems to have been replaced by *ordu:*, which means almost the same thing (residence of the ruler), except that *karşi:* is relatively more fixed and *ordu:* is relatively more mobile.[73]

Turkic *ordu:* (*ordo:*) originally signified "a royal residence"—namely, "palace" or "royal camp (N.B.)"—as the circumstances required.[74] It could also functionally imply "capital." In religious (Buddhist and Manichean) texts, *ordo:* could signify "heavenly mansions." In some Turkish languages (e.g., Osmanli), the meaning of *ordo:* is extended from "royal camp" to any "military camp," since the army was always in attendance on the ruler. In military terminology, *ordo:* signifies the largest type of military formation—namely, an "army," the only meaning of the word in modern Turkic languages. In Middle Turkic, *ordu* still meant "camp/residence/capital of the Qaghan." For example, in the medieval Russian chronicles, the rulers of Moscow are constantly "going to the Horde" (*ide v Ordu*), that is to say, they were journeying to the khan's camp/capital for some political purpose. So closely linked was the *ordu* with the idea of a mobile camp that, whenever we find the term associated with the name of a city, we can be fairly certain that the Turks had taken over some preexisting town. The Turks did not usually build cities; they Turkicized them. Nonetheless, it is natural that *ordu:* came to be used in many place names, such as Ordu:känd ("the city of residence of kings") for Kashgar.[75] Along with many other Turkic words, *ordu* was borrowed into Mongolian and became a key concept in that language. In Mongolian, the *ordu* was the residence of the ruler, his palace or camp. Mongolian also borrowed another old Turkic word *karsi:* as *xarsi* ("palace, hall"), which we have seen above as most likely deriving from Tocharian. While the word early on dropped out of Turkic in favor of *ordu*, both *ordu* and *xarsi* survived in Mongolian, with *ordu* referring more to the tribal, military, and mobile aspects of the ruler and *xarsi* more to stationary buildings of administration (it was used as a translation of Sinitic *dian*, "palace, hall").[76]

Ordus/ordos, the Mongolian plural of *ordu/ordo* ("residence of a ruler; palace; camp"), was also adopted for both the name of a particular tribe and its territory in Inner Mongolia (the Jeke Zuu, or Ike Chao).[77] The Ordos was the zone of the most intense interaction between the north(west)erners and the inhabitants of the EAH—between settled and mobile, between the steppe and the sown, between Sinitic and non-Sinitic. The embodiment of the fuzzy boundary between these diametrically opposed pairs, the Ordos is where the settled, agricultural ecology of the Yellow River Valley, through a freakish accident of geology, punches up into the soft underbelly of the steppe and encircles a part of it. The Ordos plateau, with a general elevation of about 3,600 feet and ridges that rarely rise above 6,500 feet, is itself essentially covered by steppe. Much of the plateau is covered by loess or sand and is very arid, receiving less than ten inches of rain per year. To the west and north the Ordos adjoins steppe lands, and on the east and south it borders upon mountainous areas. In a very real sense, then, the peculiar configuration of the Great Bend of the Yellow River Valley has captured a huge chunk of the steppe, making the steppe part of itself.[78] A portion of the steppe has thus been placed inside of a riverine box. By the same token, we may say that, in the form of the Ordos, the restless, nomadic ecology of the steppe has invaded the complacent agricultural body of the Yellow River Valley. As the zone of consummate interface between the settled and the steppe, the Ordos is the true homeland of "China." Ordos is a perfect name for this perennial hub of empire building in the EAH. Writ large, the *ordo* was an enormous military encampment that might be surrounded by tens of thousands of troops. The *ordo* signaled the constant state of military preparation and activity of the steppe ruler and his legions. It was through their military prowess, pre-emptive energy, and organizational skills that the north(west)erners were able to create a succession of polities in the EAH over a period of three and a half millennia.

The would-be Great Wall was a pathetic attempt on the part of "domesticated" north(west)erners to prevent wave after wave of their confrères from entering the EAH. Unfortunately, throughout most of its history, the system of defensive walls linked together by the First Emperor of the Qin was highly porous and served primarily as a symbolic statement rather than an effective deterrent. The line of the Great Wall in Shaanxi roughly follows the division between the flat steppes to the north and the mountainous region to the south.[79] In other words, the primary purpose of the Great Wall at its center was to dissect the Ordos (that part of the steppe that had been captured by the Great Bend of the Yellow River) from the body of the EAH. Not only was the gesture in vain, it was also a form of self-mockery.

North Asians (northern Chinese, Mongolians, Japanese, Koreans, and Tibetans) are genetically closer to West Eurasians than they are to southern Chinese and Southeast Asians.[80] The dividing line between these two great groups lies roughly at the thirtieth parallel (Yangzi River Valley).[81] Surnames also show a clear separation on either side of this line, corresponding remarkably well with observable differences in genes, fingerprints, and tooth structure.[82] The categorical boundary between north and south in China, then, is not to be found along the Great Wall, but rather along the Yangzi River Valley.

From the very beginning, the distinction between the north(west)ern peoples and the peoples of the EAH was by no means absolute. As we have already witnessed, the Shang—who established suzerainty over the peoples of the EAH—were not entirely settled themselves. At the same time, their enemies to the north, northwest, and west, with whom they constantly fought to maintain dominance, were in many respects mirror images of themselves.[83] Had they relaxed, they would have been swiftly displaced by other willing and able forces from the north(west), as eventually did happen when the Zhou defeated the Shang.

Although the construction of the Great Wall was ultimately in vain, there was another—much less tangible—demarcation between the north(west)erners and the people of the EAH. This intangible partition functioned as a sort of semi-permeable membrane, across which a kind of ion exchange occurred, permitting steppe elements to penetrate into the EAH and allowing features of Sinitic civilization to affect individuals and groups who lived to the north(west) of the EAH. However, since the peoples of the steppes were more active and restless, the "relative ionic weight" of the exchange appears to have been heavily imbalanced in favor of the steppe peoples. So incommensurable was the flow of human steppe "ions" across this membrane that it was almost unidirectional.[84]

The Conclusion of a Long March

> *What we call the beginning is often the end*
> *And to make an end is to make a beginning.*
> *The end is where we start from*
>
> —*T. S. Eliot, "Little Gidding," V.1–3*

Throughout history, there have been numerous disjunctures in the process of state-formation in the EAH. Yet it is striking that both the institution and the periodic reinstitution of dominant political entities in the territory of what is now called China have inordinately been the result of initiatives taken by north(west)ern steppe peoples and agro-pastoralists. The modern Chinese nation-state, by contrast, has partially broken out of that paradigm. The new pattern appears to be one of state-formation and state-maintenance from the south: Sun Yat-sen (Canton—far south); Chiang Kai-shek (Zhejiang—southeast, his *Northern* Expedition started out on July 1, 1926 from the Canton region); Mao Zedong (Hunan—south); Deng Xiaoping (Sichuan—southwest); Jiang Zemin (Jiangsu—southeast). Powerful external influences—economic, technological, ideological, intellectual—come via the ocean (and now by air) and concentrate in southern entrepôts.[85] It is telling that the last person in history who attempted to establish a new dynasty was none other than a general from the north-central region, Yuan Shikai (1859–1916), and that the person who stopped him was Cai E (1883–1916) from the distant southwest in Yunnan. The hopelessness of Yuan's enterprise is encapsulated in the sorry title he chose for his new state: Zhonghua Diguo (Central Florescent Empire). The appellation "Zhonghua" had already been taken by the southern-based republic of the Nationalist Party (KMT, Guomindang) and was also subsequently adopted by the southern-dominated People's Republic of the Communist Party. Today, most of the leaders of China are technocrats (not military men, and certainly not Confucian literati) who come from a strip of land no more than about a hundred miles on either side of the Yangzi River from Shanghai to Chongqing. Whether the EAH will shift from the Yellow River Valley to the Yangzi River Valley remains to be seen. Or perhaps it has already done so.

Or perhaps not, for there is still one more north-south tale to tell. Let us discuss briefly the celebrated Long March of 1934–35.[86] This was prompted by the retreat of the forces of the CCP (Chinese Communist Party) from the Jiangxi Soviet after the last of the KMT's Encirclement Campaigns in October 1934. Mao Zedong (1893–1976) was not in command, fortunately for him, because he thus avoided blame for the defeats that had precipitated the Long March. Mao had been sidelined, and it was Zhou Enlai (1899–1976) who gave the order to march, after agreement with the Comintern, obtained by wireless. The Communists left on October 15 with no clear idea of where they were going, except inland, where Chiang Kai-shek (1887–1975) had less direct power. After leaving Jiangxi (southeast central China), the Communist forces headed west and arrived in Zunyi, Guizhou (southwest central) in January 1935. Mao re-emerged as the main leader of the CCP at a conference held there, and the decision was made to set out for the northwest (!), against opposition from other Communist leaders who wished to flee to Sichuan or even Tibet. Led by Mao, remnants of the original force (roughly 8,000 out of over 100,000 troops, cadres, and supporters)[87] marched through inhospitable areas and arrived in Shaanxi in October 1935, a year after they had left Jiangxi. At last, they ended up in the obscure town of Yan'an. A glance at a map shows that Yan'an is situated in the mountain fastnesses not far south of the Great Wall at the bottom of the Ordos. This is ostensibly a most perplexing place for the Communists to have called halt to their year-long flight.

Why did Mao, a southerner, retreat to the remote northwest?[88] Political and geographical reality made Yan'an appealing for a number of reasons. First of all, there had been a recent victory of the Communist movement led by Liu Zhidan (a local leader loyal to the party). Second, the KMT's influence in northern Shaanxi was severely restricted because it was close to Japanese forces in the north. Third, Yan'an offered a convenient escape route to the Soviet Union. Fourth, if the Communists were dislodged from Yan'an for any reason, they could also go relatively easily from there farther west to Gansu or even Xinjiang where the KMT was extremely weak. I suspect, however, that there was a deeper and more compelling reason why Mao chose Yan'an, of all possible places, to regroup his forces. In the back of his mind, or deep in his subconscious, Mao knew well that this was where lasting EAH states are born.[89]

Part Two
Bringing the State in

Chapter 3
State-Making in Global Context: Japan in a World of Nation-States

MARK RAVINA

In the 1850s Japanese social and political institutions bore little resemblance to those of the great imperial powers. Japan lacked anything resembling a modern centralized state. It had not one, but two national sovereigns (a shogun and an emperor), and many powers of state were exercised by daimyos, regional lords. There was no national treasury, no national army, and no national navy. There was no national taxation. There was no foreign ministry: the shogunate handled foreign affairs, but it treated Western powers as "barbarians." Japan had no banks, no public companies, no bonds, and no stocks. Merchants arranged long-term agreements, but there were no contracts, no contract lawyers, and no national laws for commercial transactions. At the symbolic level, Japan lacked a national flag, a national anthem, and national holidays.

By 1900 almost all this had changed. Dedicated reformers, both in and out of government, had radically transformed Japan's social and political institutions. The emperor was now the sole sovereign of Japan. By law, his rule was constrained by a constitution and by an elected assembly, but this was in concert with European models. In practice, his actions were governed by the advice of senior statesmen, again in concert with European models. Japan had reformed its legal codes to European standards and the great powers had dropped their demand for extraterritoriality. Japan, however, had extracted colonial concessions, including extraterritoriality, from Korea. Japan had national taxation, a national currency, banks, stocks, bonds, and commercial contracts. Japan had a national flag, appropriately patriotic national festivals, and a newly composed national anthem. Japan had, by then, become "Japan," the singular and exclusive subject with which we are all familiar.

How can we explain these radical changes in Japanese institutions? Was this "Westernization" or "modernization?" What caused this isomorphism with European institutions? American historians have relied on a variety of theories. Many early accounts of Japanese history assumed the superiority of Western models. In *A History of the Modern World*, R. R. Palmer (1909–2002) argued that Japan adopted "Western ways" because of "an admiration for Western statecraft." Japan was most impressed by the "external apparatus of Western civilization . . science, technology, machinery, arms, political and legal organization." The Japanese adopted these external manifestations as a defense against Western "penetration" and in order to protect "the innermost substance of their culture." The convergence of Japanese and European institutions was thus based on Japan's acceptance of European superiority.[1] Japan specialists had a similar take when they wrote of Perry "opening" Japan and of Japan's "Westernization."

The dominant school of historiography in the 1960s and 1970s was modernization theory. Based on the work of Max Weber (1864–1920) and Talcott Parsons (1902–79), this approach assumed parallel patterns of development in all "modernizing" societies. Modern society required instrumental rationality, specialization of function, and bureaucratic organization. The most "modern" societies were those in which these features were most fully developed. The best example of the modernization school approach was Robert Bellah's *Tokugawa Religion*, which examined early modern Japanese religious practices in its search for parallels to the Protestant ethic. Japan's successful transition to capitalism and modern society, argued Bellah, was rooted in the similarities between Japanese religious traditions like *shingaku* and Protestantism.[2] Although Japanese historiography is beyond the scope of this essay, it is worth noting that while modernization theorists were hoping to emplot Japanese history into a Weberian metanarrative, Japanese historians were doing the same with a Marxian metanarrative: searching not for Weberian rationality, but for appropriate markers of class consciousness and class formation. Notably, both schools ignored what has become an important part of recent historiography: ethnicity. Both schools assumed the nation (ethnic homogeneity) and asked merely "what sort of state?"

More recently, historians have begun to focus on modernity rather than modernization. The concepts of modernity and modernization share a number of features: both focus on issues such as the rationalization of social and economic roles, the emergence of new social and economic positions. But the concept of modernity is centered on the power relations implicit in the new positions, not the functional merits of modern society. Theories of modernity also focus on the reflexive quality of modern society. The concepts used to distinguish modern social life from premodern social life, concepts such as economic efficiency and individuality, are themselves products of modernity and are enmeshed in its system of power relations. An outstanding example here is Takashi Fujitani's *Splendid Monarchy*. Drawing on Michel Foucault's (1926–84) theory of governmentality, Fujitani examines the development in Japan of a modern monarchy and a modern nation-state. His concern is with the production of new social and political spaces, new subject positions, and possibilities for political action, not with the increased ambit of instrumental rationality.[3] In a similar vein, a recent study on the invention of tradition in Japan demonstrates how the very concept of tradition is a function of modernity. Japan and Scotland, for example, both invented "traditional" life as part of the process of industrialization.[4]

Part One: World Society Theory

In this essay I would like to propose an alternative explanation based on world society theory. World society theorists find that, in the modern world system, nation-states are "structurally similar in many unexpected dimensions and change in unexpectedly similar ways." They posit that international systems require a level of uniformity among their members; in order to interact states must have a minimal set of shared institutions and concepts. Increased interaction deepens this global culture and leads to greater isomorphism. Globalization is, therefore, a cause of isomorphism.[5]

World culture theorists acknowledge a functional component to isomorphic forces. States in the modern world have similar goals so, quite naturally, they develop similar institutional solutions. From a functionalist perspective (or, in political science parlance, "realist" perspective), states are rational actors, acting logically to pursue coherent agendas. Nation-states are similar but this is only because they share a common agenda. World culture theorists acknowledge this functional aspect of isomorphism, but they counter that states adopt similar institutions even when they have different agendas.[6] The external institutional uniformity between the United States, North Korea, and Iran is far greater than rational planning would suggest: all three states have departments of agriculture and defense. Many of the rituals of statecraft are similar: military parades, national holidays, myopic history texts, flags, and the like. States are similar in their external aspect even when their ideologies and levels of development are radically different.

Global political culture, like any culture milieu, defines the identities of actors. In a world of nation-states, polities must conform to the rules of nation-states.[7] The cultural causes of institutional isomorphism are perhaps best understood through an analogy: if we treat an international order as a society and states as actors then the implications of a common international culture becomes more apparent. Actors who will not or cannot assume recognized roles within a social order cannot function. In a republic, an actor who identifies himself as a subject of the king is certainly acting inefficiently, but, more importantly, he is acting unintelligibly. In a republic, there are no subjects of the king. The issue is not functional: the problem is not that subjects of the kings vote for a losing political party. The problem is ontological: subjects of the king do not exist as voters. Actors who expressly insist on nonstandard social positions become socially incompetent and incapable. In modern society, an actor who declares his occupation as serf or knight errant is, by definition, mentally disturbed. In the modern world serfdom is a fantasy rather than a social fact. A self-declared serf will therefore likely be deemed mentally incompetent. This process of marginalization occurs in both human society and international society. The most germane international case is Korea's diplomatic stance in the late nineteenth century. As the last defender of the Chinese world order, the kingdom of Korea insisted on its status as an autonomous vassal kingdom of the Chinese empire. Korea was thus a mentally diminished actor in world society, a "hermit kingdom" in period terminology. Like a hermit in a modern society, Korea needed either to be taught a proper social role (hermit does not appear on either the Department of Labor or Internal Revenue Service table of occupations) or to become a ward of the state. Significantly, the Treaty of Kanghwa, imposed on Korea by Japan in 1876, insisted on Korean sovereignty. Japan sought to minimize Chinese influence and advance its own geopolitical agenda by bringing Korea into the modern world order as a sovereign state. When this failed to secure Japanese interests, Japan fought, successfully, to have Korea redefined as a protectorate. In this rhetoric, widely accepted by the other colonial powers, Korea was an immature state and therefore could manifest its independence only with Japan's aid and protection. Japan, as a fully realized international subject, would take responsibility for raising its fledgling neighbor.[8]

In the context of world culture theory, the construction of the Meiji state can be understood as the construction of a legitimate modern subject. The construction of modern subjects was thus both an internal and an external process. Internally, the Meiji state created new rituals and customs for its human subjects. Externally, it created a modern state-subject, the Japanese nation-state as a new subject in an international community. The two projects were clearly interconnected; Japan was a legitimate international subject (or actor) in part because it mastered the paraphernalia of nationalism (flag, anthems, processions) and used these practices to create, domestically, a nation of Japanese nationals. The "invention of tradition" was an international phenomenon because all nation-states needed similar populations: culturally uniform nationals.

World society theorists have sought to emphasize the "soft" or ontological force of the modern international order over the blunt, "hard" coercive force of imperialism. Recent research on world society, for example, has focused on the shared culture of non-governmental organizations (NGOs) in different countries. NGOs lack the coercive force of the nation-state, and their shared assumptions and values reveal, Boli and Thomas argue, that they are part of a common "epistemic community." "All sorts of actors," they continue, "learn to define themselves and their interests from the global cultural and organizational structures in which they are embedded."[9] The nineteenth century society of nations-states is a more problematic case. Clearly we cannot ignore the brunt force of imperialism, but a social order can include both blatantly coercive and more consensual sources of power. To return to the analogy between civil society and international society, that a state sends in troops to crush a general strike does not mean that it uses naked force to enforce right-of-way regulations at traffic intersections. Rather, these rules are supported and reproduced by the actors themselves. Similarly, systematic racial bias in a nation's justice system does not mean that right-of-way at intersections is determined by race.

Meiji leaders, I will argue, were fascinated by these non-coercive "rules" for international society. They were not blind to raw power and aggression, but they were also interested in how rules for international conduct both legitimized the international order and its constituent members. While there was certainly a pragmatic aspect to this interest, I want to emphasize the ontological aspects of this theory rather than the functionalist aspects. In others words, I want to look at when and how the Meiji oligarchs thought that a nation-state was necessary for Japan to exist as a legitimate subject in world society. I want to move away from the question of cultural or technical "borrowing" and look instead at a more complicated question of social production and reproduction.

Part Two: The Modern World System and Meiji Japan

The production of subject positions occurs in language, but the process is often implicitly rather than explicitly flagged. That is, actors do not necessarily declare that they are engaged in the production or reproduction of subject positions. The foregrounded question is often pragmatic ("what will the state do?"), rather than ontological ("how will the state be?"). Since the ontology of political subjectivity is often assumed rather than interrogated, the important traces are the background. Thus, we can find markers of the production of a new subjectivity for the

Japanese polity in a wide variety of *bakumatsu* and Meiji texts, but the traces are extensive rather than intensive: there are faint markers of this process almost everywhere and strong markers almost nowhere. Let us move now to examine a range of relevant texts.

The first case involves the reform of weights and measures. Because early modern taxation was largely a local affair, the Tokugawa regime had not fully standardized weights and measures. There were, for example, regional differences in the size of a *shaku* (the standard measure of length), as well as different types of *shaku*, including, for example, the *kyokushaku* (bent *shaku*), *kujirashaku* (whale *shaku*), *tatamishaku* (rush matting *shaku*), and *gofukushaku* (clothing *shaku*). The need for uniform nationwide standards in a centralized state was immediately obvious and in the fourth lunar month of 1868, before the shogunate had even surrendered Edo castle, Matsudaira Shungaku (1828–90) wrote on the reform of Japanese metrology. Shungaku, however, addressed the problem like the former daimyo he was; he called for the Shuzui house, the family invested by the Tokugawa as arbiters of weights and measures, to redouble their efforts to enforce national standards.[10]

The debate over weights and measures quickly became enmeshed in the debate over international standards and international society. The early years of the Meiji state coincided with the formal expansion of the metric system: the first international metric convention was held in 1875 and resulted in the establishment of the International Bureau of Weights and Measures. This was movement toward international norms that Japanese bureaucrats, politicians, or scientists could not ignore. But there was a countervailing impulse to reestablish Japanese uniqueness. Japanese nativists (*kokugakusha*) blamed Japan's nineteenth-century crisis on the indiscriminate adoption of Chinese, Indian, and Western practices, and believed that the reestablishment of ancient traditions, particularly rites and rituals, would bring about a revival of ancient virtues. These two approaches collided full force in the narrow field of metrology. The first director of the new Division of Metrology Reform (Doryōkō kaiseigakari) was Shibusawa Eiichi (1841–1931), a central figure in Japanese banking and tax reform and later its most successful modern businessman. Shibusawa was succeeded by Tomomatsu Ujikata, a disciple of Hirata Atsutane (1776–1843), the influential nativist scholar. Tomomatsu was then replaced by Satō Yoshinosuke, a disciple of Katsu Kaishū (1823–99), the noted naval officer and military reformer.[11]

The struggle between internationalist and nativist perspectives can be discerned in the earliest reform proposals. In 1871 the Division of Metrology Reform, then in the Finance Ministry, proposed setting the new *shaku* equal to 1/120,000,000 of a "great arc" of the earth. This curious choice of number and physical feature was a tacit means of promoting conformity with the metric system. The meter, as set by the French Academy in 1791, was 1/10,000,000 the length of a line from the North Pole to the equator, passing of course through Paris. The new *shaku* would thus have been exactly 1/3 meter. (This new *shaku* would have been 1.101 *kyokushaku*). The independent Bureau of Systems, however, presented two different proposals. The first involved using the old Tenpyō *shaku*, which was only 0.978 *kyokushaku*, but was established during the Nara era, the heyday of imperial rule. The second argued that the new *shaku* should be 1/360,000 of the circumference of the earth at the equator. This had no historical precedent but directly linked the *shaku* to an objective physical standard. The implicit logic here was the reverse of the Finance Ministry's. Rather than conform to international norms, Japan needed either to return to ancient ways or to develop a unique system directly connected to objective physical phenomena. The *shaku* could be naturalized or historicized, but not internationalized.[12]

The three competing proposals were handled with customary efficiency by the Shūgiin, the short-lived parliament of daimyos. The chamber rejected all three proposals in a vote that provided sixteen different opinions, such as "adopt neither proposal but pursue gradual reform," "implement [a reform] after the minds of the people have been quieted," "adopt the best of both proposals," "adopt neither proposal, but use the best of the existing system," and the ever-helpful "no opinion."[13] The topic was too politicized for easy resolution, but not so urgent that it required immediate resolution. Indeed, many in the government feared that an abrupt change in the units employed in tax collection would cause widespread public discontent. In this political context, the Finance Ministry opted for an incremental approach. In 1874, the government decreed new nationwide standards for weights and measures and assigned officers in each prefecture to insure smooth implementation and enforcement. The system included both the *kyokushaku* and the *kujirashaku* and neither had any clear relationship to the meter.[14]

The international convention on the metric system reopened the question of internationalization and on July 8, 1875, at the prompting of Japan's representatives to France, the Council of State requested that opinions on the merits of the convention from the Finance Ministry and the Home Ministry. Implicit arguments now became explicit. The Home Ministry argued that "as measurements are something essential to daily life, each country must have its own system." Certainly the lack of standardized measures within Japan had been an impediment to trade, but the problem had been resolved by recent reforms. Any further changes should be postponed until the recent reforms were fully implemented. The Finance Ministry disagreed; it wanted a single system of measure for both domestic and international trade, and it wanted Japan to pursue membership in the new conference. The Finance Ministry argued that the metric system was not only simple and logical; it was part of a world system which encompassed 28 nations and roughly 500 million people. The metric system was currently a Western affair, but because it conferred "benefits in general international relations" (*udai ippan gaikō eki*) the ministry believed that Asian nations would soon be applying to join.[15] The choice of the term *gaikō* bears special attention: narrowly defined it means "diplomacy," but the Finance Ministry clearly meant the term in the broader sense of "international relations." "Benefits in general international relations" thus corresponded to what Pierre Bourdieu (1930–2002), in a different context, would describe as symbolic or social capital. Adoption of the metric system would mark Japan as a civilized and fully vested member of an international order.[16]

The government elected to hedge the issue. Japan joined the metric convention in 1885 and formally adopted the metric system in 1891, but maintained the *shaku* as a legally valid system of measurement. Although the focus here is on the Meiji era, it is worth noting that metrology continued to track broader political movements. In 1909, near the apex of Anglo-Japanese and Japanese-American amity, Japan adopted the foot and the pound as legal measures. But in 1921, in the context of post-World War I internationalism, the government made plans to abandon both the *shaku* and the foot in favor of the meter. These policies were scrapped during the ultra-nationalist 1930s, although after World War II the American occupation meant the de facto adoption of the foot and the pound. Only in 1966 did Japan adopt the meter as its sole official measure of length.

Aspects of world culture can also be found in the Meiji discourse on currency. The choice of a currency system is largely arbitrary: cowry shells, copper, or non-convertible paper are all equally useful as money, so long as they are widely accepted. In an international system what matters is the interoperability of different national systems. An international trading system requires that different currencies be convertible; there must be some shared store of value. Even if a system of currency is fully functional in isolation, it must meet an international standard in order to be integrated into an international system. This need for conformity destroyed the early modern Japanese currency system. Within months of the start of trade with the Western powers, the shogunal monetary system began to collapse. By the mid-1860s the country was plagued by spiraling inflation. The Meiji reformers agreed that, in order to establish a stable monetary regime, Japan would need to adopt the prevailing world standard, a gold-based convertible currency.

The irony of this process is that the shogunal system was arguably more sophisticated and modern than the Meiji system. The shogunate had, for over two hundred years, managed to supply Japan with stable fiat money. Shogunal coins were made of gold and silver, but their face value was much greater than their precious metal value. The coins were fiat money. They were valuable to the degree that they were scarce, and this scarcity was assured by shogunal laws against counterfeiting. The shogunate regularly debased its coinage, usually by including more silver in its "gold" coins, and nineteenth-century critics often cited this reminting as a failure of the system. But debasement had not caused systemic inflation. The reminted coins were clearly marked as new issues and merchants valued them according to scarcity. The debasements increased the money supply, but the Japanese economy was growing, so shogunal policy was sound monetary policy: prices remained stable. Monetary expansion was regular and constrained. The shogunate did not have a disciplined central bank, but monetary expansion was constrained because the shogunate debased gold with silver; it did not flood the country with cheap money. The early modern monetary system even included fiat paper money, issued by daimyo domains. Some of these issues were widely accepted, while others rapidly depreciated into worthless scrip, but moneychangers managed to assess them all.[17]

The early modern system collapsed not because it was flawed, but because it was different. By the standards of modern economics, the *bakumatsu* fiscal system was more "modern" and "better" than the gold standard which replaced it. Since none of the world powers recognized the fiat money, much less the shogunal monetary system, the fiat values of Japanese currency could not be sustained internationally. Japanese money would need to be revalued according to prevailing precious metal standards. Gold and silver coins would be assessed by their metallic content at world values. Unfortunately, these values bore little relation to the fiat money value of Japanese coins. Worldwide an ounce of gold was worth fifteen times as much as an ounce of silver, but a Japanese silver *ichibu* coin could buy five times its weight in gold. Japanese gold was thus available for one-third of its world price. Trade with the West meant that Japan would export gold until its monetary system collapsed and its coins corresponded to their specie values. The shogunate tried valiantly to limit the repercussions of this monetary collapse, but the problem was unfixable. Prices began to rise rapidly in 1860, when the shogunate debased its coins to conform to specie values, and they began to spiral after 1865, when the survival of the shogunate itself came into question. Significantly, Western observers did not recognize that they were destroying a fiat money system. They were, on the contrary, alarmed by the "arbitrary" values of gold and silver that the shogunate had "forced upon the people."[18]

When the Meiji regime sought to create its own currency, it looked at international norms. While reformers sought the most advanced monetary system, they were aware that the "best" system was the most accepted system. Standard was normal and normal was normative. The decisive voice for adopting the gold standard was that of Itō Hirobumi (1841–1909). In 1870, he wrote from the United States to inform the government of the results of his study tour. Virtually all economists, Itō wrote, advocate the gold standard as the best monetary standard. Although some major nations, such as Austria and the Netherlands, still maintained a silver standard, "if a system of coinage were to be newly established by any of these countries, there is no question but that the gold standard would be adopted." Gold, insisted Itō was the "best metal for the standard of value."[19]

Although Itō was searching for the "best" system he was clearly aware that the best system was the most widely accepted system. Japan, he argued forcefully, needed to adopt metric coinage because this was the emerging world standard. It was, of course, more convenient, but, more important, it was being adopted in the United States and this would make it a world standard. Itō quoted the chairman of the American Coinage Committee: "Now that we have adopted this system the nations of the world will be compelled to adopt it also."[20]

England, Itō noted, had initially rejected metric coinage, but, he insisted, it would eventually "in light of future trends." It would be advantageous for Japan, Itō argued, to adopt metric coinage "in advance of other nations," because then Japanese coinage would "be exchanged without impediment in all nations." Itō not only understood "best" as most common, but also recognized that international standards were evolving and that Japan could adopt a world standard before an advanced power like England. Itō was not advocating that Japan adopt a Western standard; he was suggesting that Japan lend its weight to an emerging world standard.[21]

Finally, let us to turn to politics in the strictest sense: the debate over the nature of the Japanese polity. A similar sense that conformity to world standards was, in itself, a powerful legitimizing force can be found in the Japanese debate over constitutional government. A central text in this regard is Katō Hiroyuki's (1836–1916) 1862 essay *Saishinron* (literally, "Newest Theses").[22] This essay is arguably the first discussion in Japanese of modern Western law. Katō, a samurai from Tajima domain, was sent in 1860 to Edo to study at the Bansho torishirabejo, the shogunate's institute for the study of "barbarian" books. There he learned German and began the study of Western law. He wrote and circulated *Saishinron* in secret; the study of foreign political systems was controversial and technically beyond the charter of the Bansho torishirabejo, which focused on military science. Katō's essay is especially important because of his later career and intellectual development. In the 1860s and 1870s, Katō emerged as a leading political philosopher and prominent advocate of natural rights theory. He was active in the Meirokusha, a prominent group of progressive intellectuals. In the late 1870s, he began a turn towards Social Darwinism and German political theory and in 1881 banned further publication of his earlier political writings. He was rewarded by the government with the presidency of the Imperial University in Tokyo (forerunner of Tokyo University). He later served in the House of Peers, the Privy Council, and the Genrōin. Katō's understanding of natural law and human rights has been widely examined, as has his rightward turn in the late 1870s. I wish to examine, instead, the theme of global standards in Katō's writings.

Saishinron takes the traditional form of a dialogue between a student and a teacher over political systems. The context is the decline of China and the rise of the European powers. What, asks the student, should Japan do now? And why did China fail? The student and teacher agree that China failed to appreciate European advances in science. In their arrogance, the student observes, China failed to grasp Europe's great scientific advances. That is indeed true, replies the teacher, but the problem with China goes beyond merely adopting Western arms. China lacks the spirit to deploy Western arms. This weakness of spirit, the teacher declares, is an external aspect of a deeper problem: China lacks a military because it lacks national harmony.[23]

China, the teacher notes, did not always suffer from spiritual weakness. Ah yes, the student replies, China needs to return to its ancient ways: it needs a benevolent and virtuous ruler. The teacher agrees in part. Certainly, the ancient sage-kings of China ruled with impartial justice (*kōmei seidai*), but later, lesser rulers were not as virtuous and thus China declined. There is, however, a political structure that can assure benevolent and just rule under even a benighted ruler. The teacher then begins an explication of the "political systems of the countries of the world."

This discourse has an explicitly functional goal. Teacher and student wish to find the political system that will help Japan hold its ground against the Western powers. Having located China's failure in spiritual weakness and lack of unity, the teacher then explains which systems encourage spiritual vigor and national solidarity. It is here that Katō makes his singular contribution to Japanese political discourse; because autocracies enervate their subjects, weaker governments can produce stronger states. Republics work, he notes, because the division of power produces greater not lesser unity.[24]

The explicit goal of strengthening Japan is a major force in Katō's argument, but throughout the essay we can also find the subsidiary force of isomorphism. Not only is a division of powers better for Japan; it is the emerging global standard. The move towards division of powers, argues the teacher, is a global trend, literally "an inevitable trend of the times" (*jisei no kanarazu shikarazaru o ezaru tokoro nari*). The teacher cites the promulgation of a constitution in Prussia in 1848 as a part of this trend and points to three late-developing powers: Russia, Austria, and Turkey. These lands are still absolute monarchies, he notes, but this situation will change. Within decades they will adopt constitutional divisions of power. In the more distant future all the nations of the world will become either republics or constitutional monarchies. (Katō, in an authorial gloss, asserts that, within a hundred years, all the countries of the world will be republics.) The reason for this global convergence of political systems is, in part, functional. The division of powers matches "popular sentiment" (*yojō*). But the trend is also "natural" and based in "the will of heaven." The development of the constitutional division of powers as a global standard is a trend with its own ineluctable force, and this inevitability is, in itself, a reason for a constitutional regime. Since all states will eventually adopt a division of powers, why should Japan delay? The force here is more cultural and ontological than practical. Since all states will eventually become republics, resistance is nonsensical. Absolutist regimes are not just inefficient; they are disappearing as actors in global society. In the emerging global culture of states, an absolutist regime will be as marginal and incomprehensible as a feudal squire in a republic. Practically, these regimes will disappear because they will lose wars. Culturally and ontologically they will disappear because they have no subjectivity in the emerging global society.

This idea, that certain political forms are "global" and that Japan must conform to global trends, appears independently in other important political works, such as Sakamoto Ryōma's (1835–67) eight-point program from 1867. Unlike Katō's essay, Sakamoto's brief draft was not a work of political theory, but a hastily drafted proposal. Sakamoto, a samurai from Tosa domain, was active in organizing the coalition of anti-shogunal forces that later founded the Meiji state in 1868. His own lord, however, favored a negotiated settlement with the shogunate over a violent confrontation. Sakamoto's program, drafted on a ship en route from Nagasaki to Hyōgō, was designed to secure the surrender of the shogunate. Under Sakamoto's plan, the last shogun, Hitotsubashi Keiki (Yoshinobu, 1837–1913), would resign his title of shogun and become president of the upper house of a new legislature. In eight short articles, Sakamoto outlined his vision of a new state: the restoration of the emperor as monarch, a bicameral legislature, military expansion, and thorough domestic legal reform. This prescient plan collapsed because Keiki refused to surrender shogunal land along with his title, and in early 1868 anti-shogunal forces launched a coup.[25]

Like Katō's essay, Sakamoto's program assumed a trend towards institutional isomorphism. It was essential to announce this program "to the nations of the world (*udai bankoku*), and there was no other way to address the present crisis." If Japan adopts this system it will "stand equal with the nations of the world." Sakamoto does not explain how a new political system will advance Japanese interests, but this silence itself is important. Presumably, the constitutional division of powers is better, but Sakamoto does not develop this reasoning. Conformity with global standards is, by itself, a reason for political reform. Japan must adapt to the "world situation" and the "nations of the world."[26]

Even when philosophers saw adopting a constitution as instrumental, there was a great emphasis on international norms. In 1867 Tsuda Mamichi (1829–1903), for example, advocated a constitutional government with a bicameral legislature with the following logic. If Japan adopts "the so-called republican form of the Westerners, then no nation and none of the great powers will be able to discriminate against us."[27] Clearly, there is something both normative and instrumental about Tsuda's argument. The immediate goal is to avoid subjugation at the hands of the imperialist powers. But the means to this goal involves conforming to global norms that bind the great powers themselves. This is altogether different from the functionalist advantages of superior military technology. These global norms, like all social norms, are constructed. Tsuda, by advocating that Japan conform to these norms, is helping to reproduce these norms and is thereby helping to create the very global culture to which Japan must conform. This process is also evident in Katō's *Saishinron*. Katō posits that countries like Russia and Turkey will adopt constitutions. Japan, of course, would in most taxonomies fall into the same category as Russia and Turkey: late-developing regional powers. By predicting a world trend Katō was creating the need for Japan to keep pace and adopt a constitution itself.

World culture had a pronounced impact on radical political thought, but it also shaped conservative political practice. We can find clear reference to the importance of international norms, for example in the work of Saigō Takamori (1828–77). Born into a low-ranking Satsuma samurai house, Saigō rose to national prominence and, with Ōkubo Toshimichi (1830–78) and Komatsu Tatewaki (1835–70), negotiated the Satsuma-Chōshū alliance to overthrow the shogunate. In the early years of the Meiji era, Saigō, Ōkubo, and Kido Kōin (Tadayoshi, 1833–77) were the three most powerful politicians in Japan and were the principal architects of the Meiji state. But Saigō is famous also as a rebel, the leader of the Satsuma Rebellion of 1877, the largest military challenge to the Meiji government. Saigō believed in a strong central state, but he could not quite accept that such a state would collide with the traditional autonomy of Satsuma. He died leading a rebellion against a state he helped found, fighting an army he helped create. He was, in essence, the most reluctant partner in the creation of the modern, centralized, Japanese state—but that makes his understanding of such a state especially important. Saigō was not a Westernizing radical—rather, he made radical reform possible by giving it conservative support.

Saigō grew up thinking of Satsuma, a daimyo domain, as his state (*kokka*) and his country (*kuni*)—he only slowly came to support a modern nation-state. Imperial loyalism had a powerful, but limited impact on his thinking. Saigō began to use "state"—in the modern sense of refering to Japan—immediately after meeting Fujita Tōko (1806–55), the imperial loyalist scholar. Writing on the twenty-ninth day of the seventh lunar month of 1854 of his meetings with Fujita in Edo, Saigō reported that, although he felt unworthy, Fujita had taken him on as a disciple. He was thus delighted to be serving the "state." Since Saigō was from Satsuma and Tōko was from Mito domain, "state" in this context meant Japan. Clearly the Mitogaku idea of imperial sovereignty had influenced Saigō's vocabulary.[28]

This was, however, an extremely short-lived change. Only a few days later, Saigō was again using a more traditional vocabulary. In a letter dated the second day of the eighth lunar month of 1854, Saigō wrote that he wanted to "remove the calamities that plague the state." Here he was referring to his domain of Satsuma—and the "calamity" was a bloody succession struggle within the lord's house. This was an extremely traditional sense of "state"—what I have elsewhere called the "patrimonial" aspect of politics: the "state" was the lord's family.[29]

Saigō was thus a firm believer in early modern multivalent politics. Until 1867 he continued to support the *kōbu gattai* formula in Japanese politics, a union of the imperial court and the warrior houses. Japan, thought Saigō, could best be governed by a council of daimyos and the shogun, invested and legitimized by the emperor. Several factors eroded Saigō faith in *kōbu gattai*. He profoundly distrusted Hitotsubashi Keiki, the last Tokugawa shogun. Saigō thought Keiki was devious, dangerous, and immoral. Since he could not envision cooperating with Keiki, Saigō began to consider destroying the shogunate itself.

Another critical factor was Saigō's understanding of the global scene. He was deeply interested in English views of Japan, as he related, in great detail, in his conversations with the English consul-general, Harry Parkes (1828–85), and the consulate's translator, Ernest Satow (1843–1929). A constant theme in Saigō's accounts was world political standards: Japan needed a polity commensurate with other states. In his meeting with Parkes in the seventh lunar month of 1866, for example, Saigō spoke of Japan's desire for "normal international treaties" (*bankoku futsū no jōyaku*), his way of describing revision of the unequal treaties. Parkes responded that Japan's polity was, by world standards, abnormal. It had two sovereigns, a shogun and an emperor, and its laws did not conform to world standards. If Japan wanted "normal" treaties, it would have to have a "normal" polity. Saigō took these comments to heart. Months later, when advising his daimyo on national policy, he described conformity with global norms as an essential part of political reform: "if we deal with foreigners on the basis of the laws of the nations of the world, there will be no dissent in the realm and in the future the realm will recover its fortunes." Saigō was a devout imperial loyalist, but he now understood that the essence of political reform was making the Japanese monarchy conform to world standards. This idea surfaces again in Saigō's conversations with Ernest Satow in the summer of 1877. Saigō and Satow agreed that the "Japanese king would take political power, make the daimyos subordinate to him, and establish a national polity (*kokutai*) equal to the nations of the world (*bankoku*)." Then Japan would have a "solid political system" that could have regular and normal relations with the "nations of the world".[30]

Saigō restated this understanding of global norms after the Restoration in an opinion paper (*ikensho*), dated the eleventh lunar month of 1871. "The goal of the national polity of the imperial nation," Saigō declares, should be a return to the central position of the emperor as in ancient days, with "extensive consideration of various nations, even the Western lands." Saigō here uses a curious phrase: "*Seido Seiyō no kakkoku made mo*" (lit., "even as far as the Western lands to the West") He uses both the term *Seido*, which can include both India and China, and *Seiyō* which commonly means only Europe and the United States. When discussing military reform in the next paragraph, however, Saigō refers merely to the "consideration of various Western nations" (*Seiyō no kakkoku*). There is a subtle but important shift here. On pragmatic matters such as military reform, the West is clearly the standard. But on political reform, Japan must situate its ancient tradition of state sovereignty in a global rather than merely Western context.[31] Or, to return to the sociological metaphor, Japan needed a subjectivity, a persona, appropriate to international society.

This subtle shift in language points to what I consider a major difference between the concept of importing Western models and conforming to global standards. The former assumes that the West is better. Therefore, since Japan needs to import the best, it will import the West. The latter concept assumes that global standards are decentered: the

West must conform to these norms as well. Although Western nations may be the most successful in modern politics, modern international political society is not, in itself, Western. The norms of world society are socially determined, even new and weaker members of society can affect these norms. Global norms are "better" only because they are norms: commonly accepted ways of being and ways of behaving. Saigō was not naïve and he did not imagine that norms of conduct alone might restrain Western military force. Rather he understood international norms as a means by which Japan might legitimately project power against the West by redefining the Japanese state.

It is important to understand Saigō's thought as part of the framing metaphor of Meiji politics. Saigō was not a progressive, but he understood that Japan needed a legitimate subjectivity in international society. Inasmuch as Saigō was a conservative, not a progressive, his acceptance of this idea meant that Meiji political discourse was about how Japan should establish its international persona, not whether Japan should do so. The breadth of consensus on this issue was remarkable. Even Hitotsubashi Keiki, the last shogun, alluded to it is his letter of resignation (dated the fourteenth day of the tenth lunar month, mid-November, of 1867): "Now, as intercourse with foreign countries grows daily more extensive, unless the imperial court is made the sole authority, it will be difficult to maintain law and order." If, however, the Japanese polity is properly reformed, then Japan will "rank with the nations of the world."[32]

Part Three: Globalization as a Recurrent Process

The focus of this essay has been Japan's nineteenth-century transformation, but it is critical to understand that world culture is not a modern phenomenon. Japan's adaptation to nineteenth century world standards was anticipated by a parallel process 1,100 years earlier. From the late sixth to the early eight centuries, Japan engaged in sustained and intense cultural borrowing from China. The state adopted a foreign religion, Buddhism, and built a nationwide system of temples and monasteries. The state established, based on Chinese models, a new system of administrative ranks, offices, and salaries. The government organized a national conscript army, national taxation, a national census, and a nationwide system of land assessment and redistribution. A series of reformers built three different capital cities, all closely modeled on Chang'an, the capital of the Tang dynasty (618–907).

The reasons behind this importation of Chinese models have been debated widely. Chinese government models served to strengthen the Japanese monarchy at the expense of regional lords. Cultural borrowing thus advanced state building. The reforms also served a defensive purpose. Tang China was actively engaged in the wars of unification on the Korean peninsula. In 663, Japan and the Korean kingdom of Paekche were decisively defeated by the Tang and the Korean kingdom of Silla. Cultural borrowing was motivated in part by this defeat and the attendant fear of invasion.

But Japanese cultural borrowing should not be interpreted in isolation. Nearly simultaneously with the Japanese adoption of Chinese models, the kingdom of Tibet adopted Buddhism as its national religion and began a national system of monasteries. It adopted the Tang style system of administrative ranks, which, like the Japanese system, had twelve levels. The state systematized taxation, laws, and weights and measures. Some of the parallels are uncanny. Japan's Prince Shōtoku (574–622) and Tibet's King Srong-brtsan-sgam-po (581?–649) are both regarded as cultural heroes, celebrated for their scholarship and contributions to the Buddhism. Shōtoku is credited with drafting Japan's first constitution, a seventeen-article statement of government goals and principles. Srong-brtsan-sgam-po is credited with a similar sixteen-article constitution.[33]

Japan and Tibet undertook similar governmental reforms even though their interactions with China were strikingly different. The nascent Japanese state felt besieged by Tang China and had been defeated on the Korean peninsula. Srong-brtsan-sgam-po, by contrast, besieged his neighbors, expanding Tibetan authority over Nepal, western Tibet, the Tuyuhun, and other kingdoms on China's border. To pacify Srong-brtsan-sgam-po, the Tang emperor offered him a Chinese princess as a bride. Japanese and Tibetan economic conditions were as different as their geopolitical positions. The Japanese economy was based on farming, and the tax system focused on wet-rice agriculture. The economy of Tibet, from what is known, was based in wheat, yaks, and inner-Asian trade.[34] These differences do not suggest a convergence of constitutional systems.

We can best explain the parallel development in Japan and Tibet through the concept of a shared international culture. Tibet adopted Chinese political institutions even though its armies were defeating Chinese forces. Tibetan forces captured the Tang capital of Chang'an in 763 and exacted tribute.[35] Functionality does not explain this. What Chinese models offered was not a superior system of warfare or government but a common language of international interaction. For Tibet, Chinese models were not even exclusively Chinese. The Tibetans learned of Tang models indirectly through the Korean kingdom of Koguryŏ and the central Asian kingdom of Tuyuhun. The Sui-Tang administrative system meant that China, Japan, and Tibet had parallel government structures;

they could recognize each other's governments as legitimate actors. The adoption of Buddhism marked all three countries as civilized. Japan and Tibet could send scholars and emissaries to China, and China could send a princess to Tibet: Srong-brtsan-sgam-po was not Chinese, but he was cultured. As members of a common international society Japan, China, and Tibet could trade, ally, start wars, and end wars.

Conclusion

Returning to the framing question of this volume, Japan became "Japan" through interaction with its neighbors. In the seventh and eighth centuries, when Tang concepts of state formed a shared international culture, Japan reconfigured its institutions and political ideology in that context. In a world of states legitimized by Buddhism and Confucianism, Japan became a state legitimized by Buddhism and Confucianism. A parallel process occurred in the nineteenth century, but the dominant international norm was then the singular sovereignty of the nation-state. I do not here wish to argue that world culture can, in isolation, explain the remarkable transformation of the Japanese state and society in the late 1800s. The force of world culture co-existed with the logic of capitalist development and modernity. Historians should not consider world culture theory as an exclusive concept. World culture theory, however, highlights the ways in which Japan's adoption of "Western" models was rooted not in efficiency, rationality, or efficacy, but in the quieter forces of conformity and social reproduction.

Chapter 4

When Did China Become China?
Thoughts on the Twentieth Century

WILLIAM C. KIRBY

At the turn of the twentieth century, the Earth's human communities were to a considerable degree organized as empires. These were collections of diverse peoples, governed by small bureaucracies that ruled through divine legitimacy or the mantle of tradition. These multinational, multicultural spatial regimes included the Ottoman, Romanov, and Habsburg empires, which had their roots in medieval and early modern times; they included the "new" *imperia* of the British and the French, who together governed most of Africa, all the Indian subcontinent, and much of Indo-China; and they included the *Da Qingguo*, the Great Qing Empire of the Manchus. In the first half of the twentieth century, they would be joined by more cohesive states, such as Germany and Japan, that sought to be, and claimed the title of, empires.

One hundred years later, at the beginning of the twenty-first century, all but one of these empires have disappeared. The Ottomans have given way to a small and secular Turkish national state and a series of ethnic and religious states and proto-states in contemporary North Africa and the Middle East. The Romanov and later Soviet empires have broken up into a multitude of national or ethnic regimes. Austria and Hungary have long gone their separate ways, while the Habsburg lands in the Balkans can look back on nearly a century of murderous nationalisms. The British have lost their entire empire, which is feebly remembered in the form of the "Commonwealth," and even the future of the United Kingdom as a unified state is open to question. And *la France d'outre-mer* no longer crosses even the Mediterranean.

Of all the world's empires a century ago, only that of the Qing remains as a bordered political community, albeit without the Manchus. Although an empire that ruled from the Chinese lands of the Ming, the Qing had comprised much more: the Manchurian homeland, Mongolia,

Xinjiang, and Tibet, among its far-flung parts. In the twentieth century, the empire became the basis of the Chinese national state. Yet just what "China" has meant, as a state, has been more readily recognized, and less contested, abroad than at home.

If we define "China" for the purpose of this discussion as the contemporary Chinese nation-state, then in political if not geographical terms it is reasonable to date "China" from the founding of the Republic of China in 1912. To be sure, if we look at certain distinguishing attributes of nineteenth-century European nation-states, such as professional standing armies, investment in economic development, and the articulation of "national" goals promoted from generation to generation, then it can surely be argued that in its final half-century, and particularly in its final decade, the Qing was becoming such a state.[1] But, of course, it was not simply a *Chinese* state. Historically, the Qing state had borrowed freely from Inner Asian, Manchu, and Chinese political traditions. In the nineteenth century it was in the process of reinventing itself again with the appropriation of European institutions and officials (John King Fairbank's "dyarchy"). In its final years in the early twentieth century, modern "state-building" under the *xinzheng* reforms was accompanied, at least to some degree, by an effort to reassert the Manchu-ness of Qing leadership.

Linguistically, we know that China was "China" abroad earlier than at home. Whereas the Western powers would refer to the Qing as "China" or, in H. B. Morse's language, in his magisterial study of foreign relations, as "The Chinese Empire"[2] (a term that would be appropriated only later, and briefly, by Yuan Shikai's would-be *Zhonghua diguo*), "China" was not the term of currency domestically or more broadly in East Asia. Chinese ministers served the *guochao* (dynasty) and bowed to the *Da Qing*. Vietnamese, Koreans, and Tibetans had different ideas and terms for the area we know today as China, but they too dealt with the Qing, not with "China." Vietnamese rulers of the Nguyễn dynasty in the nineteenth century would appropriate Chinese political terms to call themselves "sons of heaven" (*thiên tử* [*tianzi* in Chinese], also *hoàng đế* [*huangdi* in Chinese]). But these same sons of heaven could and did pay fealty to the big son of heaven in the "northern court," and did so through the Qing Board of Rites.[3]

In the emerging system of international relations governed by treaties, foreign powers signed treaties with "Chinese" authorities of various sorts. The Treaty of Nanjing was signed by an imperial commissioner, yet it was the Shanghai *daotai* (circuit intendant) who signed the lease that would lead to the International Settlement. Foreign powers dealt selectively with various authorities in different parts of the realm (Lamas in Tibet, chieftains in Xinjiang), in fact often undermining the court in

Beijing while proclaiming support for the principle of "Chinese territorial integrity." As successful as the Qing was in appropriating international law to defend its sovereignty, the concept of "Chinese territorial integrity" was introduced as a governing concept by foreign powers less as an effort to define (let alone defend) the Qing than to govern their own, mutually overlapping, appetites in East Asia. (To this, of course, there could be exquisite modifications, such as the British recognition of Qing, and then the Republic's, "suzerainty," or paramountcy, but not exclusive sovereignty, over Tibet.) The broad point here is that in the nineteenth and early twentieth centuries, there was seldom a clear-cut, mutual (Manchu, Chinese, and non-Chinese) recognition of "China" despite all the international dealings that had taken place across what Westerners called "Chinese" borders.

In domestic political terms in particular, there was no "China" in a formal sense under dynastic rule. Nor, despite historically Chinese collective identities, did there exist concepts of "nation" and "nationalism" before the late nineteenth and twentieth centuries.[4] Thus, it is not surprising to read Liang Qichao's lament of 1900, in his essay on "China's Weakness," that the Chinese people by and large had no idea of what "country" they were living in. They referred to it by *chaodai*, by the name of the ruling dynasty. "China" (*Zhongguo*), Liang wrote unhappily but accurately, "is what people of other races call us. It is not a name the people of this country have selected for themselves."[5] John Fitzgerald takes Liang's point farther:

Before the modern period, the term *zhongguo* designated neither the nation nor the territorial state but the place of the emperor at the center of the world. Its first appearance in the formal designation of state was in the attenuated form of *Zhonghua minguo* (Republic of China) in 1912, although it was frequently used to refer to both the state and to the nation in the Republic. Even then, however, the usage was not universal. Not far from the capital, in the 1930's locals still referred to their country as the Great State (*Daguo*).[6]

China, then, may have had an ancient civilization, but with the advent of the Republic, it was in fact a new country. This was a fact recognized by good Chinese republicans and by the Republic's first president, Yuan Shikai (1859–1916), not to mention by the teams of international advisers that sought to influence what was widely seen as a great political experiment: the birth of Asia's first republic and the transition from dynastic to national state. But the Empire gave way not to one but to several Chinas, to at least four alternative conceptions of a republic, and to decades of contestation, still ongoing, as to what "China" should or would be.

Here we might reflect on several questions that were unanswered when the empire fell in 1911. Who would comprise the "Chinese" people of the new Chinese nation-state? How large would "China" be? What would distinguish the Chinese republic in forms of governance?

Who Is Chinese?

The post-imperial era may be defined in part as the quest to build a modern nation-state, in particular by extending the boundaries of the Chinese nation (in the sense of *minzu* or ethnic nationality) to be coterminous with the reach of the sovereign power of the state. The first Republic, of 1912, took a liberal and inclusive approach, emphasizing in its five-bar national flag that the Republic of China consisted of Han, Manchus, Mongols, and Tibetans—such generosity perhaps befitting a China-based government whose real political reach into non-Chinese areas of the old Qing was limited. At the same time, even a weak republic had ambitions for cultural and, especially, linguistic unity: the principle of "one state, one people, one language."[7] The reach of the later Nationalist (Guomindang) state was limited, too, yet it pursued a more strongly racial nationalism,[8] symbolized by Sun Yat-sen's (1866–1925) one-sun flag and his belief that, just as the Chinese "race" had defeated the alien Manchus, "the authority to rule China was placed back in the hands of the Han people and China's territories were all bestowed on the Han race."[9] Even though the People's Republic of China would promise to restore "autonomy" to selected "national minorities," and would in its own flag attempt to symbolize the country's diversity, its rule, too, would be marked by the overwhelming political dominance of the Han in the governance of the former Qing realm. (So much so that in recent years the great seventeenth- and eighteenth-century Qing emperors Kangxi and Qianlong could be posthumously elevated in film and textbook to the status of Chinese patriots.) In the People's Republic, after all, one could be Tibetan, Uighur, or Mongolian, and still be a *Zhongguoren*, a "Chinese," and citizen of the People's Republic of *China*. The presumption of Han dominance would extend even to overseas "Chinese" until the 1960s. Whereas *Huaqiao* ("overseas Chinese") might well include non-Han emigrants, they were nonetheless all citizens of "China"—should they wish to claim that right of return and that passport.[10]

Yet that assertion of extended sovereignty over "Chinese" the world over has been withdrawn in recent decades, and the question of "who is a Chinese?" has been re-opened by cultural and political debates across the Taiwan Strait in the 1990's. Lee Teng-hui's (b. 1923) *liangguo lun* (thesis on two Chinas) might be translated by the People's Republic as a theory of two "states," but it could be equally well understood (and was more likely intended) as a theory of the coexistence of two "nations" on either side of the Taiwan Strait. Taiwan's linguistic distancing from "China" is clear to anyone who follows official rhetoric on that island. As late as the 1980s the People's Republic would be referred to as *Zhonggong* (the Chinese Communists) or *dalu* (the mainland). Now—and for all political parties—it is simply *Zhongguo* (China), as distinct from Taiwan. We are all *Huaren*, says Taiwan's President Chen Shui-bian (b. 1951), coining a fuzzy term for anyone descended of the Chinese cultural realm, but we are not all *Zhongguoren*. So the covers of passports of the Republic of China will now tell the world, in English, that they are "Issued in Taiwan."

China's Borders

The question of who is "Chinese" is directly related to the capacity of the Chinese state to demarcate and defend borders. No *Chinese* empire had ever been so big for so long as the Qing realm of the Manchus. The first decade of the twentieth century was full of portends of its dissolution. But the striking fact of the twentieth century was that this space was not only redefined, as "Chinese" and as the sacred soil of "China," but also defended diplomatically and militarily to such a degree that the borders of the People's Republic of China today are essentially those of the Qing, minus only Outer Mongolia. In this sense, the Qing fell but its empire remained.

The legitimacy of this national project was recognized by the world at large in bilateral agreements and in multilateral organizations (such as the League of Nations). These borders have enjoyed international diplomatic recognition since 1912, because the great powers of the day continued to believe—rightly—that a divided China would be a source of international instability. But it was the job of Chinese governments, not foreigners, to defend these borders. They did so with impressive success.

Chiang Kai-shek's (1887–1975) Nationalist government held on to at least nominal title to areas that the Manchus had governed but where the Chinese Republic had little power: in Tibet, for example, where the Nationalists, like the Communists after them, would undermine a stubbornly autonomous Dalai Lama by playing up the authority of a (China-friendly) Panchen Lama; or in the Muslim region of Xinjiang (Eastern Turkestan) in the far northwest, where Chinese rule was reasserted in the mid-1940s, after a period of Soviet occupation. In each instance China used forms of what we would call the non-recognition doctrine; refusing to recognize anyone else's sovereignty until matters could be settled in China's favor.

The nonrecognition of unpleasant realities was carried to an art form in the case of Manchuria, which Japan occupied in 1931. It speaks volumes about the power of modern Chinese nationalism that China would mobilize for war—as it did in the 1930s—in defense of the *Manchu* homeland into which Chinese settlement had been permitted only since 1907. And it convinced the rest of the world not to legitimize Japan's conquest. If the case of Outer Mongolia turned out differently, this was perhaps because this was the one part of the old Qing Empire where people actually got to vote whether they would be part of the Chinese nation. Mongolians ratified their independence in the Stalinesque plebiscite of October 1945. With the Russians counting, the vote was 487,000 to 0. (Chinese leaders may be forgiven for being wary of plebiscites ever since.)

This agenda of national unification was perpetuated not only by successive political leaders but also by strong continuity among foreign policy elites across regimes. The success of this enterprise is due in no small measure to the professionalism and tenacity of a Foreign Ministry whose bureaucratic lineage dates back to the *xinzheng* era and to the first republic.[11] Anyone who has received an official protest from China's Foreign Ministry (as I recently have, in protest against Harvard's alleged "two China" policies) must stand in awe of an indefatigable sense of mission, across generations.

Here, too, as in the case of "Chineseness," the big test remains the question of Taiwan. Curiously enough, for most of the first half of this century, Taiwan was not *terra irredenta*, like Manchuria, but quite literally off China's map. Taiwan was not part of the Qing when it collapsed, because it had been ceded to Japan as the victor in the Sino-Japanese War of 1894–95. No Republican government challenged Japan's right to Taiwan until 1943, when Japan's defeat in World War II seemed likely. Indeed the second republic established a Chinese consulate on Taiwan in the 1930s, and permitted tens of thousands of Taiwanese to live on the mainland as Japanese citizens. Only when the Nationalists made it their last bastion in 1949, and when the Americans intervened to protect them in 1950, did Taiwan's "liberation" become a national cause on the Chinese mainland. Yet the tenacity, obduracy, and overall success of China's twentieth-century diplomacy, which made the most distant regions of the Manchu realm part of "China," helps to explain the People's Republic's unyielding determination to "recover" an island that it has never governed for a single moment.

China's Political Form

But what kind of "China" would dominate the old Qing lands? Indeed what would be "Chinese" about the principles and practice of successive Chinese republics?

The large majority, even of highly educated Chinese, did not have a particularly nuanced conception of what a Republic would be, once the Qing was overthrown. It is telling that in his forty-five days as provisional president of the Republic of China, Sun Yat-sen was much more concerned about what the Republic would *do* rather than what the Republic would *be*. He issued executive orders on footbinding and opium smoking; he ordered provincial governors to provide charitable relief; and he called for the introduction of entirely new designs of clothing that were "good for health, easy to move in, economic, elegant looking," and indeed Republican. To the degree he defined the Republic at all, it was as a "socialist republic" committed to the reforms of Henry George. A decade later, he would set forth the three principles—of nationalism, socialism, and democracy—that he deemed most appropriate for the development of China.

But in politics as in economics, Sun's was a vision of an *International Development of China*, to cite the title of one of his most famous works. Apart from his insistence that the Control and Examination branches of government join the executive, legislative, and judicial branches (taken from the French and American experience) of his ideal government, there is almost nothing of historically Chinese statecraft in his thought. If the Manchus had been political or cultural borrowers and synthesizers on a big scale, their Chinese successors in the twentieth century would outdo them in their appropriation of alternative international models of political organization. Chinese political leaders of the twentieth century, like the cultural critics of the May Fourth Movement, were cultural borrowers par excellence. Therefore, the twentieth century was a century of continual experimentation with political forms, not one of which was indigenous in origin: the parliamentary republic of 1912–13; the military dictatorship of 1913–16; the attempt at constitutional monarchy in 1916; the "Confucian fascism" of Chiang Kai-shek, and the several forms of communism under Mao Zedong (1893–1976) and his successors.

Of all China's republics, the People's Republic was perhaps the greatest plagiarizer of international forms. In its first years, Mao Zedong and his colleagues followed Stalin's suggestions that the PRC needed a "coalition government" as an initial façade for party dictatorship; it needed elections—sham elections to be sure—to the Political Consultative Conference; and ultimately it had to have (and would have, in 1954) a constitution modeled largely on the USSR's "Stalin Constitution" of 1936. As Stalin put it in 1952, "If you do not have a constitution and if the Political Consultative Conference is not elected, enemies can charge that you have seized power by force."[12]

It is particularly ironic, but an extension of this pattern of borrowing (and of limited domestic political resources), that Chinese leaders seeking to define and protect a new nation-state would so willingly and consistently invite foreign intervention, but this, too, has been a defining characteristic of Chinese republics. Thus, Sun Yat-sen did not think himself a traitor to "China" when he sought to negotiate a European military invasion in the context of Chinese civil wars in the 1910s. Later Sun, and thereafter the Chinese Communist Party, would welcome massive foreign involvement in Chinese domestic politics in the form of Soviet political and military assistance; and Chiang Kai-shek would court American intervention in the civil war of the 1940s and 1950s.

It must be a sign of the limited universe of shared political values in post-imperial states, that each of China's twentieth-century republics has treated its predecessor as fundamentally illegitimate, and so to resist it was not traitorous. Although today the Republic of China on Taiwan likes to date its birth from 1912, it forgets that it is the descendant of that second republic which overthrew the first by military force. When the People's Republic was established in 1949, by means of a military conquest that began when the country was under foreign occupation, it not only called an end to the "reign era" of the Republic of China, it declared a fundamental distinction between its "new China" and the "old China" of everything before it.

There are, to be sure, continuities across several republics, particularly those of the Nationalist and Communist Party-States. The Chinese Party-States have had several consistent roles in nation-building. They existed not only to lead the government, but also to forge a citizenry for the new nation-state: for example, Chiang Kai-shek's New Life Movement of the mid-1930s, aiming to discipline an undisciplined populace; or Mao Zedong's famous effort to revolutionize culture. At the same time the Party-States were military states, as both the Nationalists and the Communists fought their way to power by means of party-armies in the first half of the twentieth century. (One difference: whereas the Nationalist military took oaths to defend the nation, the People's Liberation Army swore—and still swears—to uphold the rule of the Chinese Communist Party.) The Party-States were also developmental states, aiming to mobilize and industrialize China on the basis of Party-approved plans, from the top down. And the Party-States were Leadership States, each with one paramount Leader leading the small group of men who, through the Party (Nationalist or Communist) would govern China.

But, the question may be posed: what was distinctively "Chinese" about the several Party-States of China's twentieth century, and what has been their effect on the development of a "China" that can be distinguished from the Guomindang or Communist Party? Much more work needs to be done, by historians and political scientists in particular, on the relationship of the Party-State to the development (or nondevelopment) of truly national institutions in China's several republics. But on the basis of current evidence it would seem reasonable to conclude that the lengthy dominance of single-party systems, has come at the cost of national institutions of civilian government that represented more the national interests of "China" than those of a political party. Certainly the influence and rituals of Party-State political culture die hard. When Chen Shui-bian was inaugurated as president of the Republic of China on Taiwan on April 20, 2000, ending the Guomindang Party-State's monopoly on power, he bowed formally three times to Sun Yat-sen's portrait after having joined in the singing of the Guomindang hymn that had become the "national" anthem.

As I have argued elsewhere,[13] the history of the Chinese Party-State has been marked by its inability to work together with civilian elites to erect an enduring, self-replicating system of government. Civilians could serve the Party-State, but could not govern separately from it. The Nationalists on Taiwan eventually learned to cohabit with the soberminded, authoritarian technocrats who guided Taiwan's economic miracle, and this may be happening on the Chinese mainland today. But these elites have never exercised political power independent of the Party-State, and they have never fundamentally challenged it.

Pressures for Taiwan's eventual democratization—and fulfillment of the original promise of the first Chinese republic—would come from other quarters, above all from the Taiwanese majority who had long chafed under Nationalist Chinese rule. Is this a portent for other regions? Will ethnic challenges lead the process of political change in the People's Republic as well? It seems too early to say, but the evolution of a democratic, autonomous Taiwan in the past decade allows us to recast the question of the unity of "China."[14] From the perspective of history, we may ask not how soon will Taiwan become enfolded in the arms of the motherland, but how long can the Chinese nation-state hold on to historically non-Chinese areas that were inherited from the Qing, such as Tibet or Xinjiang?

Ultimately, the key to the future of a state called "China" lies in the great unresolved question of the twentieth century: what kind of political system will, in the long run, take the place of the old empire? Chinese governments have been much more successful in defending territory and sovereignty—for which international recognition would be forthcoming—than they have been in erecting stable political systems that enjoy domestic political legitimacy. Save for the 1990s, every decade in the twentieth century witnessed a major political upheaval. If twentieth-century history is any guide, when political change comes in China, it will be closely related not to historically Chinese political traditions but to contemporary international political and intellectual currents.

"China," then, appears to have succeeded more as a geographic than as an enduring political project. In China as elsewhere in the twentieth century, an empire was replaced by the more dynamic state form of the twentieth century, the nation-state (which in China took the form of several republics and two Party-States). This became a viable, perhaps essential, regime in a world of competition thanks to the possibilities of military and communications technology: the military united and defended it; railroad, airplane, and telephone allowed it coherence; and its ideologies of ethnic and civic cohesion gave it a semblance of political unity. In purely geographic terms, the Chinese nation-state was more successful than any other post-imperial structure in the twentieth century. As an effort to define a state and a culture, however, "China" has been a work in progress, a process of becoming more than of being.[15]

Now, at the beginning of the twenty-first century, it may be that the new but poorly institutionalized Chinese state, like other nation-states, is losing its capacity to mobilize and monopolize economic and ideological resources, as the web of economic relations and the diffusion of cultural or religious values makes all frontiers more permeable and vulnerable than they ever were under the Qing. If that is the case, the history of "China" may prove to be a very short one indeed.

Part Three
Nation and Nationality

Chapter 5
Civilization and Enlightenment: Markers of Identity in Nineteenth-Century Japan

DAVID L. HOWELL

Politically significant markers of identity connected social groups to the Japanese polity in the nineteenth century. In this essay, I examine how changing conceptions of "civilization" and "barbarism," across the divide of the Meiji Restoration of 1868, laid the groundwork for the emergence of modern Japanese national identity. I argue that under the early modern state, the notion of civilization was tied to participation in the status system (*mibunsei*), which served as the institutional edifice of the polity.[1] Civilization was also connected to territoriality, so that the realm of Japanese civilization was equated with the area under the ultimate authority of the shogun. The Tokugawa regime collapsed under pressure from the Western imperialist powers and a new regime, committed to achieving diplomatic and economic parity with the West, came into power. Early modern notions of civilization and barbarism were discredited after the Meiji Restoration and replaced by new conceptions explicitly modeled after those of the West. However, the early modern equation of territoriality with the realm of civilization survived the transition into Meiji, with the result that the new regime felt compelled to impose a new set of markers of identity on the populace during the first decade or two of the Meiji period (1868–1912). The core of this essay will focus on this effort and argue that the Meiji project of attaining Western-style civilization and enlightenment should be seen as an attempt to rectify the dissonance between civilization and territoriality that emerged as a result of the fall of the early modern political order.

During the Tokugawa period (1603–1868), notions of "civilization" (*ka*) and "barbarism" (*i*) were framed within particular understandings of Japan's place within East Asia and the broader world order. The core polity—the so-called *bakuhan* state of the Tokugawa shogunate and about 260 daimyo domains—was the realm of Japanese civilization. It was surrounded by a subordinate periphery of barbarian or at best imperfectly civilized lands, consisting of the Ainu people's homeland, the Ezochi, in the north, and the Ryūkyū kingdom in the south. Other countries further afield, such as Korea and China, had their own, distinctive civilizations. Being civilized or not in the core polity of early modern Japan was mainly a question of whether one participated in the social status order, a set of legal institutions that placed all subjects into status groups with attendant obligations and privileges. Participation in the status order was signified by one's explicitly superficial attributes of hairstyle, clothing, and name—one's customs (*fūzoku*).

Within the core polity, customs served to distinguish members of different status groups from one another. The emblematic outward marker of status was the samurai's right to bear two swords in public, though some non-samurai were granted the privilege as well. In general, men who participated in the mainstream of society—samurai and commoners—wore their hair in a topknot with the pate shaved and were clean-shaven. Although there was leeway to express personal preferences and keep pace with changing fashions, subtle differences in hairstyle distinguished samurai from commoners.[2] Other men, who participated in the status system but were somehow removed from the mainstream, wore distinctive hairstyles. Thus masterless samurai (*rōnin*) left their pates unshaved, many outcastes wore their hair unbound, and Buddhist clergy shaved their heads entirely.

In addition to demarcating status differences, customs delineated civilized and barbarian realms within the archipelago. The connection between customs and notions of civilization had deep roots in Confucian thought. As Bob Wakabayashi and Tsukamoto Manabu have demonstrated, when early Tokugawa thinkers undertook the project of naturalizing Confucianism, one of the problems they faced was how to situate Japan vis-à-vis China. In particular, they wrestled with the question of whether universal notions of civilization were necessarily tied to the particular geographical space of China, an issue tied to the ways scholars before and after Zhu Xi (1130–1200) had read a particular passage in the *Analects* of Confucius. For example, Itō Jinsai (1627–1705) conceded that the Japanese were barbarians, but through the deployment of some "amazing philological acrobatics" turned that apparent handicap into a virtue and argued that Japan was in fact morally superior to China because "Japan embodied the hierarchical status order of Middle Kingdom Civilization better than China." According to Wakabayashi, "Jinsai emphasized the idea that customs disclosed whether a people were civilized or barbarian. If their customs corresponded to 'ritual and righteousness,' they were civilized, if not, barbarian."[3]

As originally articulated by Jinsai and other early Tokugawa thinkers, civilization was "where Confucian ritual obtain[ed]."[4] Centering above all on mastery of Confucian ritual and classical language, civilization was beyond the reach not only of alien barbarians but of the lower orders of society in China as well as in Japan. Yamaga Sokō (1622–85), who regarded barbarism as the realm in which "moral transformation (or suasion) does not extend," argued that commoners and barbarians had a common nature. For Jinsai, Sokō, and likeminded thinkers, the most pressing issue facing the authorities was to engage in jōi, or the sweeping away of barbarian elements in society through moral edification.[5] By the early eighteenth century, however, thinkers like Nishikawa Joken (1648–1724) and Terajima Ryōan (fl. c. 1712) had pushed the realm of the barbarian outward beyond the boundaries of the core polity and reconceived Japan as possessing a unique civilization of its own—different from, but not inherently inferior to, that of China and Korea.[6] One way they did this was by distinguishing between foreign countries (gaikoku), which, like Japan, accepted the tenets of Confucian civilization, and foreign barbarians (gaii), whose lands lay beyond the realm of civilization. Rather than equating civilization with textual erudition and ritual practice, they saw it more as a matter of everyday life. Thus, for Ryōan, barbarians were people "who write using an alphabet and do not know Chinese characters, and who do not use chopsticks, but eat with their hands."[7]

With the West an increasing concern in the nineteenth century, the concept of barbarism changed yet again. For example, Tsukamoto Manabu argues that Tokugawa Nariaki's (1800–60) enunciation of the principle of sonnō jōi—"revere the monarch [Tokugawa Ieyasu], expel the barbarian"—in 1838 was predicated on the eradication of barbarian elements within the Japanese realm. Within about fifteen years, however, the monarch had come to be identified with the emperor and the barbarian with the West, at which point the slogan became a rallying cry for anti-Tokugawa activists.[8] The shogunate implicitly affirmed this identification of the barbarian (i) with the West in documents referring to the Ainu when it assumed direct administration over Hokkaidō at the end of the Tokugawa period. Beginning in the fifth month of 1856, officials stopped referring to the Ainu as Ezo (a compound that contains the same character as i) and instead began calling them dojin, or "natives." Kikuchi Isao argues that the term dojin, which now carries a pejorative connotation of backwardness, did not take on its negative sense until after the Restoration. At the time of the shift, it was a neutral term that referred simply to the local people of a particular area.[9] The new terminology thus symbolically incorporated the Ainu as the (Japanese) local people in Hokkaidō and relocated the realm of barbarism outward beyond their homeland, the Ezochi. Just before this, the shogunate opened the Ezochi to permanent residence by non-Ainu, thus anticipating in geopolitics this shift in nomenclature.

Moreover, in the late 1850s shogunal officials attempted to secure Japanese sovereignty over the Ezochi by promoting the assimilation of the Ainu. In keeping with the identification of the realm of civilization with the territory encompassed by the status system, the assimilation policy centered on the manipulation of such Ainu customs as men's hairstyles. The idea was to bring the Ainu into the civilized core of the Japanese polity by assigning them customs that would mark them as commoners (*hyakushō*). Although officials realized that merely shaving Ainu men's pates would not immediately alter their sense of themselves as Ainu, the explicitly superficial transformation wrought by the assimilation policy was sufficient in their eyes to serve their immediate purpose of asserting Japanese sovereignty over the Ezochi.[10]

Both the Tokugawa and Meiji states concerned themselves with the inner lives and outward appearances of their subjects, but they weighed them differently. As the assimilation policy pursued in the Ezochi reveals, the Tokugawa authorities were more concerned with exteriority—the visible compliance with norms—than with the internalization of the principles behind those norms. Within the core polity, this concern is reflected in their obsession with sumptuary regulation, which centered on exhortations to people to dress and behave in accordance with their social station. To be sure, ideologues, often with the support of the state, tried hard to instill in the people the values that underlay the status order, and they succeeded to the extent that more-or-less Confucian notions came to permeate the value systems of people at every level of the status order. However, with the exception of its virulent attacks on heterodox ideologies that appeared to reject the premises of Tokugawa rule—such as Christianity, the Fuju-fuse sect of Nichiren Buddhism, and some of the so-called new religions that appeared in the nineteenth century—the state did not make much effort to police popular thought. (Matsudaira Sadanobu's [1758–1829] famous proscription of heterodoxy at the end of the eighteenth century was directed mostly at intellectuals.)

Lacking the means systematically to intervene in the inner lives of their subjects—and skeptical at any rate of most commoners' ability to comprehend the ethical and philosophical bases of governance—officials necessarily focused on the external performance of proper deportment. But the problem was not simply one of technology. Rather, exteriority was at least as important to the maintenance of good rule as the internalization of the ruling ideology. Consequently, a relatively weighty term like *customs* is an appropriate translation of *fūzoku*: for the people who concerned themselves with *fūzoku*, those practices did indeed carry the full weight of meaning that we would now want to see expressed by a wider and deeper range of practices.

The concern with exteriority survived through the opening years of the Meiji period, as the new regime targeted emblems of outward appearance that had been discredited with the collapse of the status order. At the same time, however, the Meiji state, working through its own institutions and with the enthusiastic support of ideologues, quickly evinced an ardor for the internalization of new norms through its attacks on a variety of popular beliefs and practices. It could hardly do otherwise, for it faced the pressing need to justify its own existence, which was necessarily predicated on a rejection of the bases of Tokugawa rule. The early Meiji period, in other words, was a transitional period during which the old concern with exteriority gave way to an emphasis on interiority. With the development of schools, the modern military, and the modern imperial institution, the state turned its attention from the active policing of physical appearance to problems of moral suasion and outright indoctrination. This project, which was still in its initial stages at the time of the Meiji Emperor's death in 1912, was central to the creation of Western-style modernity in Japan.

During the Tokugawa period, customs were imperfect markers of status and civilization within the core polity. The authorities attempted, often unsuccessfully, to keep them aligned with the status boundaries they were supposed to delineate, and intellectuals constantly debated the precise significance of civilizational categories. This ambivalence does not, however, weaken customs' overall significance, but merely highlights the fluidity of the feudal order as a whole. So long as institutions functioned more-or-less effectively, a certain amount of play helped to alleviate the discrepancies between a political order constructed around the regime's expropriative imperatives and a lively and diverse social order, in which social relations and economic interests encompassed much more than individuals' immediate need to pay taxes or perform military duties.

Conversely, however, when the authorities perceived a fundamental threat to the feudal order they were able to capitalize on customs' dual significance as emblems of status and civilization. Moreover, this ability was not necessarily deployed in a reactionary manner. Although customary norms could be invoked in an attempt to restore proper social relations, they could also be used in a creative response to perceived crisis. Official tinkering with Ainu customs is an example of this creativity. But the same principle held within the core polity as well, as when, for example, Owari domain offered the perquisites of samurai status, including sword-bearing privileges and modest stipends, to gangsters it recruited into its military forces during the turmoil of the Restoration period.[11] Far from a rigid or even moribund set of institutions, Tokugawa feudalism was both dynamic and responsive to change.

Customs marked individuals as civilized or barbarian and, within the core polity, as members of specific status groups. Although the particular package of practices that bore classificatory weight in early modern Japan was unique, a similar emphasis on customs as emblems of political affiliation prevailed elsewhere throughout East Asia, most famously in the Qing dynasty's insistence that Chinese men adopt the Manchu queue.[12] By virtue of their significance as markers of politically defined realms of status and civilization, customs made identities subject to unilateral manipulation by the Japanese state. Here identity refers, of course, not to individuals' sense of self but rather to the way social groups—both within the core polity and on its peripheries—were situated vis-à-vis feudal authority.

Thus, rather than signifying an essential or generic notion of civilized "Japanese" appearance, customs always located one within the core polity as a subject of the shogun or one of his proxies. This is why the Tokugawa authorities sought to assert sovereignty over Hokkaidō and its immediate environs in the late 1850s by expanding the realm of civilization to include the Ainu people. Japanese sovereignty over all of Hokkaidō could be asserted only if all of the island's inhabitants could be civilized and hence brought within the purview of the political institutions of the early modern state. In short, status, civilization, and territoriality were intimately linked.

The Meiji regime likewise asserted the Japanese identities of the Ainu and other peripheral peoples and the regions they inhabited, thereby subsuming the barbarian realm completely within the territorial boundaries of the modern state. This gave rise to a profound dilemma, for securely situating the early modern realm of civilization within the Japanese archipelago had required the existence of a barbarian sphere. Moreover, following the Tokugawa example and simply concluding that shaving the Ainu's pates had made Japan and all of its inhabitants civilized was not an option, because the early modern concept of civilization had been framed within a discredited understanding of Japan's place within East Asia and the broader world order. Abandoning the early modern world view, in other words, required reinterpreting both civilization and barbarism to make them compatible with the construction of a modern nation-state. Meiji leaders and the thinkers who rushed to their ideological defense responded by proposing a new dichotomy between Western-style civilization (now expressed as *bunmei*) and barbarism (*yaban*), or, in Oku Takenori's formulation, enlightenment (*kaika*) and darkness (*meimō*).[13]

Ordinarily, the phrase "civilization and enlightenment" (*bunmei kaika*) brings to mind the intense engagement with Western thought and institutions that characterized the most vital thread of intellectual life in the early Meiji period. I should pause here to note that I am following a well-established convention in English-language scholarship in rendering *bunmei kaika* as "civilization and enlightenment," though, as Douglas R. Howland has pointed out, the phrase is misleading: both words mean *civilization*. However, in practice "*bunmei* was routinely used as a noun—civilization—and implied the ongoing and total progress of humankind whereas *kaika* was used as an active verb (meaning 'civilizing' and 'developing') and, when used as a noun, implied the civilizing process directed toward its projected end," namely, "the public cultivation of civilization through government policy."[14] Thus, my discussion below will focus on the *kaika* part of the *bunmei kaika* formulation. However, it is important to note that by the mid-1880s, when the most aggressive attempts to manipulate customs had run their course, commentators dropped the term *kaika* and instead juxtaposed the barbarism they found in the slums of major cities with a universalized conception of civilization—*bunmei*.[15]

In any case, members of the Meiji Six Society (Meirokusha), particularly the educator and journalist Fukuzawa Yukichi (1835–1901), introduced the Japanese public to the ideas and technologies that lay at the heart of Western-style modernity.[16] As politically engaged thinkers, these men and their ideas had a profound impact on both the Meiji leaders and their main political opponents, the participants in the movement for freedom and popular rights in the late 1870s and early 1880s.[17] Civilization and enlightenment as high discourse has received considerable scholarly attention already, so there is no need to discuss the movement in detail here.[18] I would, however, like to make one or two general points before proceeding further.

There is a natural tendency to see civilization and enlightenment discourse as a stark departure from the ideas and institutions of the Tokugawa period. Fukuzawa himself stressed the idea of shedding the past in his writings, and scholars seeking to explain Meiji Japan's rapid modernization have, reasonably enough, emphasized the progressive elements of early Meiji thought.[19] However, in so doing scholars have obscured the degree to which the language of civilization and enlightenment was used to promote ideas at every point along the ideological spectrum. Indeed, even nativists—usually held up as the reactionary opponents of progressive modernizers like Fukuzawa—justified their ideas in terms of enlightenment, which they equated with a return to the ideas and practices of Japanese antiquity.[20] In short, for a thinker to be taken seriously in the intellectual world of the first decade or so of Meiji, he had to invoke the language of civilization and enlightenment. In some ways this represented the tremendous influence of Fukuzawa and his cohort, but it is also true that because the language of civilization and enlightenment was so widely dispersed throughout the intellectual world of early Meiji Japan, any attempt to isolate its particularly westward-looking and progressive elements is necessarily misleading.

Three critical differences distinguished the early modern (*ka* versus *i*) and modern (*bunmei* versus *yaban*) conceptions of civilization and barbarism. First, under the Meiji regime, the content of civilization—and hence of barbarism—was articulated in relation to the advanced industrial and military powers of the Western world. The westward orientation of Meiji civilization was reflected first in elites' enthusiastic adoption of the outward symbols of Western culture, such as clothing and hairstyles, and later in an institutionalized concern with hygiene, discipline, science, and other technologies of social knowledge. Both impulses had roots in the waning years of Tokugawa rule, but gained official sponsorship only after the Restoration. Second, the "ethnic" aspects of the opposition between civilization and barbarism largely disappeared. The Ainu's barbarism during the Tokugawa era was not really an "ethnic" quality at all: although it helped to define them as a people existing outside of the core polity, the particular customs that marked them as barbarians applied within the Tokugawa state itself and were therefore not *essentially* Ainu traits. Yet it is also true that by adopting civilized customs, one ceased to be Ainu in the eyes of the early modern state. Accordingly, while barbarism was not the exclusive domain of the Ainu, it was not possible simultaneously to be Ainu and anything but a barbarian. After the Meiji Restoration, even those Ainu who had nominally assimilated returned to a barbarian condition, in part because the distinction between the Japanese and Ainu was reconceived as an ethnic one. However, rather than making barbarism a peculiarly ethnic attribute (by linking it to distinctive Ainu cultural practices, for example), Meiji officials and ideologues discovered—to their considerable dismay—large and unruly pockets of barbarism within the core polity itself.

This relates to the final point: the internalization of civilization became a pressing issue in the Meiji period, whereas previously it had been (in embryonic form) the nearly exclusive concern of a limited community of Confucian ideologues. It is this politically charged concern with internalization that makes Meiji civilization "modern" in a way its Tokugawa counterpart had not been. Markers of civilization and barbarism came to include not only explicitly superficial customs like dress and hairstyle, but practices and beliefs at the very core of everyday life, such as religion, personal hygiene, and social interaction. Civilization ceased to be a garment or hairstyle to be worn or discarded at will, but rather became an essential element of individual identity, internalized as a habit of thought, a sense of self and of membership in the national community.

The alacrity with which the Meiji leaders embraced a conception of civilization borrowed from the West is often linked to their realization that achieving diplomatic and economic parity with the powers required adopting the West's social and political institutions along with its military, industrial, and managerial technologies. Although Western haircuts, beef-eating, and the like appear to have little connection to treaty revision or industrial development, ideologues marshaled their newfound knowledge of Western society to justify the change, sometimes in ways that strike the modern reader as ludicrous—by arguing that a shaved pate left a man vulnerable to infectious disease, for instance.[21] As we shall see presently, the state expended scarce administrative and disciplinary resources in its program of instituting Western-style civilization; it persisted despite dogged opposition—some of it violent—from diverse elements throughout society. We could take the ideologues at their word, of course, but that begs the question of why they were willing to go to such considerable lengths to rationalize changes in seemingly incidental customs.

Clearly, something very important was at stake in the rush to adopt the Western trappings of civilization and enlightenment. The imperative to see Japan as civilized was natural enough, particularly considering the concept's importance during the Tokugawa period. However, early modern ideas about civilization lost their geopolitical significance during the process of bringing Japan within the international order. Quite simply, the Western powers did not recognize the validity of Japanese customs as universal markers of civilization, nor did they recognize an organic connection between civilization and territoriality. But they did espouse a relationship between civilization and the right to sovereignty—that is, only civilized nations (whose borders were more or less self-evident, or at least negotiable) were eligible to govern themselves; uncivilized (and especially uncharted) territories required Western tutelage and stewardship before they could enjoy full independence. Western imperialism in China and India, combined with the assault on Japanese national sovereignty written into the treaties imposed on the shogunate in the 1850s, made the Meiji leadership keenly aware of this connection.

This is not to say, however, that early modern ideas of civilization disappeared along with the Tokugawa regime. The emphasis placed on the regulation of customs in the early Meiji period reflected a Japanese reading of civilization transposed onto the West—that is, officials and ideologues assumed that outward customs lay at the very heart of the Western conception of civilization, just as they had to the Japanese during the Tokugawa period, for they understood the relationship between

correct customs and an orderly realm to be a universal truth.[22] Just as
the shogunate had tried to assimilate the Ainu by shaving their pates,
the Meiji state thought it could "assimilate" the Japanese population by
unbinding the people's hair. And just as it had been obvious to Tokugawa officials that the Ainu needed to wear topknots before they could
remake themselves as civilized subjects of the shogun, Meiji Japanese
needed to wear top hats to demonstrate to the Western powers their
readiness to remake themselves as civilized moderns. The Westerners
had to see the top hats, of course, and thereby validate the endeavor. Accordingly, it follows that Tokyo and the treaty ports were the site of the
first attempts at the reform of customs. Here it is significant that the
Meirokusha thinker Katō Hiroyuki (1836–1916) was especially cha-
grined at the existence of outcaste villages near the treaty port of Kōbe
and invoked the presence of Westerners to justify the abolition of outcaste status, which was enacted in 1871.[23]

The Justice Ministry (Shihōshō) incorporated customs regulations
into a series of petty-misdemeanor ordinances (*ishiki kaii jōrei*), first
promulgated in Tokyo in 1872 and later extended throughout the country in slightly different form in each prefecture. Both *ishiki* and *kaii* refer
to infringements of the law, but the crimes included under the *ishiki* ordinances were considered more serious and accordingly carried larger
fines—75 to 150 *sen* (or 10 to 20 lashes for those who could not afford
to pay) as opposed to 6.25 to 12.5 *sen* (or one to two days' detention), as
originally promulgated in Tokyo (corporal punishment was abandoned
in 1876). As Oku has noted, the average daily wage of a carpenter was
forty *sen* in 1874, so the fines, while hardly ruinous, were nonetheless
substantial.[24] In all cases, offenders were not subjected to a legal proceeding; rather, enforcement was entrusted entirely to the new police
force.[25]

As a compilation of regulations concerning petty misdemeanors, the
ordinances were not exclusively or even primarily concerned with customs; they included prohibitions of threats to public safety (such as rid-
ing a horse at night without a light) and public health (selling spoiled
fish); petty theft (pilfering fruit from trees); and economic activity (unlicensed vendors). Nonetheless, a number of the ordinances did concern customs, and the prohibition of public nakedness included among
the more serious *ishiki* regulations was perhaps the most widely enforced.

The customs regulations incorporated within the petty-misdemeanor
ordinances fell into two general categories: a relatively small number
governing the body, and a larger group concerning public decorum. In
addition to the ban on public nakedness, which was directed mostly
against rickshaw pullers and laborers who stripped down to their loin-

cloths to work, the bodily regulations included prohibitions of tattooing, mixed bathing, public urination, cross-dressing (except by kabuki actors), and the wearing of short hair by women. Those regulating behavior generally covered public nuisances of various sorts, including the careless handling of livestock in city streets, fighting, drunken revelry and singing, and "opening lattices or climbing walls, and wantonly sticking one's face out to peer at or mock passersby from above" (*kaii*, article 56).[26] Others banned public entertainments like dog fighting, snake charming, fireworks in densely populated districts, and unlicensed exhibitions of sumo wrestling by men and women.

Although it is tempting to read into the bodily regulations a desire to inscribe the power of the state directly onto the persons of its subjects, in fact their aim seems to have been similar to the ordinances concerned with public decorum more generally. In other words, the goal of the customs regulations was to contain unruly and outrageous behavior of all sorts. In that sense, there was no essential difference between the assaults on scantily clad rickshaw men and inebriated crooners. The ban on women's cutting their hair without permission is a case in point. It appears that some young women in Tokyo—particularly students—cut their hair and wore items of men's clothing in the period preceding the promulgation of the petty-misdemeanor ordinances. At the end of 1871, a newspaper in Chiba praised the women, saying that the fashion was a commendable sign of economy and rationality, while in March 1872 another paper, the *Shinbun zasshi*, excoriated the fad—which it interpreted as either a misguided effort at civilization and enlightenment or perhaps an attempt by the women to desexualize (*iro o saru*) themselves—as both unwomanly and running counter to the customs of Japan and the West alike. The following month the newspaper ran a notice saying that the government's recent order allowing people to cut their hair was directed at men only, and that women should therefore keep their hair long as before.[27] Sharon Sievers argues that the prohibition on short hair on women reflected the authorities' desire to mark women as the repositories of tradition, a trail of bread crumbs to guide Japan back home should it get lost during its romp into the forest of Western civilization.[28] This reading has a certain appeal, resonating as it does with postcolonialist discourse on the feminization of the colonial subject. However, we should keep in mind (as the *Shinbun zasshi* reporter noted) that Western women in the early 1870s generally did not wear short hair, and so Japanese women who did so could not have been imitating their European and American counterparts.

Thus, while the students were certainly challenging traditional notions of proper women's appearance, strictly speaking we must distinguish the practice from the 1870s fad for things Western. Indeed, many men also adopted hairstyles that departed from both traditional and Western patterns during this period, and while their behavior was not criminalized, officials used the police to bully them into wearing their hair more conventionally.[29] In fact, evidence suggests that the prohibition was directed primarily against women who cut their hair either as a sign of Buddhist piety upon the deaths of their husbands or because they preferred not to bother with—or could not afford—the considerable trouble, expense, and physical hardship of wearing the elaborate coifs popular at the time (most of which were adapted from styles pioneered by courtesans and kabuki actors).[30] Indeed, in 1884 a group of (male) enthusiasts of enlightenment founded the Women's Upswept Hair Society (Fujin sokuhatsukai) to promote the adoption of "Western" (actually a mix of Western and Japanese elements) hairstyles for women. The group's manifesto marshaled the same arguments in favor of reform—that traditional hairstyles were uncomfortable, unhygienic, and uneconomical—that short-haired women a decade earlier might have made themselves.[31] Thus, it is reasonable to conclude that while the daring young women of Tokyo were no doubt a serious concern, the authorities sought more immediately to control the far more numerous group of people who found it easier to be unseemly than decorous, whether they were women who could not cope with the hassle of a Shimada chignon (*wage*) or men who could not contain themselves long enough to find a public urinal.

The concern with decorum is explicit in injunctions issued by local governments. For example, the Chiba prefectural authorities issued a notice to the residents of the communities of Chiba, Samugawa, and Nobuto in August 1874, exhorting them to good behavior. Although the document was not a legal edict, the eleven deplorable practices specifically listed (nakedness, public urination, dumping sewage into the streets, and the like) could all be found in the Tokyo petty-misdemeanor ordinances. Particularly interesting for our purposes is the preface, which stated:

It goes without saying now that it is everyone's duty to show respect and deference to others, and to improve manners and etiquette. However, it has come to our attention that people have been behaving in an unbearably offensive manner. They act without respect or courtesy and interfere with the actions of others. Perhaps they do not realize that traditional local practices (*fūshū*) are improper, or perhaps they misinterpret the recent talk of personal freedom and liberty (*jishu jiyū*) to mean that it is acceptable to act selfishly and wantonly. Are these customs not uncouth (*hiya*) and most shameful? Your communities lie near the government offices and must therefore serve as a model for the entire prefecture. It is therefore imperative that you reform your customs and allow yourselves to be guided by respectfulness. The young must respect the old and the aged cherish the young; commoners must defer to the gentry and the gentry yield to local officials; and local officials must not interfere with the people's rights (*kenri*). In all respects, from your demeanor to daily interactions, you must be careful to remain faithful, correct your manners and etiquette, and strive toward the attainment of true civilization and enlightenment (*shin no bunmei kaika*). . . . Each one of you must strive to eliminate the well-nigh barbarous (*yaban*) offenses [listed below].[32]

However strong the Meiji state's desire to get its people to think modern thoughts, it was easier to get them to piss modern piss first. The attack on indecorous behavior was thus a reasonable place to launch the project of introducing Japan to Western-style modernity. Aside from the propaganda value of presenting foreign visitors with orderly streets and a courteous populace, the basic idea of showing deference to superiors and compassion to the lower orders had deep roots in Japanese culture. No one being told to refrain from engaging in drunken street brawls would have been surprised at the admonition, for indeed the annals of Tokugawa jurisprudence were filled with cranky injunctions against disruptions of public order. And while a number of the customs regulations—the prohibitions on public nakedness and mixed bathing in particular—were indeed generally new to the Meiji period, they represented a modest, if significant, incremental step beyond earlier attempts to regulate public morality.

Despite these links to the past, two features clearly differentiated the Meiji customs regulations from Tokugawa practice. The first was the vigor with which they were enforced. For all its teeth-gnashing about the unruly masses, the shogunate had never dispatched patrolmen armed with oaken truncheons into the countryside to knock good manners into uncouth people.[33] In 1876, the police arrested 4,495 people for public urination, 2,727 for fighting, and 2,091 for public nakedness in Tokyo prefecture alone. In all, 10,960 people were punished for infractions against the petty-misdemeanor ordinances in the prefecture that year. Enforcement became even stricter in the years immediately following: the Tokyo police arrested 3,179 people for public nakedness in 1877 and 7,545 in 1878.[34] The police's energetic enforcement efforts notwithstanding, rowdy and indecorous behavior hardly disappeared from the streets of Meiji Japan. Years after the promulgation of the petty-misdemeanor ordinances, Western visitors like Edward Sylvester Morse (1838–1925) reported seeing (but not being particularly shocked by) plenty of nearly naked rickshaw men and laborers in Yokohama and Tokyo.[35] Even today, a late-night stroll in any urban area will quickly reveal that neither public urination nor drunken merrymaking was eradicated by the good officers of the police force in the 1870s. And while it is debatable whether the salaryman lying in an alcoholic stupor on the Umeda station platform sees himself as an agent of resistance against official meddling into the lifeways of the people, it is nevertheless reassuring that even the contemporary state, with all its technologies for instilling discipline, has never been able fully to attain its vision of an orderly modern society. Still, the die was cast: whereas Edo townsmen had taken pride in their ability to urinate whenever and wherever the urge arose, no taxi driver in his right mind—however pressing his need—would ever consider relieving himself against the wall of a police box.[36]

The second major departure from Tokugawa practice was the explicit labeling of indecorous behavior as barbarous (*yaban*). There was an early modern precedent for seeing the unrefined practices of rural people as backward—the countryside was the repository of remnant barbarian customs in the eyes of many Confucian ideologues[37]—but during the Meiji period the locus of barbarism generally shifted from remote country villages to the urban core of Japan, where manual laborers, prostitutes, and other elements at the margins of the developing capitalist economy tended to congregate.[38] In other words, economic activity, rather than preexisting cultural norms, became the key criterion of Meiji barbarism.

This reorientation of barbarism was anticipated by policies like the establishment of the Kyoto workhouse for vagrants in 1868 and similar facilities set up in Tokyo in 1869 and the years thereafter.[39] Japanese travelers' comments about the islands south of Kyushu reflect the changing notions of barbarism as well. The Restoration leader Saigō Takamori (1828–77), who was exiled to Amami Island in 1859, mocked the local customs, particularly the women's make-up and tattooed hands, and on that basis likened them to the Ainu. (His opinion of Amami improved markedly, however, after he had two children with a local woman.) Sasamori Gisuke (1845–1915), who visited the Sakishima Islands south of Okinawa in 1893, also invoked comparisons to the Ainu, but applied economic criteria in doing so. Thus he condemned the local residents for their "laziness" and lack of will to "exert themselves through work," characteristics that left them so desperately poor that they barely better off than "the aborigines of Hokkaidō."[40] It is no surprise, then, that the tendency toward economic determinism manifested itself in policy toward the Ainu, as civilizing the Ainu came to be seen mostly as a question of providing them with the means to lead "stable" lives as cultivators, rather than "unsettled" existences as laborers in the fishing, lumber, and construction industries.[41] This shift meshed nicely not only with the reorientation of political identity from status to imperial subjecthood but with contemporaneous Western notions about the alienness of the urban poor, and as such was a logical outcome of the push to impose Western-style civilization on Japan.

The effort to institute the new standards of civilization from above met with all sorts of resistance, of which stubborn noncompliance may have been the most pervasive but nonetheless the least threatening. The Satsuma Rebellion of 1877, and other samurai uprisings and peasant movements like the Mimasaka Blood-Tax Rebellion of 1873, often included demands that the state rescind customs reforms such as the ban on sword-bearing for samurai and the encouragement of unbound hair among all men. The 1876 prohibition of sword-bearing was part of the state's policy of gradually dismantling samurai status, a program that culminated the same year in the forced commutation of samurai stipends into bonds payable over the course of several years. As with the commutation of stipends, the government first issued a call for the voluntary cessation of sword-bearing (paired with unbound hair in the Ministry of State's official notice of the eighth month of 1871) before banning the practice outright. Given that the prohibition on swords was part of a broader package of reforms designed to encourage the samurai population to take up independent livelihoods, it is not surprising that it was frequently listed as a complaint by samurai rebels. In particular, the participants in the Shinpūren Rebellion of 1876, one of the half-dozen or so samurai uprisings to seriously threaten the regime, made sword-bearing one of their central issues. The rebels were so earnest in their attachment to the symbols of samurai status that they refused to use firearms, with the result that the uprising amounted to little more than a mass suicide mission.[42]

Strictly speaking, the government's granting of permission to men not to bind their hair was not a direct call for the adoption of Western hairstyles. Although the term used in the Ministry of State's edict, *sanpatsu*, means a haircut in contemporary Japanese, at the time the term referred to unbound hair. Accordingly, commentators insisted that the policy was not aimed at imposing Western styles upon the populace, but rather represented a return to classical Japanese practice.[43] However, the new hairstyles were commonly known as *zangiri* (or *jangiri*—"cropped" hair), which conjured up images of the loose, roughly cut hair of many outcastes.[44] Conversely, a song popular around the time the Ministry of State issued its edict included a line, "Folks with [long or bound] hair are barbarians—ain't it so? I guess so!"[45] That particular issue was sorted out in March 1873, when the emperor adopted a Western hairstyle, but it took another decade for short hair to spread throughout the male population. Although the encouragement of unbound hair (and soon, of Western haircuts) was just that—an exhortation, not a law—in fact local officials frequently took it upon themselves to pressure the men under their authority to adopt more or less uniform hairstyles. In such cases the object of their attack was as likely to be new, unconventional styles as the traditional topknot. Oku Takenori cites a series of increasingly irate injunctions issued by officials in Aikawa (later part of Niigata) Prefecture between 1873 and 1875, including a warning that the police would haul in anyone without an orthodox (short) haircut.[46] As a result of the imperial example and efforts like this, the practice of wearing short hair spread quickly (if unevenly) through the country. In May 1873 a Nagoya newspaper estimated that about 80 percent of men in Tokyo had cut their hair, while the following summer the *Shinbun zasshi* reported wide variation (though a tendency toward short hair) in prefectures in central Japan, with the variation mostly reflecting differences in the ardor of local officials. Thus, about 80 to 90 percent of men in Shiga Prefecture had cut their hair rather than pay a monthly tax (the proceeds of which were earmarked for education), while Aichi boasted nearly total compliance, thanks to the fact that the police were empowered to cut the hair of any shaggy maned prefectural resident they happened to encounter. By contrast, in nearby Mie, only thirty to forty percent of men had short hair, while further to the east a variety of traditional styles were still common.[47] Although Morse saw many men still wearing traditional styles in Muroran, a port in Hokkaidō, during his sojourn in Japan in 1877–78, in Tokyo only the aged and rustics failed to sport Western haircuts.[48]

Aside from armed resistance, the government also had to contend with individual attempts to manipulate the new standards in ways that did not jibe with official understandings of civilized behavior. We have already seen that some young women in Tokyo attempted to take advantage of the enlightenment fad to cut their hair. In that case, neither public opinion (at least as given voice by the *Shinbun zasshi*) nor the authorities were on their side. But for men, a haircut could similarly serve as a daring statement of one's aspirations for the new order. Men enjoyed a great deal more leeway than women in making public statements of their individuality. Although this is a complex issue that should not be subsumed completely within the realm of economics, it did have an economic aspect, insofar as it was up to individual men to guide Japan into the modern world order. The following anecdote from an 1874 book by Oka Sankei, although certainly apocryphal, illustrates the relationship between entrepreneurial individualism and the customs of Western civilization quite clearly.

Under the Tokugawa, members of different status groups wore their hair in a style appropriate to their station, but now one can wear his hair however he pleases. Barbers eager for business accordingly go to great pains to accommodate their customers' tastes, sometimes even dividing their shops into two rooms, one for those who prefer traditional styles, the other for enthusiasts of enlightenment (*kaika*). One day a young man of perhaps twenty-two or twenty-three—from his looks and demeanor, obviously a student—came into a certain barbershop. The barber clicked his scissors and leaned over to ask the customer what sort of haircut he would like. "The French 'Napoleon' style is all the rage right now, but perhaps the gentleman would like something a bit different—say, a 'Victoria' or a 'Washington'?" The student laughed derisively and replied a bit roughly, "Victoria is the queen of England. I am a stalwart fellow (*tenka no daijōfu*). Why in the world would I want to model myself after a barbarian woman (*ijo*)?" The barber scratched his head and apologized for his error. "Well, then, a 'Columbus' it is." The student grinned and replied, "I am a great man of the world (*tenka no gōketsu*)—those styles are all beneath me. Give me a 'Tamerlane,' or maybe a 'Genghis Khan.'" The proprietor was fed up but did not show it. Instead, he asked the student to wait a moment while he ran over to a nearby photographer's studio [presumably to find a picture to model the haircut after].[49]

The student's (or perhaps the author's—Oka was a Sinologue) ambivalence toward Western civilization is clear from his derisive comment about Queen Victoria and his desire to model his hair after an Asian hero's. But even if Oka intended the anecdote as a critique of the Westernization fad, he nonetheless had to accept the departure from earlier standards, which opens the door to a reading of the story as a call for Asians to beat the West at its own game. In either case, if it were not for the government's encouragement of unbound hair, the student would not have had the opportunity to express his ambitions so forcefully in the first place.

The manipulation of Western standards of civilization for private purposes extended beyond the realm of hairstyle. An attempt to subvert the association between outcaste status and meat-eating can be seen in a memorial submitted by a prominent Ōsaka *eta* (outcast) on the eve of the Restoration. In the fifth month of 1867, Mataemon, the headman of Watanabe village and hence the most influential outcast in western Japan, submitted an extraordinary request that the term *eta* be abolished. He began the memorial with an intriguing inversion of the popular understanding of the outcasts' origins. Rather than presenting his people as the descendents of foreign immigrants, he said that they were in fact the progeny of Japanese who had accompanied the Empress Jingū (trad. r. 201–69) on her (legendary) invasion of the Korean peninsula in the third century. There they adopted the Koreans' custom of eating meat, a practice they took back to Japan with them. This habit rendered them ineligible to serve the court as other Japanese did, giving rise to the distinction between themselves and the rest of the populace. Unfortunate though their situation was, they had served the nation by performing defiling duties and by maintaining the imperial tombs. Now amicable relations have been established with the foreigners. Mataemon noted, however, that "although the foreigners all eat meat and thereby defile our august country (*mikuni*), they have not been distanced from the 'four estates' (*shimin*). Only we have been so distanced, which is a truly lamentable state of affairs. We would be most grateful if, in your boundless compassion, you would remove the two characters *eta* from [the name of] our status." To add a bit of punch to his rhetoric, Mataemon closed his memorial by assuring the authorities that "we shall bankrupt ourselves to raise the funds (*goyōkin*) you have requested of us."[50] Here, too, we are presented with an appeal to economic utility over pre-existing status, though Mataemon did not go so far as to request outright that the outcasts be made into commoners. At any rate, he got his wish eventually—not only did the Meiji state abolish outcast status in 1871, but the emperor himself began to eat meat early the following year.[51]

The leadership of the Meiji state managed to keep the country on the civilization turnpike despite persistent popular resistance. Sometimes they had to yank the intransigent masses into line for their own good. Although Meiji officials no doubt saw the military, schools, and other institutions of the modern disciplinary regime as serving the public interest, let us illustrate this point with a brief examination of the attempt to deal with major cholera epidemics in 1877 and 1879.[52] In both cases, outbreaks in China warned the authorities to expect the epidemics before they actually arrived; in the absence of an effective treatment they did the best they could by ordering the construction of temporary hospitals to house the ill and thereby curtail the spread of the disease. However, not only was the death rate among patients admitted to the hospitals generally higher than those kept at home, rumors spread that the facilities' true purpose was to "remove the living livers" (*ikigimo*) of the patients "to sell to those Chinaman Westerners" (*Seiyōjin no Tōjin*).[53] Moreover, the policy ran directly counter to popular responses to the pestilence, which generally centered on mass prayer meetings at which food, drink, and—too often—the cholera bacterium, were shared. As a result, a wave of protests swept through the country in response to the containment effort, particularly in 1879. These protests—not to mention the deaths of an estimated 105,786 people in the 1879 epidemic—prompted the government to establish a public health bureaucracy over the course of the remainder of the nineteenth century.

For our purposes, two features of the cholera epidemics are particularly noteworthy. The first is the authorities' denigration of popular fear of the temporary hospitals as evidence of their barbaric backwardness, a response reinforced both by the rumors of forced organ donation and by a condescending attitude toward the popular religious practices the hospitals sought to supplant. The second is the relationship between the concept of hygiene (*eisei*) and civilization, a connection made explicitly by Nagayo Sensai (1838–1902), who coined the term *eisei* after a period of study in Germany in 1871, where he realized that existing words for in Japanese for "health" (such as *kenkō* and *hoken*) did not adequately express the linkages between private matters of diet and personal grooming and the state's need to keep the populace healthy.[54]

The introduction of Meiji standards of civilization and enlightenment entailed a synchronous process of expanding the notion of civilization so that it gradually penetrated into the core of everyday life, while linking barbarism to the urban poor and others whose livelihoods were marked as unsettled. Although the institutions of the modern state and the technologies at its disposal to order society were fundamentally different from those of the early modern regime, the linking of livelihood and civilization as emblems of the individual's place in society were the same. During the Tokugawa period, that link was mediated by the status system, while in modern Japan, the individual was cut loose from the bonds of status and allowed to be as civilized or barbarous as his ambition and ardor for honest labor dictated. In this way, the transition from Tokugawa to Meiji marked a revolutionary transformation of the relationship between the state and the individual, while at the same time articulating that transformation in terms of criteria with more than two centuries of institutional history behind them. Continuity and disjunction were one and the same.

By forging a direct connection between itself and individual subjects, the Meiji state in effect recruited individuals as active participants in the modernization project; through their adoption of the outward customs, inward discipline, and other accoutrements of civilization, its subjects signaled their readiness to join. Consequently, although the state decidedly retained the initiative, the people themselves needed an incentive to cooperate—they needed to feel they had a stake in the Meiji reforms. That incentive was the promise of freedom from the bonds of the status order and the prospect of autonomy in matters of occupation, residence, and demeanor. Not everyone cooperated, of course—but without a broad consensus on the desirability of attaining some sort of "modernity" (as defined vis-à-vis the Western powers), the state could not have bludgeoned the recalcitrant into submission.

Becoming modern was a question of both livelihood and customs. Insofar as occupation and livelihood as previously mediated through the status system were fundamentally reinterpreted after the Restoration, it comes as no surprise that customs as markers of status similarly had to be reinterpreted. Quite simply, people could not maintain their old customs and still be modern because the social and political relations those customs signified had been discredited. This explains why the authorities in Kyoto appended to their announcement of the abolition of outcast status the exhortation that former outcastes abandon "backward customs" (rōshū)—without, however, explicitly stating which customs counted as "backward."[55]

The modernization of customs through the linkage to livelihood was possible only because the political boundaries of the state had been clearly demarcated. The nation's boundaries marked off a uniform field in which some people were civilized and others barbarian, yet all Japanese nonetheless. In other words, the barbarian (iteki) Ainu of the early modern era were essentially different from the barbarous (yaban) residents of Shiba Shin'amichō, one of Tokyo's most notorious slums, during the Meiji period. Even aside from the differences in the emblems of their distance from civilization—the Ainus' unshaved pates and the slum dwellers' unwashed hands—the people of Shin'amichō never had to justify their Japanese identities. The poor were barbarous because they did not contribute to society, but that did not prevent them from contributing (and hence becoming fully civilized) at some time in the future. In other words, the barbarous peoples at the margins of Meiji society could civilize themselves in a way that the Ainu during the early modern period could not, for the Ainu had been exogenous to the status system and hence to the Tokugawa polity. Moreover, because modern civilization was generated from within, it follows that the state and its ideologues tended to rely on moral suasion rather than on unilateral attempts to impose civilization from above, particularly after the first, tumultuous decade of Meiji.[56]

The locus of agency was thus a central feature of the transformation of civilization across the divide of the Meiji Restoration. Whereas the intervention of the shogunate had been necessary to civilize the Ainu in the Tokugawa period, under the modern regime civilization and the full membership in the polity that accompanied it was available to anyone who cared to adopt it. Needless to say, the state and its hordes of freelance ideologues were only too happy to offer guidance in the form of positive moral suasion and negative denunciation of barbarism, but ultimately civilization was a matter of individual agency. The individual bore responsibility for being civilized or not because of the modern emphasis on livelihood. The poor were barbarous because they did not have the ambition or ability to embrace a productive livelihood and the markers of civilization that went along with it.[57]

Yet, barbarism in fact transcended livelihood in ways that the Meiji regime was often unwilling to face head-on. The poor were told that their customs made them barbarous, when in fact it was their poverty that placed them into that category. And while some of the residents of Shin'amichō and other slums no doubt ended up there of their own volition, it is also true that their poverty itself was in part a product of the development of capitalism in the late nineteenth century. Insofar as livelihood in a burgeoning capitalist economy is inherently perilous and thereby produces a steady stream of winners and losers, it stands to reason that some of the casual day-laborers, rickshaw men, and unemployed residents of the slums were there out of bad luck as much as an unwillingness to embrace civilization. However, according to the logic of the modern politics of the quotidian, they were marked as losers through their own agency.

This point is clearer when considering the Ainu, Burakumin (former outcasts and their descendants), and Okinawan and Korean workers in Ōsaka and Kōbe in the early twentieth century. Their impoverishment was the product of a combination of capitalist development, imperialism, and the dismantling of the status system—and of the modernized discrimination that accompanied Japan's transformation in the nineteenth century. The modern state took over the Ainus' homeland, negated their identity and their livelihoods, then labeled them as barbarous not only because of their (negated and hence officially nonexistent) alien ethnicity but because they could not support themselves. Similarly, Burakumin who lost their monopoly over leather-working and other traditional occupations, and Okinawans and Koreans who sought employment in the Japanese mainland after losing the ability to support themselves at home, became and remained barbarous through an odious combination of capitalist economics and officially tolerated discrimination. All were Japanese because they could not be anything else; but being Japanese left them stranded in a realm of discrimination from which there was no escape.

Chapter 6

Nationality and Difference in China: The Post-Imperial Dilemma

PAMELA KYLE CROSSLEY

To talk about the past is inevitably to slip into the ideological distillation of "then" from "now." As Joseph Levenson (1920–69) showed so brilliantly in his *Confucian China and Its Modern Fate,* this "then" and "now" consciousness was part not only of the intellectual discourse but the daily lives of people in "modern" China.[1] As in Russia, Turkey, India, Japan, and other societies that have already gone through their "modern" passage—and as in countries now undergoing the trauma, as in Mongolia and Afghanistan—the "then" and the "now" pushed against each other in urban architecture, in legal reform, in educational disputes, and in dress and transportation. The now-men dressed in trousers, with short hair and mustaches, and read newspapers while waiting for the trolleys. The then-men sat beside them in robes, beards, long hair or turbans, resting up before walking home or leading a donkeycart to market. That was modern China (and modern Taiwan and Hong Kong); it is decidedly past, though its echoes are still discernible in the countryside. Levenson referred to the early phases of the first two decades of the twentieth century as the "museumification" of the past. It was physically present, but held at arm's length, inanimate, scrutinized as one would a mineral that had fallen from a passing meteor. We might call it a self-orientalization: the splitting off of a culture condemned as "traditional," the reduction of the recent past to an object to be viewed and judged as if it does not, in fact, suffuse the present and the subject attempting to do the scrutiny.

It is surprising that until the last few years writers on Chinese history have tended to brush aside the fact that the Nationalist Republic of China claimed all the territories of the Qing empire (with the exception of Tibet) and received remarkably little international interrogation on that. Indeed, of the great Eurasian land empires disintegrating in the early twentieth century—the Russian, Ottoman, Austro-Hungarian,

British Raj, and Qing—only one persisted in its geographical form under a revolutionary national government. It is obviously different from the case of Turkey emerging from the ruins of the Ottoman empire, but it is also different from the case of the Russian empires. From the time of the revolutions of 1917, the former Russian empire was organized into regional entities that were surely under the governance of a central power in Moscow, but nevertheless developed internal coherence and external balances that have allowed them to survive the USSR. By contrast, post-imperial China was explicitly intended to be a centralized government, working with provincial entities with no independent claims to sovereignty (in many instances, not even the limited sovereignty they had enjoyed under the Qing). The lesser Eurasian empires of the early modern period also followed a general pattern of distilling into smaller, ostensibly national republics or falling under the domination of the expanding powers of Europe and of the United States. Only China was led by military and political leaders—possibly supported by a significant public consensus—determined to yoke the former imperial territories into a vast but centralized republic. In the simplest terms, China's nationalist leaders proposed an empire without an emperor. Their reasons were practical and in many ways remain persuasive. But the decision appears to have created a contradiction in basic assumptions of political affiliation that are tightly interwoven with many other destabilizing forces in contemporary Chinese society. A consideration of the problems of identity, and particularly of "ethnicity," suggests both the sources of this contradiction and its effects.

All polities deal with the problems of defining common elements of a political culture that are expansive enough to define a general unity, while limited enough to keep the consenting majority large. In most cases, the majority must agree that the basic form of the polity is good—under an emperorship they must affirm that emperorship is a righteous tool of government, and under a presidency or a parliament they must affirm that these, too, are beneficial. But other elements may or may not be added to the political culture, depending on where the slopes lie that would slide a majority of participants into some culvert of dissidence. In most cases, some agreement on the basic pattern of economic relationships must be at least tacitly affirmed. It may be possible to add a much longer list of items. A religious or linguistic conformity might be enforced, or strict standards of public behavior, or certain forms of historical indoctrination. What is important here is that emperorships tended to require a minimum scope of political commonality, while republics have tended to require a maximum. This is not an issue of "liberty" or "freedom" or "civil rights," but merely a focus on the index of cultural conformity necessary to maintain a political community. Indeed individual liberty, and what we tend to call "privacy," depends upon extensive political participation by the individual, with a minimum of coercion, and therefore requires a maximum scope of shared political assumptions. In contrast, emperorships required—or permitted—little individual political participation, and therefore tended toward little concern for maintaining a wide array of shared assumptions, standards, and behaviors.

The Qing emperorship as it existed at the height of the empire was peculiarly well-suited to accommodate tremendous variegation in the cultural, spiritual, and political hues of the empire. I have argued in *A Translucent Mirror* that the Qing emperorship was "simultaneous" and able to be manifest as regionally authentic in its communion with diverse histories, languages, natural environments, and religious ideologies.[2] The cultural orientations of most (not all) individuals in facing the emperorship was of little importance. All that mattered was that emperorship was affirmed to be good, that the emperor was a unique point of integration between the present and the past, between the supernatural powers and the human world, and among all the varieties of culture within the realm. The corollary was that the emperor was insightful, empowered, and righteous in a way that no other individual could be, and therefore no individual could presume to political enfranchisement in competition with, or rejection of, the emperor. By contrast, the People's Republic of China (PRC) was, at the height of Mao Zedong's (1893–1976) power, ostensibly based upon the complete political enfranchisement of every individual, which meant that the range of common assumptions within which individuals operated had to be total. In this arbitrary comparison of the periods of the Qianlong emperor (1711–99) and Mao Zedong, an inverse relationship between political enfranchisement and conformity is suggested, and many more examples could be added to extend the same theme. In contrast to emperorships, republics do not rely upon a single, personal, transcendent power to integrate all the diversities that compose any society. They depend upon the internalization of a complex set of assumptions and affirmations, which allows a maximum portion of the population to be politically participative without the society disintegrating upon the strain of unlimited, irreconcilable, intractable frames of reference.

Republics, then, must put a premium upon cultural transformation. They must use public education, military conscription, constant ideological conditioning and an ever widening theater of standardization and consistency to persuade a critical majority to assent to the state's continuation, perhaps even to make large sacrifices out of fear that without them the state might not continue. This assent required by the abstract republic under discussion might be contrasted to the consent demanded and usually extracted by emperorship. Because the assent is conscious and willed, it is an aspect of political enfranchisement. It is unprecedented personal political participation, at the price of unprecedented personal conformity. Historically, not all emperorships accommodated unlimited cultural diversity, and not all republics have demanded total conformity. But with respect to the "ethnic" complex of local affiliation, to conscious alienation from a perceived majority, and to distance from the dominant historical narrative, emperorship (not to say "empires") can be associated with a liberal central posture toward local essentialisms, while republics can be associated with a centralizing, radical transformative agenda.

There is an important connection between this transformationalism and something that is often described as "universalism." Both depend upon a notion that human nature is fundamentally the same everywhere, and that humans may therefore be reshaped in thought and behavior in such a way as to benefit society—that is, to benefit themselves by means of state intervention. Those who advocate transformationalism tend to see history as a large and mostly forward process, in which profound forces work to affect the lives of a majority of people in a generally similar way. As Joseph Levenson pointed out long ago, both Confucius (c. 551–479 B.C.E.) and Karl Marx (1818–83) were universalists or have been understood that way, and for this reason Levenson suggested that Communism exerted a power over Chinese thinkers that really owed more to its universalistic similarities to Confucianism than to any special charm of Communism itself. The great anti-universalist idea of Levenson's work was nationalism, which he suggested could never have been expected to satisfy the universalistic values of Chinese thinkers for long. Of course, Levenson was aware that in the 1930s nationalism and Communism were synthesized in Stalinist thought, and in this form "Communism" enjoyed its greatest influence, both direct and indirect, throughout Asia and parts of Europe. But Levenson's interpretation implies that the amalgamation of universalism and particularism in Stalinist thought (of which Mao Zedong Thought was an interesting variation) was an unstable one, which must eventually decompose into a predominantly transformationalist or a predominantly essentialist mass.

The dichotomy between transformationalism and essentialism is more than a little heuristic, and need not be belabored here except as it reflects upon the contemporary problem of whether the trajectory of social and cultural differences in China will follow a "liberal" or a "radical" path. Levenson already demonstrated the flaw in the opposition of "liberal" to "radical" by relating Confucian and Communist universalism to one another: one appears mild, rational, and liberal; the other radical, coercive, and totalitarian. But their similarities are more pronounced than their oppositions when their perspectives on cultural difference are compared. Confucianism and Communism are among that set of historical philosophies that hold differences among humanity to be temporary, superficial, irrelevant to concepts of justice or rectitude, and destined to be eradicated by the mill of historical change. Nationalism is an implacable challenger to such notions, since it posits sources of justice, freedom, and cultural value that are not universally derived or necessarily subject to universal forces of historical change. In a similar way, theories based on the particular "nature" of thought and behavior, whether related to gender, genetics, or religious conditioning all defy the fundamental transformative assumptions of more universalistic policies. What is at issue here is not what causes historical change, but what basic ideas have been evinced in twentieth century policy and discourse on "ethnic" minorities and their place in a modern Chinese society.

Though the Qing empire did not formally end until the abdication of Puyi (1906–67) in 1912, the end of the history of the emperorship comes much earlier. After the death of the Daoguang Emperor in 1850, a remarkable decline in the personal effectiveness of Qing emperors has been noted by all historians of modern China; successors to the Daoguang emperor (b. 1782) were invariably weak in power, sometimes weak in body, frequently intimidated by eunuchs, by imperial princes, by the Empress Dowager Cixi (1835–1908), occasionally imprisoned by their bullies, and possibly even murdered by them. This does not have to be seen as an episodic melodrama of intrigues, corruption, and high-level mayhem. There were striking structural and ideological changes in the emperorship in this period, profound enough that the history of the Qing emperorship may be considered to have ended here. The general changes were related to a steep decline in the revenues directed into the control of the emperor and his personal offices, the resurgence of institutions of princely governance that had been integral to early Qing political culture and never entirely destroyed, and a long-term reaction against the style and content of imperial rule under the Qianlong emperor. The emperorship clearly also was affected by a succession of crises that damaged both its charisma and its institutional efficiencies. The explanation for these large changes is not germane to this discussion. What is important is that the war from 1850 to 1864 to quash the Taiping Rebellion and its coeval disorders took place in an environment in which the emperorship no longer functioned.

Seventeenth- and eighteenth- century Qing emperors had been forced from time to time to defend the ideological sources and contemporary legitimacy of the Qing emperorship itself, but never before the Taiping War had Qing rulers been required to fight a comprehensive ideological battle against a rebel state. This was partly because the challenge from the Taiping leaders and propagandists, particularly before 1859, was itself cultural. The Taipings argued not merely that the Qing emperors as a lineage were illegitimate, corrupt, or unjust, but that China's elite traditions were generally invalid. A thoroughgoing cultural offensive against the Taipings was also required by the fact that the Qing emperorship was no longer the final argument for the integration of society and narration of history. In the military struggle of the 1850s and the subsequent struggle for economic recovery and political revitalization in the 1870s, a progressively programmatic "Confucian" orthodoxy was set against putative heterodoxies, a "benevolent" imperial rule was posed against "wild," "chaotic," or "violent" rebel organizations, and an emerging "Chinese" civilization was offered in preference to superstitions, delusions, deviations, and crudities of ethnic cultures. The transformative assault from the Taipings was met by a transformative assault from the Qing government, a struggle that presaged successive struggles in the twentieth century.

Mary Clabaugh Wright's (1917–70) argument in *The Last Stand of Chinese Conservatism*, more implied than direct, was that the period of reconstruction after the suppression of the Taipings was an attempt to return to earlier (in her characterization, "traditional") social mores and political institutions.[3] Certainly, this was the character of state expression during the war and through the reconstruction period, but a close examination of earlier Qing political culture suggests that there was little about the anti-Taiping government exertions that was actually "traditional" or established. It was tradition by invention, a broad-based, conscious use of communications and educational institutions to forge a novel ideological conflation of the Qing empire with "China," and of putative Chinese traditions (foremost "Confucianism") with the Qing court. A similar hypostatization of tradition was implicit in Levenson's *Confucian China and Its Modern Fate*, which dealt with a slightly later period. Though Levenson seemed to be considering the confrontation between "tradition" and "modernity," his tradition was "New Text" Confucianism, a late Qing phenomenon that had a very problematic relationship to scholarly assumptions of the earlier Qing, and of more remote periods. Kang Youwei (1858–1927), a focus for Levenson, was in fact one of the great precursors of twentieth century transformationalism. He envisaged a society without an emperor, in which the internalization of social concepts and personal values informed by Kang's interpretations of classical texts would create a polity in which "independent" (but, in fact, conformative) personal actions would enrich a stable, rational, utterly just society.

It was this late, amended, post-Taiping ideology—not "tradition"—against which revolutionary nationalists were staunching themselves at the conclusion of the Sino-Japanese War in 1895. In their rhetoric they were at least partly dependent upon the literary output of the Qianlong court, but a far more important point was that essentialism (and its contemporary manifestation as racial thinking) was the fulcrum upon which radical, nationalist, republican, rejectionist rhetoric of the last years of the nineteenth century turned. In contrast to defenders of the Qing, nationalists claimed that foreign invaders would not equate themselves with civilization, that they could not be sincere defenders of Chinese people and their interests, they could not bring a national "China" into a world dominated by national entities and national economies.

In order to make their claims even minimally coherent, nationalist propagandists had to unglue "Confucian" values from a Chinese nationalist identity. This was best done by rejecting the transformationalist ethic in late Qing Confucianism, which had proposed that all individuals "and all cultural groups" were equally receptive to the civilizing influence of Confucianism. This was the logic that had allowed the Qing to characterize itself as the greatest champions of Confucian civilization in opposition to the Taipings, though their own origins were outside China and thus outside the Confucian domain. So long as the anti-Taiping logic was allowed to stand, nationalists could not argue that the Qing ("the Manchus") had to be displaced as China's rulers. Nor could they argue that the Mongols, who had distinguished themselves in the forefront of the Qing conquests, should be, indeed must be, excluded from Chinese civil life. So long as late Qing transformationalism based on allegiance to Confucian values prevailed, the grounds nationalists were seeking for uniting those identified as "Chinese" against those identified as "Manchus," "Mongols," "Uigurs," "Tibetans," and others could not be found. But rejection of Confucianism, and of the dynasty, and of the Manchus needed to be bound together in the rhetoric of "nationalism."

Propagandists for national revolution had some very complex historical trends to deal with. One was that the form of a post-imperial polity in China had not been prescribed. A second was that as the empire decayed, more national entities than one threatened to emerge. The geography of identities at the end of the Qing period exposed deep fractures in the Qing empire, fractures which the Confucian transformationalism of the late Qing had been intended to heal but which remained. Central China, particularly in those areas that had been materially devastated in the Taiping conflict or urban areas suffering the traumas of war-related refugee problems, was beset by sharp differences in local economic conditions as well as profound status differences within the localities; this frequently came to be expressed as hostilities among religious groups or groups with variant geographical origins. In southern China hostilities between Hakka and Cantonese, or between

Cantonese speakers and Fujianese speakers were widespread in the countryside. In the cities of Shanghai and Guangzhou (Canton), merchants cooperated with those whom they regarded as sharing their local place (or their religion, as in rivalries between Muslims and others), and migrants from rural regions or poorer provinces were expected to do the menial labor.

Outside the central provinces, more overt and more threatening chasms began to yawn. In the aftermath of the Taiping War local leaders—many of them Muslim—attempted to establish an independent state in Yunnan, suppressed only in 1872 with the execution of Du Wenxiu. Shaanxi and Gansu provinces were wracked by a variety of Muslim uprisings between about 1856 and 1873, culminating in the attempt of Yakub Beg (1820–77) to establish an independent Muslim regime in the Northwest. Zuo Zongtang (1812–85) expressed the consummate post-Taiping imperial ideology in insisting that the differences to be distinguished were not between the nationalist affinities of "Chinese" and "Muslim" but between the universalist values of "good" and "evil." In practice, of course, his suppression of the Yakub Beg movement was brutal and specifically targeted against Muslims. Perhaps the lasting impression it made on later nationalist thinkers was that the Yakub Beg episode had explicitly risked the alienation of major stretches of Qing territory should a distinct culture and distinct stratum of leadership become alloyed with a northwestern identity. Zuo's attempts to disentangle Russian political interests from those of Yakub Beg and other Muslim rebels were adroit and prolonged, culminating in the agreement at St. Petersburg in 1881 and the subsequent creation of the Qing province of Xinjiang, "centrally ruled and militarily governed," in 1884.

The Chinese nationalists debated, as did their counterparts in Turkey, Russia, Austria, and elsewhere, about creating a purely "national" state within the "passes" (that is, south of the Great Wall and east of Xinjiang) that would be "Chinese" and in which only Chinese would be welcome. As in the other national schemes of the era, this involved the requisite discussion of racist ideology, the displacement and disenfranchisement of aliens. But the first decade of the twentieth century showed the folly of such a notion. Surrounded by imperialist and still expanding powers in Russia, Japan, and the Raj, how could a small China surrounded by hostile and easily subverted states really maintain its independence, let alone become prosperous and strong? These fears were reinforced by Japanese interference in Manchuria and Mongolia, Russian in Mongolia and Xinjiang, and British in Tibet well before the fall of the Qing was even imminent. Security considerations forced Chinese nationalists to insist upon integration and defense of virtually the entire Qing territorial corpus. The leaders of the PRC insist that this is still the case today, and that for security reasons they were forced to absorb Tibet even though it had been independent in the (disastrous) Republican era.

By the first decade of the twentieth century, Liang Qichao (1873–1929) had parted ideological company with others of the nationalists who continued to adhere to a radically essentialist line. Liang's new interest in constitutional monarchy, in mass education, and in gradual political change are often considered "liberalizing" in contrast to the stark racism that continued to animate much nationalist discourse. Liang was indeed liberal, in the sense that liberalism at the turn of the century meant the extension of education, industrialization, and limited political enfranchisement through imperialism. He saw that if Zhang Binglin (1869–1936) and others were correct, and Manchus, Mongols, Tibetans, Muslims, and others could not and should not become culturally Chinese, then China's expansion could not be justified and its historical mission would come to a halt. In his short essay, "Feudalism and Its Effects," Liang explained that the two great phenomena of the later Zhou had been the "dissemination of civilizing influence and assimilation of aliens." Liang saw himself as both a contemporary of this process and a participant in it. "The rulers of Zhou undertook the tremendous task of colonization by dispersing civilized groups among the aboriginal semi-barbarous tribes. There was great opposition to this by the aborigines. It took several hundred years of persevering struggle to civilize the region between the Taixing Mountains on the north and the Yangzi River on the south. This cultural expansion is one of the greatest and most difficult undertakings recorded in the history of China."[4] Its next greatest advance would be due to national imperialism (*minzu diguozhuyi*). What Liang foresaw (and here he remained a disciple of Kang Youwei) was a modern transformationalism that he regarded as different from the exploitative, opportunistic semi-assimilation of imperialism. Indeed, his "national imperialism" was not an abstract theory, but was his own characterization of the kind of expansionism being vigorously pursued by the United States of America— a progressive, liberal, if self-congratulatory program for improving others by making them more like oneself. His transformationalism would be the antecedent to full political participation by all adult men in the society (and perhaps, in the long run, adult women too). Only by becoming internally, authentically similar, could citizens become free.

The conclusion of the Nationalist Revolution of 1911–12 was a compromise in which the Republican forces based in the south called a draw with the diffidently loyal forces of the north. It was agreed that the last Qing emperor, the child Puyi, would abdicate as ruler of the Qing empire, and the empire itself would be dissolved; these were accomplished on February 12, 1912. In return, the imperial lineage would continue as an institution, and imperial properties in the Forbidden City as well as parts of the northeast would be protected. There was also, as part of the compromise, a set of laws protecting the property and the safety of certain minority groups. These Laws of Favorable Treatment, ratified by the new Republican parliament in 1912, specified that Manchus, Mongols, Uigurs, Muslims, and Tibetans would enjoy the same property and personal safety rights as the Chinese. In other words, the leaders of the Republic were stipulating that, contrary to the rhetoric they had assiduously promoted for twenty years, the peoples who had been fundamental to Qing rule in China for almost three hundred years would now be legally incorporated into a Chinese republic. The Laws of Favorable Treatment were promulgated in the aftermath of violence against identified "non-Chinese" that had been intense in many localities, particularly the northeast and northwest. As a political gesture it was important, but the power of the Republican government was not such as would actually prevent further violence by mobs intending to harm non-Chinese or destroy their property. Equally important, the Laws were no general protection for non-Chinese, and peoples not specifically protected by the Laws—for instance, the Zhuang, Miao, Kazakhs, Koreans, or Russians—had no avenue for seeking equality except under the general criminal statutes. In sum, the Laws of Favorable Treatment were more an artifact of the compromise that ended the civil war of 1911–12 and less an emblem of a society that in any way embraced universal civic values over particular essential criteria of identity and status.

After the formal demise of the emperorship in 1912, the ability to articulate cultural spheres without claiming cultural content for the state itself was lost. Successive Chinese republics were forced to deal with a state rhetoric that in one form or another founded itself on an ideology of heritable Chinese identity. With respect to ethnic zones of northern China and Inner Asia, this policy considerably narrowed—in comparison to what had been available in Qing times—the rhetoric that could be used in claiming dominion by the Chinese republics. The choices were in fact two: the rather brutal claim of Chinese superiority as a mandate for the subordination and control of local populations, or the ostensibly more benevolent transformationalist ideology which had a long history as a Confucian discourse in imperial history and underwrote the socialist transformation ideologies of the ethnic policies of the People's Republic of China from 1949 to the Great Leap Forward.

Revolutionaries of 1911–12 adopted—with minor alterations only—the geographical contours of the despised Qing empire to define their "China." As suggested, the proximate inspiration for this policy was strategic. During the last decade of Qing rule, atrophied governance from the center and outright colonization had allowed Japanese, Russian, or European influence to become dominant in Korea, Manchuria, Mongolia, Xinjiang, Tibet, and Taiwan. Whether to chance the instabilities of divergent historical, cultural, and political assumptions with the new Republic, as Liang Qichao advocated, or whether to exclude such destabilizing internal influences and instead risk competing as a smaller nation among many jostling neighbors, as Zhang Binglin advocated, was a serious strategic as well as philosophical issue. Equally profound was the influence, in the 1910s, 1920s, and 1930s, of educators, journalists, and historians (many of them government advisors) who were fixated upon the idea of the "nation" (in this case the Chinese nation) as the natural beginning and end of political narrative. Chinese writing in this vein drew upon a complex range of sources, from early modern scholars such as Lü Liuliang (1629–83) to major international intellectuals such as Oswald Spengler (1880–1936). It was easy, from this perspective, to argue that historical injustice arose from the distortion or suppression of national energies, and that historical rectitude could be found in the resurgence of untrammeled national states. Chinese writers arguing the necessity of destroying the Qing empire had at their backs both material evidence—Chinese society's injuries at the hands of Qing and subsequently European invaders—and the abstract international consensus equating national sovereignty with justice. Clearly, any independent national government was better than any imperial administration, and the more "national" the government, the better. The problem in China (again, contrasted to Turkey, or Greece, or Russia) was that in order to be secure from its historical bullies, this national entity must be vast and control areas that the empire had controlled (for the same reason that the empire had controlled them). With or without explicit acknowledgment of Liang Qichao's prescription, leaders of nationalist China began to pursue his "national imperialism."

The claim to these territories could be framed in national terms, but only if the Qing empire was retroactively nativized. Thus, China could legitimate rule over the former Qing territories in northeast Asia on the basis of the idea that the Manchus were sinicized, beginning in the Ming period (never mind that this was logically inconsistent with the nationalist rationale for overthrowing the Qing as dynasts). It could claim Mongolia and Inner Asia on the basis of Mongol submission to the Qing, Tibet on the basis of Yuan and Qing dominion, Taiwan on the basis of outright conquest by the Qing armies. In these cases and more, the absorption of the Qing dynasty into the history of "Chinese" rulers facilitated argumentation for political incorporation of these areas in the post-imperial period, and as a corollary nationalist rhetoric in the early years was argued strongly and simplistically that the Qing rulers had been "sinicized."

One way to continue the story is to look at the period of political dis-
union in China, at least prior to 1931, as one in which the impossible
contradictions of the national republican political culture were obscured by the overwhelming problems of high-level rivalries, local social
dislocation, economic imbalances, and constant pressure from a preda-
tory Japan. But the obverse is also true: the irresolvable contradiction in
the national republican political culture precluded centralization, general economic reforms, and true national security. And, it may not be a
coincidence that as national reintegration began to be achieved by force
after 1928, the large-scale conflict between the Nationalists and the
Communists took hold. At bottom, it was the search for a national political culture that could address the anomalous geocultural entity that
was modern China.

The Nationalists had no answer to this that could have made any
sense. They eventually found a niche for themselves in the discrete and
relatively homogeneous geographical entity of Taiwan, and that is probably not coincidence either.

"Warlordism," as it is generally understood with respect to this era,
enabled the loose federation of regions and the midlevel negotiation of
regional and sub-regional interests. But the authoritarian federalism of
the period also permitted the growth of local interests that were inimi-
cal to centralization of the state. Many of these trends had distinct "ethnic" and regional undertones. Mongolia and Tibet were nominally
independent in this era; though the Nationalists were acute in their attempts to gain friends in the high ranks of the local political leaders, it
was not a prominent part of the national Chinese agenda to gain control of these distinct zones. But the margins under nominal Chinese
control were subject to constant disturbances from separatists, often ag-
itated by Japanese (in Mongolia and the northeast) or British (in Tibet)
encouragement. In 1917 alone, the uprisings of the Mongol nobleman
Babojab and of the Manchu prince Shanqi (1863–1922) disturbed
northern China, the two-week restoration of Puyi to his throne by the
bannerman Zhang Xun (1854–1923) diverted the capital, and a border
conflict with Tibet escalated to warfare. In combination with warlordism
throughout the former Qing territories, threatened or gradual foreign
interventionism provided leverage to highly localized, distinct regimes,
including the two Muslim republics (Kashgar in 1933, Yining in 1944).
Other warlords, such as Yan Xishan (1883–1960), provided hospital employment and political encouragement to young participants in the
Mongol home rule movements in Inner Mongolia.

As in the 1930s, the Nationalists attempted to tighten their control
over ethnic zones, the struggling Chinese Communist Party (CCP) pursued a policy of recognition and qualified regional autonomy. The divi-

sion of the Chinese territories left them open to Japanese aggression, and to the violent struggle between the Nationalists and the Communists that was resolved in 1949. The decades of guerrilla fighting necessary to secure the People's Republic made the Party beholden to many of the peoples of the southwest, northwest, Mongolia, and the northeast, some of whom were enfranchised as early as the promulgation of the constitution of the first soviet republic in Jiangxi.[5]

But for "China" the Communists had an answer—not necessarily the only answer, but at least a possible one. "National minorities" in the south, west, and north were early and critically important supporters of the Communists who in 1931 had specifically guaranteed minority cultural and property rights in the constitution of the Jiangxi Soviet. The political culture prescribed by Mao and his interpretation of Communism had the capacity to define goodness and justice in ways that had nothing to do with whether an individual was Chinese. Justice was an international proposition again, and class enemies were more dangerous, more to be universally feared, than barbarians of the old days or foreigners of the present. Joseph Levenson saw the appeal of Communism to intellectuals as the presentation of a universal moral philosophy that filled a void left by the rejection of traditional universalism. I think there was more that was offered, and that Communism was the only political culture that could have prevented the Qing corpus from breaking rapidly into mutually destructive parts.

On looking at the effects of the CCP campaigns to unite China between 1931 and 1949, one is struck by the degree to which transformationalism, rather than nationalism, returned to Chinese discourse and eventually to policy. The fall of the empire had discredited conventional Confucian universalism in most quarters, and nationalism was overtly enshrined as official thought. This nationalism was exclusivist, and in all probability managed to thrive for the primary reason that Nationalist China was not expansionist; on the contrary, it struggled to maintain the vast boundaries of the Qing empire and to prevent extension of foreign influence within those boundaries. Its exclusion of non-"Han" minorities from all but the basic political protections made it, in fact, a contractionist regime—rendering its realm of inclusion and dominance smaller than its borders. In combination with the military decentralization of the period between 1900 and 1928, this contractionist ideology meant in practice that the ostensibly non-Han communities of the remoter regions of China were able to function without great interference either in their practical affairs or in their modes of self-definition. And though those decades of relative self-reliance and self-definition were respected by the constitution of the Jiangxi Soviet, in practice a growing Communist movement had to have the same basic transformationalist dynamics as late Qing Confucianism before it. In the long run, the goal was eradication of material differences and the unification of all in the struggle for the realization of socialism.

Following the reunification of the country in 1949–50, the CCP stipulated no large policy for dealing with regional cultures. The constitution of 1954 famously enunciated the principles (still preserved in Article 4 of the present constitution) that all "people" (*renmin*) in China are equal—an important difference from the language of the Laws of Favorable Treatment, which had only specified the property and personal protections of the groups who had been recognized and historicized under the Qing empire. Official policy toward minorities was designed under the guidance of Li Weihan (1896–1984), promulgated in 1956, and given public debut in August in an article penned by Fei Xiaotong (b. 1910) and Lin Yuehua in the *People's Daily*.[6] The establishment of a policy for identification of minority nationalities (like the concurrent policy for the identification of intellectuals) was antecedent to the application of graduated political pressure that culminated in the Great Leap Forward, though there is no reason to suppose that participation in the construction of identifying criteria were cognizant of the fact. Indeed, Li Weihan was later punished during the period of radicalization for his lack of support for transformational policies.

It may appear ironic that the creation of all the main autonomous regions was accomplished in the late 1950s. On the surface this may appear to have been the culmination of the movements for home rule for which Ulanfu (1906–88), among others, had been a distinguished advocate. In fact, the contexts in which these autonomous regions were created reveals not a liberalizing but a radicalizing dynamic. Dru Gladney has termed the process of Uigur containment in their autonomous zone as their "minoritization"—the end of aspirations to sovereignty and national independence, and the beginning of formal identification as a subordinate "minority nationality" within the People's Republic of China. There are echoes of the ways in which the creation of the province of Xinjiang in 1884 followed the devastation of the several independence movements of Turkestan in the mid-nineteenth century. The creation of the Tibetan Autonomous Region was even more extreme, following the actual military occupation of Tibet by the People's Liberation Army in 1959.

What this sequence suggests, against the backdrop of the Great Leap Forward, is that the creation of the autonomous regions and the rising of a new, radical, transformative political wave shared some logic. The apparently liberal developments by which Muslims, Yi, and other regional minorities were encouraged to form their own mutual aid teams in the early 1950s, the apparent granting of formal recognition to deep and enduring differences among cultures marked by Li Weihan's pronouncements, and the welcoming into the Party ranks of Mongol, Yi, and Tibetan members in 1956 and 1957 would appear to have its culmination in the granting of autonomy to the large "ethnic" regions. But, in fact, the creation of the regions opened the period of stringent political and economic pressure on the minority eras during the Great Leap Forward. Many topical explanations can be found, including the utility of creating separate statistical mechanisms for the minority areas that would eventually show them to be less "productive" and less "socialist" than the non-autonomous regions. But there is a deeper logic, too. Transformationalism thrives on the identification of its targets—from the Taipings in the late Qing, to the monsters, outcasts, and subversives of the Cultural Revolution. The hallmark of transformationalism is not the conceit that everyone is the same, but the proposition that all correct historical forces have the potential to make everyone the same.

It should be remembered that the Soviet and Chinese intellectual communities were severed after 1960 and that Chinese scholars and bureaucrats were encouraged to pursue putative Stalinist interpretations in order to legitimate the Chinese system, not to bring it closer to the post-Stalinist Soviet system which was perceived to be in condition of deviation. During the Cultural Revolution, the decentralized, essentialist posture of the Common Program toward local and ethnic identities was specifically rejected as insular and partisan. Instead a centralized ideological program was sternly proposed, one that would insist upon the transformation of all peoples under the guidance of a legitimate despotism—in this case, the "broad revolutionary masses." In 1968, the new constitutional committee resolved:

The old party constitution stresses only the special characteristics of the nationalities and the conducting of social reforms, according to their own wishes, but not the party's leadership and the social revolution. . . . By emphasizing nationalism (*minzuzhuyi*) to the exclusion of patriotism (*aiguozhuyi*) and internationalism, it in reality creates national schisms. The broad revolutionary masses maintain that the following directive from Chairman Mao should be stressed in the new party constitution of the Ninth Congress: "National struggle is, in the final analysis, a question of class struggle." The unity of all nationalities on the basis of the thought of Chairman Mao Zedong and on the socialist road should be stressed.[7]

In periods of political radicalization—the anti-bourgeois movements of the early 1950s, the Great Leap Forward, the Cultural Revolution, and the more current campaigns against spiritual pollution and bourgeois decadence, "minority nationalities" have systematically come under overt or covert attack. The brittleness of the "minority nationalities" concept in China is the state's most aggressive policy against what it fears. By construing minorities as definitionally backward, by attempting to control them through preferential policies, the state hopes to prevent the maturation and spread of ethnic consciousness. This is a subject that has received extensive comment with respect to Islamic fundamentalism, and is self-evidently relevant to the new prestige and power of Kazakhstan (religion quite apart) and the potential for development in Mongolia.

What I am trying to suggest is the specific link between political structures and concepts of identity, whether essentialist or transformationalist in character. In the *fin de l'empire* scenario, race was essential to the formation of oppositionalist ideas. Its appeal seems to have resulted from the mixture of Huxleyan and Spencerian rhetoric with a widespread sense of political outrage, which ignited a dynamic rereading of the anti-Qing tracts of the seventeenth century. Race quickly became the only persuasive concept of identity in an environment in which all other identity structures were rapidly decaying. An idea like Zhang Binglin's that the next century's "China" would be founded upon the sympathetic cooperation of people with their own "kind" led gracefully to his advocacy of a small, culturally monistic republic governed by autochthonous institutions firmly founded on the history, language, and lineage structures of the historical Chinese. A different idea, like Liang Qichao's, that the next century's "China" would be a tutelary monarchy conducting the people toward parliamentarianism, citizenry, and national imperialism led gracefully to his advocacy of a large, cosmopolitan empire governed by institutions adapted from the most successful liberal empires and improved by Chinese practice.

The overriding transformationalism in state ideology after the Qing period frames this very striking problem of empire without emperorship for the People's Republic of China. As with all republics, a unitary identity within a monolithic political culture is a necessity, but with regard to the former imperial territories in the northeast, in Inner Mongolia, Xinjiang, and Tibet, this is accompanied by an imperial (that is, transformationalist) agenda. Though China is now emphatically without emperors, its ideology of dominion remains underwritten by the transformationalism which—whether in Confucianist, liberal imperialist, or socialist armor—has historically opposed the essentialism that has underlain the definition and enfranchisement of local identities in China's periods of relative decentralization.

This is a disturbing thought when put in the context of the contemporary pronouncements by the Chinese government. Though socialism is still the official ideology, nobody is being encouraged to practice it. This means nobody is being overtly socially transformed. What is the basis, then, of unity in contemporary Chinese political culture? According to government spokesmen, it is "Chinese culture"—not a set of values, as Confucianism or Mao Zedong Thought had aspired to be, but merely the particulars of Chinese culture as they might be defined at any particular moment. There being no universalistic appeal in this supposedly "unifying" theme, one is left to understand that the true unifying dynamic is the overwhelming numerical superiority and economic clout of the "Han" Chinese, who still enjoy a ratio of dominance vis-à-vis their "minorities" that is not only quantitatively different but qualitatively different from those in other major nations. Chinese culture, in this scenario, unites only because it dominates and intimidates.

A great deal of venerable discussion of China's social and cultural history has revolved around the opposition of "public" and "private." These have been variously defined, usually in connection with the context under discussions—"sphere," "spaces," values, and the like. The usual conclusion is that the "public" in China is easy to translate and easy to identify, while the "private" is subtle, elusive, and perhaps an alien intrusion of foreign observers. I would like to suggest that public and private be considered in the context of political culture and cohesion. Public may be considered that area of shared assumptions that define political unity, while private would be everything else. Private in this heuristic means not secret, or concealed, or silent, but discretionary. What is private may be universally known. The question is: Are private choices made on the basis of personal values and preferences or on the basis of public prescriptions that underlie political unity? In this sense, the private realm in imperial China was relatively large and the public relatively small, while the opposite has been the case in China under the People's Republic. Privacy would manifest itself as choices made for personal reasons, and not subject to public judgment even if they are universally known. For instance, in the United States an "ethnic" identity is to a large extent a private matter. This does not mean it is a secret; it means that whether one goes about labeling oneself as being a given ethnicity is a matter of personal sentiment, personal values, and personal perceptions. The choice is understood to be threatening to neither the basic unity of the political culture nor to the material safety of other citizens. In theory, a society that could tolerate (that is, understand as private) such diversity of ethnicity could also tolerate diversities of religious faith or affiliation, or gender identification. This contrasts to China, where choices regarding ethnic identification are limited to the legal ethnic identification of one's own parents. The standards are "objective," shaped by state criteria and not by the sentiments, imagination, or historical sense of the individual.

Many who see a general liberalizing pattern in contemporary China hypothesize that values of privacy, and perhaps even a legally encoded privacy concept, will be the eventual basis for reconciling cultural difference (primarily religious practices) with political unity in China. This idea is frankly derived from a model of European and American "civil" societies and seems to beg the question. Though limited property rights now have a respectable history in the PRC, and though religious choice has had a limited protection in Chinese law since 1954, there is no evidence that "privacy" in any coherent form is creeping into either Chinese law or Chinese civil values. To the extent that religious diversity has taken public, civil forms, it has not been welcomed by the government or naturalized in public practice. Indeed, while the government of the PRC is hardly threatened in any real way by the extremist, violent movements for independence or secession in Xinjiang, Inner Mongolia, or Tibet, it is much threatened by the movements for religious choice, diverse public behavior standards, and liberalization represented by, for instance, the Muslim street marches in Beijing of March 1989. Similarly, the relative mildness of the Falun Gong demonstrations elicited an inversely violent government response. It is not extremism that can threaten the government, but the tendency to incorporate movements for cultural diversity into normal, peaceful, civil action. This would mean the normalization of diversity, something to which republican thought in China—socialist or not—has never found a practical approach. The continuing response of the government, one expects, will be to insist upon this role in the licensing, endorsement, and limitation of minority identities. To understand the reason for this, we should remember that, though at present the government of China appears content to permit a good deal of political decentralization and economic disparity, it cannot permit the process of local differentiation to go on indefinitely. There will eventually come a recentralization, and these centralizing phases in the past hundred and twenty years have been accompanied by strongly transformative political campaigns. The relegation of cultural difference to a "private" realm would eradicate the ability of the state to identify the targets necessary for that process to occur.

Historically, all societies must insist upon at least a minimal transformative agenda, and evolve institutions—primarily legal and educational, but often also linguistic, religious, commercial or sumptuary—that will support it. The scope of transformational requirements varies almost infinitely. In ancient China, the group retrospectively characterized as "Legalist" in the Han period hypothesized that so long as the population obeyed the dictates of the government, other transformations would be either secondarily derived by necessity or unnecessary altogether. The "Confucianists," by contrast, insisted that total, ongoing programmatic transformation of each individual, family, village, region, and finally the whole nation was necessary for civilization to continue. In modern times, virtually all polities have had to require that individuals be brought to a point of consent on the basic nature of the polity itself—subjects of monarchs must affirm that monarchy is good, citizens of republics must affirm that republicanism is good, and so on—but beyond that societies have demonstrated that requirements can differ greatly. The scope of transformation varies from polity to polity, and moreover in the vast majority of cases has historically varied within regions and societies. "Ethnicity" as a value, as an expression, as political dynamic, is clearly one of the many elements in any society's transformative agenda at any particular time.

What is striking about the case of contemporary China is that transformative requirements are both unusually visible—meaning in practice intrusive, coercive, and superficial—and unstable. Beginning in 1949, the government has consistently found it necessary to announce the agenda and to require changes in unusually rapid vogues. With respect to regional, historical, and personal cultural variation, the government's original orientation was what its spokesmen termed "Stalinist." It envisaged socialist transformation as an inevitability of the near future, but posited a finite field of acceptable variation in the near term. Among the acceptable variations were phenomena most writers consider "ethnic," or described in Chinese by terms associated with *minzu*. Not everything foreign observers would consider "ethnic" was tolerated, but language use, some religious conservatism, social deviation (even slavery, in the case of the Yi), and physical segregation were recognized as tolerable. Indeed, it has been a hallmark of CCP policy on ethnicity not only to tolerate these differences but to insist that they are invariably the definition of "ethnic" phenomena. While "folk" customs such as costume, dance, and some traditional economic activities are objectified and celebrated, they also are made the impassable barriers of ethnic identity itself. Since 1949, to live outside the autonomous areas, speak Chinese exclusively, be educated, urban, and progressive have not been recognized as "ethnic" except in the few and easily identified party members who function as tokens of inclusivity, and in fact of the inevitability of ethnic dissipation. As, in the late 1950s, policy became driven by the leap "forward," the program to eradicate ethnicity was accelerated, and continued overtly and coercively through the 1960s and most of the 1970s. In the era of Deng Xiaoping (1904–97), the transformative agenda has narrowed slightly, and the ethnic criteria of the early 1950s have by implication recaptured the discourse on historical and contemporary ethnicity.

What the CCP has never tolerated, even in its most liberal periods, is a criterion of ethnicity that would take it outside the Stalinist standards of language, residual religion, vicinage, and highly limited economic segregation. An individual who speaks only Chinese, lives in a city, works in an office, has no folk customs or superstitions, and yet considers himself or herself "ethnic" makes no sense either in CCP policy or in Chinese social discourse. It is true that the simplistic heritage lines of paternal or maternal transmission of ethnic affiliation are usually recognized in policy, but the evidence is manifest that individuals who invoke these associations to assert ethnic status in the absence of gross manifestations of clinically ethnic behavior are considered opportunistic (or even sociopathical) frauds. It is possible to attribute the simplifications and stolidity of state ethnic criteria to a lack of imagination or absence of flexibility. It is probably more important to see this approach not in terms of unnecessarily ossified conservatism, but in terms of positive and pointed control. An acknowledged ethnicity that found expression in individual behaviors, beliefs, historical perspectives, or political ideals would constitute a cache of privacy, potentially subversive of not only state policy but social stability.

Within the terms established in this essay, the remarkable point about the period of the nationalist revolution in China—roughly 1890–1930—is that it did not fall within one of the periods of centralizing, radicalizing, transformative trends. That is, it was based upon a profoundly decentralizing notion, of exclusivist nationalism, and civic participation for ancestral "Chinese" only. And it was unsuccessful. "China" as framed by the geographical contours of the Qing empire was not in fact united, nor was the government centralized. This is a remarkable difference from the post-Taiping period, and from the period of rising dominance of the CCP after 1931. It also contrasts to the period of the Cultural Revolution, when, despite many other catastrophic events, power was indeed recentralized under the more radical, nationally-oriented factions of the CCP. This suggests that Levenson's early hypothesis that the universalizing faculties of Confucianism or Communism are prerequisites to national integration in China may actually be inverted to provide another interpretation entirely: that national integration requires a universalizing rhetoric and nurtures a universalization of culture.

The proposition that universalizing political culture is required by a nationalist agenda is superficially ironic, but historically demonstrable. In the French Revolution, universalizing rhetoric about liberty, fraternity, and equality produced an integration of regions into a geographical France, but did not further integrate France into a global community (despite the Napoleanic conquests). American universalization of democracy and capitalism fostered American national unity, but did not in itself make that nation "universal" in its appeal. Stalinists had a very direct insight into this dynamic and openly condoned the propagation of a universal rhetoric of Communist transformation in the service of national integration. But today we rarely give Stalinists credit for the obverse insight: that without universalist pretensions, national integration cannot be secured.

This much is a commonplace of political science and modern historical study. The more specific point to be made in relation to China is that this universalizing of political culture that is the staple of modern republican state organization is the modern cognate of emperorship. It works the same way, representing the articulation point of diverse histories, cultural orientations, and religious realms. It transcends the limits of statutory time and provides the wellspring for changes in constitutional or legal institutions. From the time that the Qing emperorship in China ceased to function during the Taiping War, universalizing rhetorics and transformationalist agenda have been the *sine qua non* of true national integration. This being the case, it is not surprising that China's present leaders cling to a rhetorical "Communist" mission while working day and night to make the country capitalistic. Until a new universalizing rhetoric can be put in service of Chinese national integration, the old will still be used to keep privacy in check and a coherent political culture obscured.

Part Four
Locale, Nation, Empire

Chapter 7

Cultivating Non-National Historical Understandings in Local History

LUKE S. ROBERTS

This essay explores how discourses of national history dominate the writing of regional history of early modern Japan. Regional history is a strong field among Western historians of Edo-period Japan.[1] Yet regional history has been unable to free itself from national studies in significant ways. I shall argue that creating histories which are not framed by discourses about modern nations is a useful method to understand certain important issues relating to the history of the nation itself, and also, more directly, may create new ways of understanding human history to set alongside the nationalizing history which is so prevalent in our profession today.

I wish to make clear here at the outset that I am not arguing that national history as such is wrong or should be abandoned, but rather that the creation of a parallel intellectual space for non-nationalized histories is desirable. Modern historians live in a highly nationalistic environment and its discourses shape our thought and expression as well as our understandings of what information is meaningful and important. One of our most important and widely accepted functions in society is to create national narratives, a task in which we participate perhaps not fully consciously or with intention but with great effectiveness nevertheless. At a basic level these narratives reaffirm in our minds the importance and the very existence of national political identities in general and thereby also contribute to a sense of national communal identity in the reader. At other levels such narratives create specific national identities which are used in politics, society, and culture, influencing how people of one nation relate to other nations. As such, the national narratives we create are expressions of our participation in nationalism. Such participation as historians is, in my own judgment, not in any fundamental sense morally good or bad. However, it is merely one framework of understanding, and it is therefore intellectually limiting when we are unable or unwilling to leave this understanding. In this way, my general argument goes well beyond the situation of the historiography of early modern Japan. The points made in this essay should be applicable to the histories of regions within almost any modern nation, but the evidence I shall use comes from my own field of study and personal experience.

Modern regional history in early modern Japanese studies is strongly tied to or imbued with nationalizing discourses. First, let us look at the primary titles of works of Edo era regional history published in the 1990s: *Central Authority and Local Autonomy in the Formation of Early Modern Japan, Capitalism from Within, The Making of a Japanese Periphery, 1750–1920, The Meiji Unification Through the Lens of Ishikawa Prefecture, Fishing Villages in Tokugawa Japan, Japan's Protoindustrial Elite, Land and Lordship in Early Modern Japan,* and *Mercantilism in a Japanese Domain.*[2] What are they about? Ishikawa is the only regional name to emerge, and the author apparently felt constrained to make explicit in the title that Ishikawa is not the object of his study but merely a lens by which to view the national tale of Meiji unification. The titles assert that they are all narratives about Japan.

The last of these titles is my own book, and a description of how that title came to be illustrates some of the forces which nationalize the regional histories we write. My professor Marius Jansen (1922–2000) once told me that he ceased encouraging graduate students to study local history because such students had difficulty finding publishers for their revised dissertations. No publishers wanted something that was "only" local history. Indeed, one early reviewer of my own manuscript wrote: "Roberts faces a dilemma common to those who study localities within Japan, which is that we foreigners aren't really interested in sections of Japan; we want to get the poop on the country as a whole." Indeed, when it came time to publish my reworked dissertation on Tosa domain, I was eventually turned down by four presses, three with essentially the same reason, "the scholarship looks nice, but it won't sell." Finally, and most fortunately for me, Professor Jansen provided me with an introduction to Cambridge University Press, which was receptive to my project and finally decided to publish the manuscript.

The negotiations over the eventual book title reflect what I call the nationalizing values in our field. My original title was *Imagined Economies: Economic Nationalism in Eighteenth Century Tosa.* In the hopes of improving my chances with presses, Professor Jansen was the first to suggest that I change my title, and he offered *Economic Policy in Tokugawa Japan: Merchant Contributions in a Samurai Domain.* I tried to stick to my own title early on but ended up with four failures. My tenure case was looming and I had no book contract. When the Cambridge acquisitions editor wrote, "I'd like the title to be as descriptive as possible, and to include 'Japan' in the main title," I quickly agreed, and the final result was *Mercantilism in a Japanese Domain: The Merchant Origins of Economic Nationalism in 18th-Century Tosa*. The pressures that led me to bring Japan into the title are those that incessantly work throughout the field. They are not merely intellectual and political but also economic and institutional: The press quite reasonably wanted to sell as many books as possible, and the editor knew that putting "Japan" in the title would increase its marketability. The library entries for my book and all the other regional histories noted above repeatedly highlight "Japan" as the national frame of reference essential to organizing our knowledge in familiar and accessible ways.

Most powerful of all are the purely intellectual constraints against writing non-nationally framed history. I would like to say that my book is really about Tosa and only incidentally about Japan—that my new title lied—but that would not be true. Although, while writing, I had consciously formed the thought that Japan should enter into the story only insofar as it helped me to understand Tosa, a quick reading shows that in addition to arguments concerning Tosa, I make many arguments concerning Japan as a nation. Reading reviews of my book, I see that readers understand and judge it almost completely as Japanese history, with Tosa either being a "case study" of the Japanese institution, the "domain," or more generally its history as an example of what was going on in the larger Japan at the time. This makes me recognize once again the tremendous discursive power of nationalism on our consciousness. I feel a certain sense of failure in not achieving my aim of writing a non-nationalized regional history which would be of interest to people who are not specialists in the region. As a result one of my major projects since the publication of the book has been to understand more deeply the influence that nationalism has on the discourses we produce.

The main titles of the regional history books noted above indicate the most common strategy for getting regional history published and read in English, which is to argue for a Japan-wide relevance to the topic. This relevance can be created in a number of ways. One is to make an argument that this region played a special role in the national narrative. This is the strategy of such excellent works as Marius Jansen's *Sakamoto Ryōma and the Meiji Restoration* and Albert Craig's *Chōshū in the Meiji Restoration*.[3] They discuss regions that jumped onto the national stage in the mid-nineteenth century and by influencing the nation "earned their place in history" as special locales which contributed to the national story. There is also the approach influenced by the social sciences such as seen in John Hall's classic *Government and Local Power in Japan 500 to 1700: A Study Based on Bizen Province*. Hall does not argue for Bizen's special place in Japanese history but rather "to draw connections to the wider flow of national history or to read into observations made at the local level implications for a broader understanding of Japanese history."[4] This involves two related strategies: One is to see the region in terms of how it experienced the national story, and another is to look at the local history as somehow an example of a national story. These are indeed the dominant strategies seen in the monographs of recent years, including my own. A concomitant demand made of this type of regional history is that the researcher must establish whether the history of the region is representative of national characteristics or not. This issue has recently been analyzed by Philip Brown in his "Local History's Challenges to National Narratives." Brown recommends that the recent increase in the practice of regional history by English-language historians of Japan is an opportunity to correct current national narratives or to highlight the diversity of experience within what is too often a homogenized national narrative of Japan. If somehow we can compare enough regions then we can understand Japan better, creating a geographically complex and thereby more accurate national narrative.[5] Brown's observations are an important statement of the possible contributions of regional history within national narratives, but distinct from what is being argued here, because his essay is about the quality of the national narrative itself, not about the national framing of history as such. Based on the evidence of work to date, what one has to do to make a work of regional history perceived to be important is have it somehow convincingly alter a narrative of the nation.

The need to make the nation the category of history which confers upon research narratives significance is to be found in the origins of the modern academic discipline of history itself.[6] In a recent forum in the *American Historical Review*, entitled "Bringing Regionalism Back into History," European history scholar Celia Applegate summarizes the effect on regional history: "The devaluation of regions and their pasts in the nineteenth century thus emerged naturally alongside the triumph of the national historiographies."[7] The prevalence of this phenomenon is echoed by the other historians of the forum representing the historiographies of East Asia, Southeast Asia, and the United States. There is a curious disjuncture between the comments of the historian of the U.S. South, Michael O'Brien, and others. He writes:

So a historian of the American South comes to the articles on European and Asian regionalism with mixed feelings, greatly pleased to see such intelligent synthesis, but mildly puzzled at the notion that all this is news. In Mississippi, regionalism is not "a less-than-familiar perspective." . . . So it is tempting to say that Southerners have been there, done that. . . . In fact they might be slightly dismayed to discover how trendy Southern understandings might be.[8]

Actually, there are great differences between the uses of, or politics of, regional history as practiced from within a country and that as practiced from without, a point not sufficiently considered in the papers in the forum. The papers make the now customary, and for the most part accurate, criticisms of modernization theory and area studies, but do not systematically discuss the divide between regional history as generally practiced within a nation and that produced without. One generally creates narratives of internal others and negotiates the directions and process of incorporation into national identity, and the other generally creates narratives defining foreign "nations" and how we (nationals) should relate to them. There are similarities as well: Both create "others" to the national narrative, thus reinforcing national identity, but the imagined audiences of these literatures and the interests creating internal and external others for the national narrative are usually altogether different. Indeed, the O'Brien essay fully enacts possibilities of the internal perspective: After establishing his region, the U.S. South, as the place within the United States where regional history has long been practiced at its best, he then makes it the key to his narrative of U.S. historiography itself. His conclusion then moves to establish national specialness and difference for the U.S., when he writes, "I suspect that the new availability of the language of regionalism in Europe and Asia may be partly due to the cultural influence of the United States. . . . Applegate and Wigen are certainly discerning an indigenous movement in foreign cultures, but they may also be listening to an echo of American ideology."[9] I need not comment on the national parochialism of the statement, but it is instructive for this paper to note how what I will call an "internal regional historian" first defines his nation by the qualities of his region and then uses his nation as the medium through which to relate his knowledge to those somehow conceptually outside his nation.

Three of the papers in the AHR forum also highlight the role of modernization theory in deemphasizing regional history or subordinating it to the nation, but I doubt that it had a particularly distinctive role in this regard. Histories written long after the heyday of modernization theory and informed by diverse theoretical perspectives still consistently create national narratives and grant regional history its importance in terms of what it says about nations. Even when the intent of the author is to complicate an identity, to retain inconclusiveness and open-endedness, when one asks "of what?" the answer is always the nation. At the beginning of our new millennium, the vast majority of history professors continue to be hired to teach national histories and write national narratives, because we continue to live in an era of nation-states. It could be stated as a truism that whatever the era, histories create narratives which hold political import for the authors and readers. Indeed "regional history" itself has long had a vigorous and essential (while frequently denigrated) subaltern role within modern national history. In a certain sense, it could be said to have been invented along with modern national history.

To bring a longer historical perspective to this point, it is worth reflecting for a moment on history writing in times and places in which the nation was not as politically potent a concept as it is today. Most of Japan during the Edo period was strongly ruled under the overlordship of the Tokugawa clan, but it was not governed along the lines of a nation-state. In the Edo period there was a complex network of coexisting and somewhat overlapping spheres of (and concomitant discourses of) governmental authority. Most prominent among these were warrior household governments and their associated territorial state governments.[10] The Tokugawa samurai household was at the apex of a feudal polity and economy based upon ideologies of service, grants of prerogatives, and status privileges accorded to household heads. The ruling warrior houses were certainly the most powerful form of political organization on most of the islands in that day. Although today we would normally think of household matters as something beneath or subsumed within government, in the Edo period the samurai household itself was a dominant form of government. Thus, *kahō* (house laws) and *kasei* (house government) were major sites of political and ideological struggle and the governmental household an important anchor of personal identity, much in the same fashion that the nation is an important anchor of identity today.[11] It should come as little surprise therefore that "house histories" were one of the most common forms of history writing in the Edo period.

The *Tokugawa jikki* (True record of the Tokugawa, 1843) is the annals of the Tokugawa clan, overlord of all of the samurai houses who ruled the territory of most of what we call Japan today.[12] The original title of this history was *Ojikki* (Reverent true record), and the absence of the Tokugawa name is both enabled by and reinforces the supremacy of the house within the discursive and political space of its intended audience. There was no powerful need to situate it within the discursive space of Japan by specifying the Tokugawa name. The implied community of readership in such a title perhaps is akin to giving popular U.S. history books titles such as *The Story of Our Country* or *Our Great Country*.[13]

The *Ojikki* is a "family" history recording births, deaths, and household rituals, and simultaneously a "public" history creating political messages about good and bad government.[14] Within the *Ojikki* events and people gain importance in the narrative to the degree that they affect or are involved in the Tokugawa household. A branch house or retainer house has a position in this history analogous to that of "regional history" in modern national narratives. Thus, for example, the Hayashi clan, retainers of the Tokugawa (and in the fortunate position of being the appointed authors of this history) asserted their importance in terms of their contributions to the Tokugawa.[15] The births and rites of passage of every child of the Tokugawa clan are recorded but not those of other samurai houses, however important. Likewise, though major Tokugawa government appointments, retirements, inheritances, and punishments of all major retainers, including lords who ruled their realms, are recorded, the governmental issues of domains were not recorded. For example, Tokugawa "reforms" (*kaikaku*) are described, but the reforms of government within various lord's domains were not. Likewise commoner protests which occur in Tokugawa demesne are recorded but similar events occurring outside are not. The hierarchy of importance of historical information is informed by the political hierarchy of the household. This same ideology is revealed in another Tokugawa sponsored history, the *Kansei chōshū shokafu* (Histories of the houses, compiled and edited in the Kansei era), a compilation of the house histories of all of the retainers of the Tokugawa house with right of audience. The histories of thousands of retainer households are included, and with the exceptions of the "pre-fealty" histories of the first generation sixteenth-century founding member of some houses, the content of the histories are almost completely records of service to the Tokugawa and consequent recognition and reward.[16] The point here is to indicate that the political order of the day had tremendous influence upon the narrative strategies of the histories. The common discursive frame of these histories was the household, and the hierarchy of importance of (retainer) households within (ruling) households was analogous to the hierarchies affecting the role of regional history within the national region.

Most daimyo lords and governments also commissioned household histories as a normative form of history writing. For example, the Yamauchi household, who owned and ruled Tosa domain, commissioned the *Otōke nendai ryakki* (Abridged annals of our household, 1849) as such a history.[17] The historiographical choices made within it are similar to those of the *Tokugawa jikki* but with the Yamauchi family as the center hub through which other historical facts gain significance. Even when dealing with the Tokugawa, it is primarily Yamauchi service to the overlord which is described and not events important to the Tokugawa themselves. Yamauchi centrality in their own narrative is evidenced in the naming of the household itself. In the *Tokugawa jikki*, the Yamauchi clan appear under the name Matsudaira. This was the discarded Tokugawa family name which had been granted to the Yamauchi as a sign of favor by Tokugawa Hidetada (1579–1632) in 1610. This "sign of favor" also was a means to weave the Yamauchi more tightly into the Tokugawa household and reduce autonomy.[18] However, within Tosa and their own household, the Yamauchi retained their clan name—and indeed granted the Yamauchi name to many of the households of its retainers such as the Andō, the Inui, and the Hayashi who are known as Yamauchi in the *Otōke nendai ryakki*. As is the case with the *Tokugawa jikki*, the starting point of the history is the birth of the dynastic founder rather than the acquisition of ruling authority itself. In this way it is separate from a "country" history of Tosa. In addition to annals of service to the Tokugawa overlords, there are annals of the government of Tosa and the Yamauchi household. Within the *Otōke nendai ryakki* all individuals, retainer households, and events appear and are important to the degree that they affect the narrative of the Yamauchi household. Thus, in the same way that today the nation confers importance on the facts of regional history, in the early modern part of the archipelago ruled by households, the ruling household conferred importance upon the facts of the histories of lesser, subsumed households.

Country histories as opposed to house histories also existed in the Edo period, but they were generally of a highly dynastic sort. The main inspirational sources for such histories probably were the Chinese dynastic histories. The *Dai Nihon shi* (History of imperial Japan, an early draft completed in 1720) was more a history of the imperial clan than of Japan regionally conceived, but the title does center upon the country rather than the clan, and perhaps it is not too far off from early "great man" types of national histories. It certainly was a major influence on the first widely popular history of Japan, Rai Sanyō's (1780–1832) *Nihon gaishi* (An unofficial history of Japan, 1827). The Yamauchi lords of Tosa also commissioned a history of their domainal country of Tosa. It was divided into two parts called *Kokushi naihen* (An internal history of the country, 1869) and *Kokushi gaihen* (A history of the external relations of the country, never completed). It also reads as a heavily dynastic (Yamauchi) history of the domainal country, taking as its starting point the entry in 1600 of the Yamauchi rulers into Tosa, rather than dealing with the history of earlier Chōsogabe lords of Tosa.[19] More truly regional histories and historical document collections were compiled in Tosa but by common people rather than by government scholars.[20]

A most interesting fact is that, just as the *Kokushi naihen* was completed in 1869, it was renamed *Hanshi naihen* (An internal history of the domain).[21] This was in recognition of the fact that the new Meiji government, beginning in 1868, had ordered lords to change the designation of their realms from *ryō* and *kuni* to *han*. This was part of the unification process of the modern nation-state. The term *kuni* or *koku* (which I and some other scholars such as Mark Ravina choose to translate as "country" when referring to domainal states) had become a politically potent concept in the developing nationalist order of the Meiji state, and therefore the Meiji leaders had an interest in monopolizing the term as well as related terms such as *kokumin* (subjects/citizens of the country), *kokuhō* (law of the country), *kokusei* (government of the country), and the like which had previously been employed by domainal countries as the language of their territorial state rule. Although the domains and household governments were not abolished by the Meiji government until 1871 when the prefectural system was instituted, the process of terminologically erasing the "countryness" of the lord's domainal countries began in 1868.[22]

Most relevant here is the fact that this three-year interim period between 1868 and 1871 has had a surpassing influence upon the way modern historians term and view the previous 267 years of lordly domainal rule. *Han* is the standard term for domainal countries in modern history books, rhetorically situating them as mere domains within an timelessly national Japan. Furthermore, since the usage of the word *han* rhetorically unifies the daimyo household and its ruling territorial state apparatus, it also leads to a view of households not as being polities in themselves but rather as being subsumed within a state polity. This safely nationalizes the past at another level by making the territorial state the presumed or natural form of government.

There exists a brilliant deconstruction of how the use of modern terminology to describe the past projects back into time the emperor-centered nationalism of Japan. The historian Watanabe Hiroshi pointed out in 1997 that a number of terms now used to denote the Tokugawa and their government, such as *shōgun* (military general) and *bakufu* (military government), were uncommon terms in the Edo period but were popularized by the people who created the Meiji state in order to emphasize the subordination of the Tokugawa "general" to the "emperor" who was becoming the center of Japan's past and present. In the Edo period the Tokugawa were officially and most commonly styled the *kubō* or "ruler" and their government the *kōgi* or "government."[23] Watanabe also notes (based upon the research of Fujita Satoru) that the modern posthumous Japanese title for emperor, *tennō*, had been revived in 1840 after a lapse of more than six centuries. A forceful and assertive *kinri* (an earlier term for "emperor") named Kōkaku (r. 1780–1817, d. 1840) had engineered the revival in preparation for his own death. The political climate of the 1840s included a slowly destabilizing Tokugawa authority which permitted this break from six centuries of tradition.[24] This revival is thus part of the collapse of the Tokugawa and hints at the shape of the new order to emerge soon afterward. Nevertheless this interesting history has been unknown to nearly all historians of Japan.

This is not the result of a conspiracy of the right wing, inasmuch as the information has been available all along; it is simply that the discursive force of nationalism makes us blind to disruptive realities. Learning of these various events of renaming helps us better to understand the process by which Japan was created into a nation-state when confronted with the Western dominated imperial world order. All of these *linguistic changes* happened in the era of the Meiji Restoration because language usage was a fundamental part of reshaping political consciousness to what became a modern national mode. This has been and will continue to be a meaningful way of seeing the past. What is undesirable is that it should have such a monopoly upon how we try to understand and narrate that past.

I have suggested above how we can better understand the origins of national modernity by not blanketing the past with nationality. Let me suggest here briefly how we can better understand some aspects of the Edo period past by playing closer attention to the language use of the day from a regional perspective. Watanabe is mainly interested in the thought and politics centered on the ruling Tokugawa who were overlords of nearly all of Japan, and he has not evinced interest in regional history or perspectives. His narrative is mainly about the relative balance of authority and power between the Tokugawa and the *kinri* in Kyoto. The 'emperor' is pushed farther from center but the image of Japan itself as a national polity and enduring entity is not in question. For this reason, he takes *han* as a term which identifies domain governments and does not note that *han* was neither an official term nor anything but an uncommon pedantic word in the Edo period. Why? Perhaps it is because Watanabe can thus ignore that within domainal discourse the term for the government of domainal countries is *kōgi*—the very same word as that which he argues we should use to describe the Tokugawa government because of its standard use in the Edo period.[25] His new terms are ostensibly taken from the Edo period usage but they do not quite reflect Edo period meanings. This is because Watanabe has his new terms take on meaning within an assumed discursive space of Japan. It is, of course, common modern practice to have terms immediately locatable within a national framework, but this practice misses the way words were used and manipulated in the Edo period. Modern terminology must fit hierarchically within—and take on meaning within—the assumed discursive space of "Japan." Within an Edo period domainal country the unspoken frame of reference for most political terms was the domain and not Japan, or the daimyo household and not the Tokugawa household.[26] This means that when a person in a domain spoke to another and said *kōgi*, "the government," he normally meant the government of his lord and domain, not that of the Tokugawa, and when he said "*kuni*" he meant his domainal country, not Japan. However, in modern formulation the country-like aspects of large domains as seen in discourse incorporating such terms as *kuni, kokka, kokusei,* and *kokushi* become rhetorically invisible, and the user of the term *han* can thereby conveniently obviate the issue of the unspoken modern national frame of modern words describing pasts on the archipelago.

Perhaps most fascinating and troubling, because it is difficult to describe within a nationalist vocabulary, is that the language of lord, government, and country would be completely different when a domainal person spoke to a representative of the Tokugawa. For example, the *kuni* (country) would become *ryō* (territory), the *kōgi* would become *jibun shioki* (personal management), the *kō* (public authority) would become *watakushi* (personal), and as we have seen in the case of the Yamauchi, even the family name might change. This language use reflects the politics of the day. All lords were personally subject to Tokugawa rule and, facing him, were nothing but "private" servants. However, facing their own households and domains they were the supreme public authority. They ruled their own households as absolute—indeed in certain contexts of local understanding divine—rulers, and ruled their fiefs with nearly untrammeled authority. From a national perspective this situation appears mutually contradictory, and the seeming contradictions have traditionally been resolved by putting primacy on the Japanese national framework of understanding. However, political consciousness and action in the day are arguably better understood by realizing how people then appreciated and tried to manipulate the complex network of identity boundaries.[27]

Furthermore, as noted above, government was not merely the territorial state but also the household. Domain territorial governments coexisted with but did not fully overlap with the samurai house governments which ruled powerful people and the economy largely under a metaphoric structure of the household, and this was sometimes at odds with the ideology of the domainal "country." The lumping together of household and country into the one term "*han*" makes it difficult to perceive the dynamics of interaction between house government and domainal country government. Because political struggles are often struggles about perceived relationships which are formed by rhetoric, I would assert that a clear perception of how the participants saw or described their world is necessary to understand their motivation and strategies of engagement. In my analysis of the merchant origins of *kokueki* (national prosperity) mercantilism in Tosa, perceiving these two governmental forms as dynamically separate is (among other things) necessary to understanding commoners' struggles with their samurai governments in the eighteenth century. Local merchants gradually con-

vinced samurai rulers that preservation of the economic domainal country was more important than devotion to the household economy of
service, using a rhetoric of what today would be called economic nationalism scaled to the domainal country. This history is nearly impossible to describe using modern nationalizing frames of knowledge.

The compartmentalized nature of politics in much of the region of
Japan in the Edo period was something which early modern scholars described as *hōken*, perhaps best translated as "polity of sealed off spaces of
authority."[28] Each political space was relatively independent when it
came to internal matters and was also to a certain degree a discursive
space. This is only noticeable and analyzable through practicing early
modern local history in its own terms, taking its own view as the central
perspective on an issue. Only when we do that can these histories be free
to reveal logics separate from the national, to become direct lessons on
humanity and its history, rather than lessons mediated through the nation. If we nationalize the terms of understanding by which we view the
past, much is tamed to be less disruptive of the modern national narrative but much of the past thereby becomes invisible.

In the process of appropriating regional history for its own needs, national history makes it difficult to understand regional histories on their
own terms insofar as they detract from national narratives. Indeed, if
they do not contribute to national narratives, they thereby become
unimportant. I have suggested above that, if we practice history from a
regional point of view, we may understand the historical development
of the nation more fully, and we may understand various types of pre-
national consciousness more accurately and thereby better perceive the
logic of political action and engagement. The former of these two is, of
course, a form of national history, and asserts within our modern national context the value of history from a regional standpoint. The value
or significance of the latter is less obvious. If the "big picture" which be-
stows significance upon our narratives is not national, then what can
it be?

If modern history writing is framed by modern political concerns,
then the trick should be to identify current political interests and groupings and somehow make a relevant story out of the past history of a region. If currently, for example, the struggle for women's rights and
gender expectations is a political issue, then a history of merchant
women in the eighteenth century city of Ōsaka need not make claims for
them to represent Japan but merely the experience of a class of women
in one city. This would free the writer from the need to argue the rep-
resentativeness or non-representativeness of these women vis-à-vis merchant women in other Japanese cities, who might live under entirely

different expectations and conditions, and to make most improbable comparisons with samurai women in the city or with women in poor rural families. Concentrating on their immediate environment, one might then find something about the experience of these women in their mercantile society comparable to that of shopwomen in sixteenth- or twentieth-century Paris, for example. There indeed might be perceptions that one would miss if one were constrained—as I believe we are—to make it a narrative about the early modern "Japanese women," or early modern "Japanese merchant women."

Ultimately such history rests upon the author making a simple narrative choice. "What if I wrote a history which deliberately made no reference to the nation? What would I find? What logic would emerge?" It could be done using historical methods of which Ranke could be proud, and at worst would be a small adventure in narrative.

Chapter 8

Where Do Incorrect Political Ideas Come From? Writing the History of the Qing Empire and the Chinese Nation

PETER C. PERDUE

In this essay, I address two paradoxes. First, despite nearly two centuries of violent upheaval, culminating in one of the world's most radical revolutionary movements, social institutions from China's imperial past are showing vigorous signs of life today. Second, despite the key role of nationalism in the history of modern China, major theorists of nationalism consistently ignore East Asia. Are these two phenomena connected, and is there an explanation for them? The two paradoxes have a common answer, related to the difference between theory and practice. Although Chinese nationalist ideologies ferociously attacked the institutions of the past, and the Communist state destroyed many of their formal structures, everyday social practices survived to regerminate the institutions when the pressure relaxed. Theories of nationalism have focused excessively on nationalist ideologies, which claimed to be "modern," while neglecting the lived experiences that often generated community solidarity before the intellectuals arrived. Pre-nationalist China did not have a single set of coherent, consistent "traditions," but it did create a template on which the new nation was built. Post-reform China today relies for its economic vitality on the same social institutions that radical nationalists tried but failed to eradicate. Everyday life has won out over theory.

The Resistance of Everyday Life

Evidence of the revival of pre-modern institutions in China is abundant. Popular religions in the Daoist and Buddhist traditions are flourishing. Festivals banned under the Maoist regime have returned. Overseas Chinese capital and local donations have sponsored the rebuilding of guild halls and lineage halls. The Cantonese have renovated lavishly the tomb of an ancient local king, while officials in remote regions celebrate the "traditional" virtues of their area in order to encourage the tourist trade.[1] City walls are being restored; the temple of the City God is no longer a warehouse. Even "secret" societies have re-emerged, and popular religious traditions have blended into a dizzying array of new sects. Uneasy officials have openly attacked conspicuous ones like the Falun Gong, but many others enjoy official approval, or at least tolerance. Any Qing magistrate would smile ruefully at seeing local cadres attacking only a selected number of "heterodox" teachings, while allowing many others to breed undisturbed.

Commercial institutions have proved especially resilient. Since the economic reforms provided legitimacy for private economic activity, markets, restaurants, and shops have proliferated in China's major cities. They are still only a small percentage of the national economy, but they have conspicuously reinvigorated the life of the streets. Peasant marketing of agricultural goods has been the most active generator of commercial activity since the reforms began.

To what extent do these activities have links with the past? It could be argued that the new commercial activity is entirely a product of reform policies, and that peasant marketers and shopkeepers are only responding to individual incentives of economic gain. Yet the location of the new economic activity shows uncanny links with the past. A comparison of the economic centers of the Southern Song (1127–1279) and the People's Republic of China (PRC) shows remarkable overlap. Clearly individual economic actions are strongly constrained by the inherited geographical structures that characterized both the empire and the modern nation. The actual forms of commercial organization also do not display simply individualistic behavior, but coincide quite closely with the organizations that were most dominant in the nineteenth century: the family firm, the artisan's guild, the labor boss. *Guanxi*, or personal connections, still significantly affect social interactions in post-reform China, as they did in the Qing.[2]

Of course these practices have not simply bounced back intact. The modernization programs of the twentieth century have transformed them substantially. We should avoid, whenever possible, speaking of a "traditional" China comprised of a specific set of constant, coherent institutions that endured over centuries. Here, I refer primarily to the social institutions prevalent in the Qing period (1644–1911), even though many of them had earlier origins.

Communist ideology attacked the major social institutions of the Qing dynasty as products of a backward, feudal system. They repressed lineages, guilds, religious sects, and private markets in the interests of creating a new society based on class alliances. If we focus on ideology alone, we find little sympathy among revolutionary cadres for the central cultural and economic institutions that continued to be vital through the mid-twentieth century. Mao Zedong (1893–1976), for example—like Sun Yat-sen (1866–1925) before him—saw secret societies as useful supporters of a tactical alliance against his enemies, but in his appeal to the Gelaohui secret society he called for its members to join in solidarity with the revolutionary proletariat against the oppressors of the nation. He claimed that "our views and our positions are . . quite close," but he did not guarantee or recognize their autonomy.[3]

Despite the ideology, however, some of these practices not only survived, but were reinforced during the Maoist period. In the realm of everyday life, many structures continued in a new guise. The state structure inherited the imperial bureaucracy, from the highest level of regions down to the county level. Because the PRC took over the boundaries of the Qing state (minus Taiwan, Hong Kong, Macao, and Mongolia), the frontier regions kept nearly the same boundaries created in the eighteenth century. The number of counties and their boundaries also did not change much from 1800 to 1950. Below the county, of course, the PRC added new units of communes, brigades, and teams, but many of these mirrored existing sub-county administrative units. After the end of the turmoil of the Great Leap Forward, mutual-aid teams often mirrored the organization of natural villages, and many teams included all the members of one lineage.[4]

Maoist policy damaged the marketing hierarchy much more severely than the state structure. The abolition of private marketing, the centralization of grain supply in state organizations and the distribution of grain by rationing instead of by price mechanisms tore up the long-standing channels that moved primary commodities around the country. Forcing a "cellular economy" of autonomous collectives on the highly commercialized countryside obstructed agricultural production and marketing, and fastening peasants to their villages with the household registration system blocked their incessant mobility to regions offering more opportunities.[5] Yet, after the reforms, much of imperial China's pre-Communist structure reemerged intact. The old channels returned, following paths that offered the lowest transport costs, with the old marketing structure partly modified by the impact of railroads and paved roads. Farmers once again specialized in crops that suited local weather, soil, and demand, often abandoning the grain crops that the collective system had forced on them. Interregional grain flows, featuring the Yangzi River trunk route, again mirrored the Qing pattern, modified only by the impact of foreign imports and coastal trade. Peasants freed in practice from registration and rationing regulations that bound them to their villages recreated heavy internal migration flows as they flooded into cities for seasonal labor.

Religious organizations had long been a target of attack before the Communist takeover. The Guomindang campaigned intensively against the "superstition" and "waste" produced by religious ritual activities.[6] Merchant guilds were attacked for extracting illegitimate profits from the masses, and lineages were criticized for enforcing the patriarchal authority of landlord interests over their members. But all of these organizations proved to be resilient enough to re-emerge in the 1980s.

What accounts for this surprising continuity over many decades of revolutionary change? How did these practices contribute to holding China together, or ripping her apart? The general answer is that these protean, elusive practices of everyday life proved to be remarkably tenacious in the face of open assault.[7] The state and its cadres could attack the formal institutions that expressed their public face: the guild halls, lineage halls, and their written constitutions. In the extreme period of the Cultural Revolution (1966–76), they could even attempt to tear apart the family relations that undergirded them and literally demolish the buildings and deface the graveyards. But they failed in the end. After tremendous pain, many social ties survived the Cultural Revolution's assault. Once the storm had passed, children sought forgiveness from their parents, students looked for absolution from teachers they had attacked, and much of the tension was submerged by silence. Of course, there was never total reconciliation. If we look only at the "wounded" literature of the post-Cultural Revolution, or many memoirs published in English, we have ample testimony to the brutality and anarchy of the period. But these accounts need to be balanced by the stories of how ordinary Chinese people reknit their communities in the wake of conflict. They had to struggle to keep ordinary life going in the face of attack by the revolutionary state.

Communist mobilization failed because its new names did not match social realities. Class labeling, for example, was an essential element of revolutionary mobilization. Attaching a label to a person put him into a homogeneous class to which was ascribed a political function. Proletarians were necessarily revolutionary, while landlords were reactionary. Even though they claimed to be derived from "scientific Marxist" analysis, the labels never corresponded closely to the actual relationship of any given person to the mode of production. They always had an irreducibly subjective element. In land reform campaigns, personality and reputation among the villagers counted for as much as actual landholding in determining a person's label. The revolutionary state could not analyze each production relationship too closely, because it aimed to homogenize and standardize the multifarious agrarian relations so as to simplify tasks of extraction, control, and mobilization. Class warfare was a state simplification project, designed to create unmediated relations between the state and society.[8] It failed because everyday life, consisting of complex, overlapping interactions, fought back against the effort to line people up in opposing camps under the banner of class struggle. The revolutionary legibility project defeated itself. Efforts to mobilize the masses against a small number of class enemies dissolved into an indecipherable welter of local feuds and factions. Continuities with the past did not come from an invisible "cultural consciousness" beneath the surface of conformist behavior, or "feudal thinking," as the revolutionaries put it. Resistance, almost an unintended byproduct of conformity, sabotaged the radical projects.

Linking the Present to the Past

Even if strong continuities are apparent, however, we should avoid invoking simplistic analogies between the present and past. Some political scientists, for example, have pointed to resemblances between Communist cadres and Qing local officials. The Qing historian Pierre-Etienne Will finds these analogies "laughable" because they only talk of static essences. As he states, "Complex long-term evolution," not "binary oppositions or parallelism drawn out of context," is the appropriate way to "reintroduce history in a serious manner."[9]

Rather than looking at the superficial similarities of structure, we should examine specific administrative practices. Here I will give two examples: tax collection and border defense. Philip Kuhn argues that China's imperial regime had a consistent problem with eliminating intermediaries between the taxpayer and the state. Officials constantly denounced *baolan*, or "proxy remittance," in which powerful agents paid reduced taxes on behalf of peasants, in return for rights of patronage. They blamed "clerks and runners" for peculating revenues and turning fiscal charges into illegal "customary fees." But efforts to enforce individual tax payment—for example, by requiring every taxpayer to journey to the county seat to deposit his taxes in a sealed box—ran up against unavoidable practical limitations. The low allotments for administrative expenses given to local officials prevented them from hiring enough staff to supervise such an ambitious revenue collection program. Numerous intermediaries between the magistrate and the village had strong interests in preventing his direct access to the peasant taxpayer, and even the most well-intentioned magistrate had few means to avoid them. "Disintermediation" was a persistent goal of the Qing state, but limitations on bureaucratic size and efficiency prevented its implementation.

Collectivization, in Kuhn's view, was one more effort to eliminate disloyal intermediaries between the state and the peasant. Socialist agriculture was a "curious amalgam of the statist fiscal program of the ancien régime and millenarian visions of Mao at the end of his life."[10] Collectivized peasants now gave a large share of their production to the state, while sharing the remaining surplus among their members. Like Qing officials, Communist cadres were local representatives of the state, to be sure, but their relationship to the state and the subject society differed vastly. Local cadres, unlike Qing intermediaries, depended entirely on the state for their authority. Many of them had risen to their position from the poor peasantry, so they had reason to be grateful to the Communist regime. In any case, they had little room to maneuver between the demands of the state for revenue and the limited output of their collectives. Most important, cadres had no independent source of textual authority from the demands of the center. Marxist-Leninist-Maoist texts provided divergent interpretations for policy issues, but the principle of "democratic centralism" provided that the "line" decided at the center determined an unequivocal answer. This left no room for remonstration or renunciation.

Two key economic features also distinguished collective agriculture from the Qing: the decommercialization of society and the endorsement of a productivist ideology. The most radical achievement of the PRC was to remove money from society as a meaningful factor in economic transactions. Collecting taxes in kind put back agrarian fiscal relations to the anomalous situation of the early Ming dynasty. Ming agrarianism of the fifteenth century briefly reversed a trend of increasing monetization of tax collection that had begun in the Song dynasty. By the sixteenth century monetization spread again.[11] Collection in kind favored the newly established Ming and Communist states, because it allowed no alternative uses for the agrarian surplus. Instead of choosing which crops to grow, marketing the most profitable ones, then paying taxes in cash, peasants had to give up their grain crop immediately. The state received guaranteed grain supplies which went to support the urban population.

If state demands had been stable, this might have been a viable solution, but the collective system contradicted the other principal ideology of the PRC: the intense dedication to industrialization as the means of raising productive capacity. Unlike the Qing, grain surpluses had to support not a slowly growing agrarian and commercial population, but a rapidly rising industrial working class. China faced the same scissors crisis that hit the Soviet Union, where the demands of heavy industry contradicted the needs of peasant farming. The result was the Utopian efforts of the Great Leap, which ultimately destroyed the collective system.[12]

The collapse of collectivism put the PRC state back in the fiscal situation of the high Qing: rapid commercialization of agriculture, increasing mobility out of agriculture, and relative decline of revenue as a percentage of national product. The post-reform state has not given up the productivist ideology, which heavily favors urban industry and commerce, but it has given up, de facto, the effort to tie peasants to the land and extract a fixed revenue in kind from them.

The Will-Kuhn approach links imperial practice to that of the PRC by tracing specific approaches to enduring administrative challenges. The underlying structural continuity is that of a large bureaucratic state attempting to extract sufficient revenue from recalcitrant villagers for large-scale projects of social reform or social control. In both cases, the state's reach exceeded its grasp. Qing fiscal institutions did succeed for over a century in providing enough revenue to support major military campaigns and grain relief for a vastly expanded empire, but in the nineteenth century they were inadequate to support either domestic repression or military responses to foreign attack. The PRC's structure failed even faster, because the goal of crash industrialization on the Stalinist model ran up against the severe ecological limits on the productivity of mono-cropping collective agriculture. Since structural constraints inherited from the past continue to operate in China today, officials choosing from a limited repertoire find themselves returning to methods that many have used before them. None of them work perfectly, or even well, but few alternatives exist.

Let me apply this approach to another example: border defense. Here, too, there are strong structural continuities between empire and nation, and equally enduring problems, centered on logistical limitations which inevitably produced ineradicable intermediaries. The Qing and the modern nation-state both promoted bureaucratic penetration over the long run to bind the frontier territories to the center, but neither succeeded more than temporarily. Like collectivization, the nationality policy of the PRC aims to resolve the Qing problem of uniting multiple peoples under a single authority.

Like every state, the Qing, Republic, and PRC all had to define their boundaries and ensure their protection against foreign incursion and domestic unrest. This task required effectively combining diplomatic, military, economic, and cultural projects. The Qing goal in the eighteenth century was to create and stabilize an empire containing many peoples with vastly different cultures under a single hegemon, an emperor who claimed legitimacy on the basis of universal principles of benevolence and Heavenly grace. Nationalists in the twentieth century chose to take on the same task after the Qing fell. Few of them even questioned the idea that China's state boundaries should include all the territories conquered by the Qing emperors. Yet carrying out this goal in the era of nation-states proved even more problematic than it did for the Qing rulers.

The Kangxi (r. 1662–1722), Yongzheng (r. 1723–35), and Qianlong (1736–96) emperors pursued a continuous policy of unification by conquest, and after the conquest they wrote a coherent narrative to explain their success. The basic elements of their program were, first, the elimination of rival state builders and military forces among the Mongols, their most formidable enemy; second, the definition of a sharply delimited border along the Russian frontier, replacing an ambiguous frontier zone; third, the promotion of economic integration of the newly conquered regions into the empire by expanding the role of Han merchant capital and agrarian settlement; and fourth, the legitimation of the conquest by invoking Heaven's will as the supporter of emperors with nearly divine foresight. These four elements were closely linked together. To name only a few connections: military victories depended heavily on the logistical support provided by the commercialized agrarian economy of the interior; and Russian agreement with Qing diplomatic aims also depended on access to the profitable markets for fur in Beijing. Subordination of the Mongols relied on combining economic incentives (such as grain relief in time of famine) with invocations of the emperor's role as victorious Khan and the deployment of kinship relations between Manchus and Mongols. By the end of the eighteenth century, the high Qing program of imperial expansion seemed to have been crowned with success.[13]

But the inability to exclude all intermediary powers, economic, social, or cultural, inescapably limited Qing control. In Southwest China, native chieftains (*tusi*) ruled with near total autonomy until the eighteenth century and maintained considerable freedom of action thereafter. Control over Mongol lands depended on the loyalty of tribal leaders, given titles as *jasaks* and nearly complete autonomy within carefully delimited pasture lands. Likewise, *begs*, or oasis chieftains, fulfilled dual roles in Xinjiang as local officials and Turkic notables. In Tibet, the entire administration was in the hands of local nobility and clergy, and the Qing only maintained a small garrison in Lhasa and controlled the succession of major Lamas. These were fragile, indirect means of control, typical of many agrarian empires, including British India.

Indirect rule, however, conflicted with another principle of Qing imperial control: economic integration, specifically the expansion of Han or Hui (Muslim) Chinese mercantile capital and peasant settlers to the frontier. Qing officials had great ambivalence about migration on all frontiers. In Taiwan, for example, they vacillated between all-out colonization and protection of native peoples against exploitation. Frontier settlers were often the most unruly elements in any jurisdiction; there were good reasons to limit migration. But in Xinjiang, the Qing promoted immigration more actively than on any other frontier. On this frontier, state policy supported actively the construction of commercial networks and the clearance of land aided by state investment in roads, water conservancy, and agricultural means of production (tools, seeds, animals, and labor).

The ultimate result was an explosion of violence in the nineteenth century, first in the Jahangir revolt of the 1820s and later outright secession by Yakub Beg (1820–77) in the 1870s. Both revolts grew from severe hostility between native Turkic peoples and Han immigrants, allowing Sufi orders and military adventurers to join under the banner of Islamic *jihad* against the infidels. Xinjiang also became a major center of opium production, facilitated by the near independence of the *beg*s, and their connections with trade routes to Central Asia and India.[14] Still, after suppressing the revolts, the state pursued further integration of the region, culminating in Xinjiang's incorporation as a province in 1884.

Holding on to the frontier regions has been a major preoccupation of the Chinese state in the twentieth century. Xinjiang activists revolted twice to establish an independent republic in the early twentieth century; Outer Mongolia freed itself from Qing domination by joining the Soviet zone; Tibet declared its independence but was never recognized internationally. The Guomindang and later the PRC were forced to give up claims to Outer Mongolia, but they both reconquered Xinjiang and never yielded on claims to Tibet. It is worth noting that the relative alienation of China's northwest frontiers from Beijing today mirrors their position at the end of the eighteenth century: Manchuria, the home of the Qing elite, is now fully part of China; Inner Mongolia, whose inhabitants had the closest ties of all Mongols to the Manchu ruling elite, is closely integrated with the PRC today, because of heavy Han immigration and the end of nomadism. Xinjiang has renewed the cross-border trade routes to Central Asia giving it an alternate orientation, and its Uighurs resent the influx of Han immigrants, a process whose roots lie in the eighteenth century. Even within Xinjiang, the oasis of Turpan in the east finds the most profit in Chinese connections, and Kashgar the least, just as they did under the Qing. Tibet lies the farthest from the center in distance and culture, with strong links to India, and only belongs to China because of the latter's heavy military presence and Beijing's claim to control the legitimacy of succession to the titles of the high Lamas. The Qianlong emperor, who established the "golden urn" system of selecting reincarnations by lot that Beijing now claims as the "traditional" method, would smile to see a revolutionary state carrying on his "feudal" innovation.[15]

These examples indicate briefly how we may trace the evolution of administrative practice from the Qing to the present, to show how the Republic and the PRC before and after reform have addressed enduring problems of frontier control. In practice, despite divergent ideologies, emperors, republicans, and Communist revolutionaries have repeatedly chosen similar solutions to the same problems from the limited set of options available to them. The paradox of "feudal" persistence in the face of revolutionary onslaught derives from structural constraints and the resistance of everyday life.

Erasures and Silences in the Theory of Nationalism

> . . . The clan tartans
> Invented by mill-owners inspired by the hoax of Ossian,
> To control their savage Scottish workers, tamed
> By a fabricated heraldry: MacGregor, Bailey,
> MacMartin. The kilt, devised for workers
> To wear among the dusty clattering looms.
>
> —Robert Pinsky, "Shirt"

Let me now turn to the second paradox: the relative neglect of East Asia by theorists of nationalism. As Prasenjit Duara has pointed out, nearly all of the prominent theorists of nationalism begin with the presumption that nationalism is a radically modern development, originating with Western European intellectuals.[16] They may disagree on when the first nationalist ideologies appeared, but they regard these ideologies as sharp breaks from the past. Liah Greenfeld finds the source of English nationalism in Elizabethan England; Hobsbawm focuses on the period after the French Revolution; while Benedict Anderson looks to the creole elites of the early nineteenth century in Latin America.[17]

Explanations for the rise of nationalism are closely tied to the assumptions of modernization theory that begin with a binary division between characteristics of "traditional" and "modern" societies. These assumptions are revealed in various specific hypotheses, like Ernst Gellner's (1925–95) claim that the functional differentiation required by industrial society requires the homogenizing ideology of nationalism, or Anderson's link between "print capitalism" and the consciousness of an imagined community created by nationalist intellectuals.[18] Anderson's theory, like Karl Deutsch's (1912–92) theory of social integration based on communication, sees the masses as passive receptors of messages broadcast from the elite centers. Inasmuch as China, of course, had "print capitalism" at least as early as the Song dynasty without any corresponding nationalist ideology, and since cultural integration was quite high in imperial China, Gellner's stress on nationalist integration and Anderson's focus on print technology do not apply well to China.[19]

It is certainly true that nationalists claim to create new collective identities for their people, rejecting outmoded and oppressive organizations that block their development. Yet the modernization theory of nationalism fails to explain the other side of nationalist ideology: the invocation of timeless essences of a people's past, and it does not explain the many contradictions in nationalist ideologies. Duara coins the term "discent" (dissent/descent) to characterize the multiple, inconsistent efforts to trace the lineage of a people and to use these new stories as a means of mobilizing a new community. Nationalist narratives do not create histories out of whole cloth; they mobilize selected elements of an existing historical repertoire in the effort to construct a new, consistent story.

But as Ernest Renan (1823–92) pointed out, nationalists must suppress as much as they create: "Yet the essence of a nation is that all individuals have many things in common, and also that they have forgotten many things. No French citizen knows whether he is a Burgundian, an Alan, a Taifale, or a Visigoth, yet every French citizen has to have forgotten the massacre of Saint Bartholomew."[20] The erasures, though, are never total; they may survive in the memories of marginalized groups as spores waiting to be reborn under different conditions. Hue-tam Ho Tai, in her review of Pierre Nora's *Lieux de mémoire*, points out that "Renan's claim . . is dubious, given its central place in Protestant memory."[21] Particularly at the margins of the nationalist community—its geographical frontiers and social peripheries—lurk the disturbing shadows that communities need to forget in order to highlight their unity. "Enlightenment," the great watchword of national liberation movements, brightens the center, but it also throws sharp shadows. "We see those, bathed in light; those in darkness, fade from sight" (Berthold Brecht, 1898–1956).

As Duara puts it, the central "aporia" of nationalist narratives is the contradiction between the claim to be modern and the manufacturing of primordial essences. Benjamin Schwartz (1916–99) expresses the same idea more simply: "Here we find the ubiquitous dilemma of modern nationalism. On the one hand, the achievement of national wealth and power may require a radical break with the constraints of tradition. On the other hand, a vital sense of national identity seems to require faith in the intrinsic worth of the nation's cultural accomplishments of the past."[22] We should take neither claim at face value.

Many theorists of nationalism rightly debunk the false claims to discover a unified "ancient" race in the misty roots of the past, whether it is the highland Scots, the Slavic soil, the Sons of the Yellow Emperor, or the Sun Goddess Amaterasu Ōmikami. The "invention of tradition" literature demonstrates how recent these primordial traditions are.[23] Yet the opposite danger is to believe that nationalism really is as new as it claims to be. If nationalism is only a result of the "uneven diffusion of modernization" in a tidal wave across Europe and the rest of the world after 1800, it appears merely to be a reactive phenomenon, stimulated primarily by the impact of European industrialization and imperialism on the globe.[24] Asian nationalism then appears as only a very late phase of the process, since explicitly modernist nationalist ideologies directed against European imperialism did not flourish until the 1870s self-strengthening movements in China and Japan.

These misleading assumptions about East Asian unity, by Chinese ideologues and Western theorists alike, derived from their excessive focus on ideology at the expense of practice. The Central Asian Republics of the Soviet Union supported the coup against Gorbachev, rejecting reforms that threatened Soviet centralized power. But in the age of the "Former Soviet Union," they had no difficulty in quickly creating nation-states with the full panoply of symbols, flags, official histories, languages, and ethnocentric ideologies. Practice led ideology, not the other way around. Olivier Roy states that "the poverty of ideological production (in both the Soviet and post-independence periods) . . . shows that nationalism can perfectly well develop outside any sophisticated elaboration, as a *habitus* and not as ideology. . . . [T]he national level of things derives more from a practice than a declaration."[25] Roy alludes to Pierre Bourdieu's (1930–2002) concept of *habitus* as a "system of enduring dispositions," or tendencies to act in accordance with understood rules of the game.[26] The lived experience of communities, more than the pontifications of intellectuals, ultimately generates the most powerful feelings of belonging to a larger whole.

But this is too narrow a definition of nationalist consciousness. Duara rightly roots the nationalist phenomenon in the wider issue of the forging of political identity. He does not, however, examine how political identities were transformed in Asia before the twentieth century, and how these transformations laid the groundwork for the rapid outburst of nationalist movements after 1900. I argue that the eighteenth century, in fact, created all the major elements, ideological and institutional, required for the generation of nationalism in the twentieth century. The spores (the ideological germs) had been formed and the soil (the social *habitus*) prepared. All that was needed were the disseminating devices—newspapers, intellectuals—to spread the epidemic.

This does not mean, however, that united Asian peoples were simply lying in wait to be discovered by intellectuals. Such nationalist myths infect even the most intelligent analysts. Eric Hobsbawm, in his otherwise excellent study of nationalism, makes the extraordinary statement that "China, Korea, and Japan . . . are indeed among the extremely rare examples of a historic state composed of a population that is ethnically almost or entirely homogeneous."[27] This is a perfect example of the power of nationalist myth not only among members of the nations themselves, but on supposedly more detached observers. The "Han" Chinese who claim to comprise 94 percent of the PRC are, of course, just as much an invented tradition as any other nationality. They are not homogeneous at all, divided by separate spoken languages (mythically dubbed "dialects"), cuisine, histories, and customs. Scholars of China know well the artificiality of this construction of "nationality," but they struggle against a tenacious myth of Han "homogeneity."

Hobsbawm would like to deny that ethnic or racial mobilization plays a large part in generating national consciousness, so he puts nearly all of East Asia (a mere 20 percent of the world's population) aside as a special case. If he recognized that in fact the East Asian ethnicities were also just as constructed as others, it would undermine his claim about the insignificance of ethnicity. This question of ethnicity's relationship to nationalism is related to the artificial separation of "civic" (good) nationalism (French, American) from "ethnic" (bad) nationalism, seen in Greenfeld and other theorists.[28] If East Asia becomes a comparable case to the rest of the world, and we recognize that creating ethnic identification was a critical element in generating its nationalist movements, then we cannot ignore the vital role of ethnicity in all nationalist movements. Yet, this critical link between nationality and nation-state was already embedded in the Qing imperial project.

Borders, Empires, and Nations

Establishing fixed borders was the first crucial step. By negotiating a boundary with the Russian empire in 1689, the Kangxi emperor eliminated the unbounded freedom of action of the peoples in this frontier zone and began the construction of "nationalities" with fixed territories, genealogies, and collective identities. To illustrate the evolution from Qing empire to Chinese nation, after sketching this classification project, let us look at nationalist interpretations of the border negotiations between Russia and China that led to the signing of the treaty of Nerchinsk in 1689.

After conquering and incorporating a multitude of peoples into the empire, the Qing rulers legitimated their authority by speaking, and writing, in many tongues. First, they classified the peoples they ruled as distinct cultural formations. This required mobilizing scholars to carry out large projects of systematic historical normalization. After eliminating the Zunghar Mongols militarily in 1760, the Qianlong emperor demanded that Mongols surrender their genealogies to state officials, so that they could write an imperially sponsored history of the Mongol clans. He had his own version of Mongolian history inscribed in the opening section of the vast official campaign history, the *Pingding Junge'er fanglüe* (General plan for the conquest of the Zunghars). (Since, by contrast with Chinese records, no Mongolian genealogies survive, one is strongly tempted to believe that the originals were destroyed). The *Fanglüe* and other official histories imposed a simplified, coherent narrative of Mongolian descent on an ambiguous, multifarious reality. Before the conquest, each lineage had its own version of the relations among the different tribes; now the differences were smoothed over to create a much more legible historical view.[29]

Mapping also sought to provide the emperor with a "comprehensive view" of his domain, based on a combination of local knowledge and new technologies of surveying introduced by the Jesuits.[30] The famous "Jesuit Atlas" (*Huangyu quanlantu*, or "Comprehensive View of the Imperial Domains") of 1717–21 was in fact a collaboration between Jesuit advisors and local surveyors, closely connected to the strategic interests of the state. As the empire expanded, new territories, like Xinjiang, were "entered on the registers" (*ru bantu*)—placed on the maps—in order to make the entire realm accessible to the view from above.[31] Ethnographic atlases likewise put the peoples of the empire in distinct categories.[32] Hundreds of these atlases were published in the eighteenth century, covering many of the peoples of the south and southwest, Taiwan, and the northwest. They provided pictures, descriptions of customs, and discussions of local ecology. Over the eighteenth century, they grew increasingly detailed, as the effort to gain a comprehensive view (*quanlan*) of all the peoples of the empire expanded.

Each of these imperial projects created a space of structured homogeneity and difference. The new "peoples" were categorized as uniform units with terminology that invoked empirical research. Thus, they became embedded in a "scientific" discourse implying natural divisions of the human species. At the same time, imperial administration adapted its techniques to these local particularities, in the interest of efficient tax collection and social control. The Qing had created proto-nationalities and proto-autonomous regions long before Sun Yat-sen or Vladimir Lenin (1870–1924) came along to name them.

Benedict Anderson singles out the census, the map, and the museum as key colonial impositions on Southeast Asia that constructed the categories under which new nation-states and peoples built their identities.[33] By stressing only the European colonial background of new nations in

Asia, Anderson unduly restricts his scope. He too, implicitly, seems to accept the nationalist myth that China was not a colonial power like the others, but something altogether different. The Qing empire concurrently implemented the same strategies as the British in India, the Dutch in Indonesia, or, later, the French in Indochina. It was a colonial empire like its contemporaries, with many of the same concerns for revenue, control, and visibility of localities to the administrative gaze. Putting China back in the picture with the other colonial powers helps to rescue our view of Qing history from nationalist distortion, and modifies the assumptions of the prominent theorists of nationalism.

If the current territorial claims of the People's Republic resemble closely the boundaries achieved by the Qing rulers around 1800, and China today includes within its borders fifty-six nationalities, contemporary China's ruling ideology and practice are as much imperial as national in content.[34] It is hardly surprising, then, that uncanny echoes of Qing imperial rhetoric still ring in governmental prose. The controversies over the nomination of the Panchen Lama in 1995 and the escape of the Karmapa Lama in 2001, for example, are only the latest in a long line of events that reveal striking analogies to Qing efforts to intervene in Tibet. Once again, on the frontiers, claims to incorporate clearly defined "nationalities" under a multinational nation-state have met great resistance.

Has the Empire Really Become a Nation at All?

The inadequacies of Chinese nationalist ideology derive from its inheritance of the claims of the Qing imperial rulers, without their legitimating appeal to a universal cosmology. Architects of a Chinese nation did not look to more Han-centered models of Chinese territory and polity, like the Song or Ming dynasties. Instead, nearly all of them took for granted that the boundaries and peoples included in the maximal period of Qing should belong to the nation. The construction of the Han as a distinct "nationality" (*minzu*) in the late nineteenth century merged distinctive groups like the Cantonese, Hakka, Taiwanese, and Hunanese into a seamless whole, and the promotion of China as a "multi-nationality nation state" (*duo minzu guojia*) in the twentieth century incorporated non-Han peoples under a single national ideal. Both ideologies tried to resolve the conflicting claims of empire and nation, legacies of the Qing's frontier expansion, but they could not remove all contradictions. For Lucian Pye, China has only a "relatively inchoate and incoherent form of nationalism," because it is a "civilization pretending to be a nation state."[35] Pye has put his finger on the correct syndrome, but given the wrong diagnosis. It is not Chinese civilization that is the problem, but Chinese empire.

The contrasting perspectives of Zhang Binglin (1869–1936) and Liang Qichao (1873–1929) in the first decade of the twentieth century highlighted this contradiction clearly. Zhang, supporting a strictly racial construction of nationality, argued that the non-Han peoples could never be completely assimilated, and China could only unite against the West when the Manchus were expelled:

Today five million Manchus rule over more than four hundred million Han only because rotten traditions make the Han stupid and ignorant. If the Han people should one day wake up, then the Manchus would be totally unable to rest peacefully here, like the Austrians in Hungary or the Turks in the former Eastern Roman Empire. It is human nature to love one's own race and to seek gain for oneself. . . . If the Manchus are not expelled, however, we cannot expect that the scholars will perform well or that the people will share a bitter hatred of the enemy in order to reach a realm of freedom and independence.[36]

Although he believed that Mongols and Tibetans had enjoyed friendly relations with the Han for five hundred years, he admitted that the Muslims of Xinjiang might hate the Chinese as much as Chinese hated the Manchus: "If the chieftains of Xinjiang, because their hatred of the Manchus pierces their bones, generate such resentment against the Han people that they want to separate from us and restore the Turkish lands, we must allow them to do so. We can see that our relation to the Manchus is like that of Xinjiang toward us." Although he did not support independence for Muslims under Chinese rule, he did propose that China and Xinjiang could form an "alliance" against Russia if it suited Muslim interests. If not, Muslims in Xinjiang could go their way separately from the Chinese state.[37]

Liang Qichao, by contrast, insisted on maintaining the Qing imperial territories, while transforming the empire and its peoples into citizens of a constitutional monarchy. Kang Youwei (1858–1927) had argued for "no divisions between Manchus and Han, with rulers and people united" (*Man-Han bufen, junmin tongti*).[38] Liang also tried to overcome the divisions between Manchu and Han, in order to promote unity against Western imperialism.[39] For him, "protecting the race" (*minzu*) was "not as critical as protecting the nation."[40] Sun Yat-sen after 1911 converted from racialism to Liang's civic monarchy because he could not allow the division of Chinese territory by claims for autonomy from separatists. The problem for Sun was that "the word 'Han' failed to accommodate the variety of ethnic communities now thought to comprise the 'race'." He constructed a "philosophically empty" vision of five nationalities unified under Han dominance so as to maintain China's claim to the frontier territories.[41]

Neither Liang, nor Sun, could respond adequately when other peoples of the former empire, besides the Han, found their own voices as nationalities. Because of his intense racialism, Zhang more than other nationalists was willing to face the possible consequence of ethnic nationalism: the breakup of the Qing empire. Few others could accept this. But even Zhang took for granted the loyalty of Mongols and Tibetans to the Han-centered nation. He thought that the many distinct nationalities of China could get along much better than, for example, blacks and whites in the United States.[42] Like the Western theorists who assumed the existence of Chinese "homogeneity," the Chinese nationalists assumed that the loyalty of the multiple peoples who had submitted to an emperor's divine will would naturally transfer to a nation-state endowed with a new sacred mission of unification, this time backed by science instead of Heaven. They could not face the obvious logic of racial nationalism: if the Han people deserved their own state because of their genetic unity, why should not the Manchus, Mongols, Uighurs, and Tibetans deserve the same?

The idea of enlightened intellectuals bringing modernity to benighted masses is yet another highly flattering self-conception that nationalist intellectuals hold of themselves. Considering the disasters that so many of them have produced, some skepticism is in order as to who was really enlightened: the intellectual terrorists who attacked "enemies of the people" in the name of a higher goal, or the "ignorant" peasant farmers who could not quite figure out what the fuss was all about. Historical study of the empire may give us greater respect for pre-nationalist practices, both as generators of the forces unifying the nation and as productive resistances to the destructive power of high modernist nationalism in its most arrogant forms.

We need to go well beyond the fantasies of nationalist elites to examine why certain of their ideas did strike roots in local communities, generating powerful social movements. Genuine social histories of nationalism are still quite rare, as Geoff Eley and Ronald Grigor Suny note,[43] but at least we know that it is misguided to view nationalism as a simple one-way transmission of "modern" ideas of the nation by enlightened intellectuals to societies "buried in feudal and absolutist slumber."[44] The mass response to nationalism arises out of transformations in these societies themselves.

Removing the Middle Ground: or, What Really Happened at Nerchinsk

Let me turn from these general considerations to two specific examples of the breeding of the *habitus* of nationalism in the soil of empire: the fixing of borders and the weaving of community networks. By agreeing to define their border with Russia, the Qing rulers decided what space would define the empire. It was the same space, ideally, that would define the Chinese nation. The imperial ideology that legitimated control of this vast expanse tied distinct peoples to the universal emperor. Though it differed from the nationalist invocation of popular masses, the two ideologies shared the same spatial and ethnic claims. Within and beyond this space, many associations formed dense linkages of economic and social interaction that held together distant peoples with common bonds. The ties of locality, or *guxiang*, defined a network space which provided fertile ground to encourage the spread of nationalist ideology when it arrived.

In 1689, Manchu and Russian negotiators agreed on a treaty defining the borders between the two empires. At Nerchinsk, for the first time, an empire ruled from Beijing drew a permanent boundary with a large Central Eurasian empire. By marking the frontier with a definite line, the treaty removed many of the sources of dispute in the region of Siberia and Manchuria created by the incursion of Russian fur traders and military garrisons since the end of the sixteenth century. In return for access to profitable markets for furs in Beijing, the Russians yielded control of the fortress of Albazin, which was destroyed, and gave up claims to territories along the Amur River. The Qing negotiators had originally claimed much more, but they accepted a smaller territory, because they feared a Russian alliance with the rising power of the Western Mongolian Zunghar state.

Interpretations of Nerchinsk have varied widely ever since the treaty was first signed. Most modern historians focus only on the treaty as an event in Sino-Russian relations or as one element of Chinese relations with Western powers. They tend to ignore the role of the frontier peoples between the two empires in determining the negotiating stances of both sides, and they do not recognize the most important consequence of the treaty: the closing off of intermediate space that allowed for multiple identifications in this borderland zone. Fixing the border prepared the way for a territorially defined nation-state, but nationalist historians on both sides focus only on the damage inflicted on their own country, not on the intertwined interests of the many actors of the time. The Nerchinsk treaty was the outcome of a marvelously complex interplay of many state and cultural interests, and its outcome was by no means predictable in advance. A comparison of later accounts of Nerchinsk with the story in the archival sources helps to illustrate how nationalists constructed and erased facts to serve their narrative purposes. It also will serve as one example of how the Qing empire's institutional achievements laid the groundwork for the Chinese nation.

Plenipotentiary ambassador Fedor Alekseevich Golovin (1650–1706) arrived at the frontier town of Nerchinsk in July 1689.[45] With his entourage of about one thousand, he met with seven Qing ambassadors, led by the Manchu high official Songgotu (d. 1703), and a supporting cast including the two Jesuits Jean-François Gerbillon (1654–1707) and Thomas Pereira (1645–1708), and military regiments and Buddhist clergy numbering at least ten thousand.[46]

No Mongols attended Nerchinsk, but their hidden presence critically affected the negotiations. The key issues in dispute concerned the loyalties of the tribes of the frontier, both Tungusic and Mongol, and the impact of the dynamic military leader of the Western Mongols, Galdan (1644–97). The tribes, like weathervanes, had switched their loyalties depending on pressure from the surrounding empires. Many of them paid *iasak*, or tribute, to both the Russians and the Qing. One of the most powerful Tungusic chieftains, Gantimur, had first served the Russians, then joined the Manchus, then returned to become a subject of the Tsar. Having formerly been a banner captain, he was later baptized an Orthodox Christian.[47] Qing demands for the return of Gantimur and his followers had hung up negotiations with the Russians for nearly twenty years. Now, however, the rising influence of Galdan forced the Qing to realize that they could not afford to alienate the Russians. Eliminating frontier mobility meant giving up claims to those who had crossed the border, but the threat of a Zunghar-Russian alliance was much more serious.

The delegates first had to choose a language of discussion. Neither side could use its native language, because preserving the illusion of equality was essential to success at the negotiating table. The two parties had open tents side by side, with equal numbers of men. The Qing officials did have Russian translators available, but did not use them. As high ranking Manchus, they excluded participation by any Chinese in border negotiations. Both the Russians and Manchus, however, were familiar with Mongolian, which had been the most common language of communication between different peoples in this frontier region. And yet the primary language of the Treaty of Nerchinsk became not Mongolian, but Latin, a language known only to one or two Russian representatives, and the two Jesuits serving the Qing.

Because the Jesuits inserted themselves as crucial mediators, they could decide the terms, and the language of communication. On the first day of the meeting, August 22, the envoys agreed in principle to communicate in Latin.[48] According to Golovin's report, they believed that there were not enough Mongolian translators, and they were not reliable, so both sides agreed that it would be more "objective" to rely on the Jesuits' Latin. The Pole Andrei Belobotskii acted as the Russians' Latin translator. Discussions, however, soon became hung up on the question of where to draw the border. At first, the Manchus claimed all the territory up to Lake Baikal, basing their claim on the fact that all the Mongolian tribes of this region had paid tribute to the Mongols' Yuan empire. The Russians held out for preserving Albazin and Nerchinsk, suggesting the border be drawn along the Amur River. They heard the Manchus threaten them with military activity if they did not concede immediately. When they realized that the Jesuits were "inserting words" in their translations, they asked to communicate with the Qing envoys in Mongolian.[49] After a long discussion among themselves in Manchu, the Qing envoys said that they had "only directed the Jesuits to speak of the border issue, and not of military matters."

Each time discussions deadlocked, the Russians tried to communicate directly with the Manchus, using Mongolian translators, but the Jesuits opposed them, on the pretext that the translators were incompetent. The Jesuits also told the Russians not to speak to the Manchus in between negotiation sessions, and they told their own interpreters and Manchu official assistants (*jargochi*) never to speak to the Russians alone in Mongolian.[50] Mongolian could certainly have served as a bridging language just as easily as Latin; by excluding it, the Jesuits put themselves in the position of getting better terms for the propagation of their religion from both sides. They enticed the Russians into promising favorable treatment from the Tsar by pretending to be able to dissuade the Kangxi emperor from war, and they obtained an Edict of Toleration from Kangxi in 1692 by taking the credit for successful treaty negotiations. In the time-honored tradition of powerful mediators up to Henry Kissinger today, they were determined to exclude any communication channels outside of themselves.[51] Monopolizing the language and access of each side to the other, they successfully kept out any Mongolian interests from the negotiations.

The conflict over where to draw the border line was ultimately settled by the threat of force and by the ambiguous loyalty of the Mongols between the two empires. When Golovin resisted Qing demands to destroy the fortress of Albazin, without compensation, Songgotu induced Russia's Mongol allies to switch to the Qing side, and mobilized an army of 12,000 men to surround Nerchinsk, while Golovin with his 1,500 men prepared a last-ditch defense.

Two days later, knowing that his position was hopeless, Golovin gave in to most of the Qing demands. The Qing would pay no compensation for Albazin, but would allow traders access to the region; the border would be drawn north of the Amur River along the nearest mountain range, determined by stone markers.

Golovin thus succumbed to an adroit use of military threats and enticements by the Manchus. Losing his Mongolian tributaries would have cost him nearly all control of the Transbaikal region. At the price of giving up Albazin, he preserved access to lands north of the Argun, and he kept control of the tributaries currently under Russian control. The Qing gave up claims to land which they never controlled in the first place, and by offering trading access ensured that the Russians would not support Galdan.

The terms of the treaty have elicited highly divergent interpretations in both Russia and China ever since.[52] Golovin, on his return home, was congratulated by the Tsar for successfully resolving a dangerous frontier conflict in a region in which the Russians were heavily outnumbered. Russia needed peace in the Far East as it prepared for war with Crimea and the Ottoman empire to its south. Golovin himself bitterly complained that Russia had made all the concessions, while the Manchus never yielded. Nationalist criticism of Golovin and Nerchinsk persisted through the nineteenth century. Vasil'ev in 1900 accused Golovin of having panicked under threat of force, allowing the Manchus to take control of large territories along the Amur River which they had never controlled before. Others, however, like the Buriat Mongol Sychevski, writing in 1846, praised Golovin for making the best of a bad situation: using clever diplomacy in a position of weakness, Golovin held off further Qing penetration north of the Amur and gained access for fur traders to the Beijing market.

Qing writers in the nineteenth century praised the treaty as a just settlement. He Qiutao (1661–1722) argued that the Russians yielded because they recognized the justice of Qing claims to peoples along the Amur. He neglected to mention the heavy military pressure that Songgotu put on Golovin. As China was forced to negotiate more unequal treaties under military pressure from Western powers, Nerchinsk stood out as a shining example of an "equal" treaty. Guomindang historians praised Nerchinsk as the only triumph of Chinese diplomacy in recent centuries. They saw no need to conceal the use of military force to gain the result: Chinese now realized that force prevailed in international relations over justice. In the 1950s, during the years of the Sino-Soviet alliance, Chinese historians praised the treaty as an outstanding example of Sino-Russian friendship, negotiated on the basis of equality. Once again, the use of force faded from view. After the Sino-Soviet split, Chinese historians struck a more celebratory tone, praising the achievements of Kangxi in expanding China's boundaries and congratulating the Mongols for joining with the Chinese to hold back Russian aggression. Leading PRC historians, like Dai Yi, accuse Russia of having given substantial aid to Galdan, viewing the treaty and Kangxi's Mongol campaigns as victories over Russian aggression. In recent times, apparently, popular Chinese views have diverged from the official history. Many Chinese now regard Nerchinsk as the first of many unequal treaties. The sources of this view are unclear. It may be a result of historical ignorance, driven by a rising sense of victimization, fueling the feeling that all agreements with Western powers, especially Russia, must be "unequal."[53]

The Soviet view is summarized in the *Great Soviet Encyclopedia* as follows:

The Manchu dynasty had ruled in Peking from the middle of the seventeenth century and had subjugated the Chinese people. A military conflict broke out early in the 1680s when the Manchus attempted to conquer the Amur region, which had been settled by the Russians. Negotiations between a Russian delegation, led by A. Golovin, and representatives of the Ch'ing government, led by Songgotu, took place beneath the walls of the Nerchinsk *ostrog* [fortified settlement]. At the same time Nerchinsk was virtually besieged by a Manchu army that had invaded Russian territory. The territorial clauses of the Nerchinsk treaty, contained in the first three articles, were forcibly imposed on the Russian representatives, who were compelled to give up the vast region of the Albazin Voevodstvo. . . . In the middle of the 19th century, Russia finally concluded its long diplomatic struggle to revise the Nerchinsk treaty. This aim was reflected in the relevant clauses of the Aigun treaty of 1858 and the Peking Treaty of 1860.[54]

The editors of the archival documentary collection *Russko-Kitaiskoe otnosheniia* support this argument, claiming that by the mid-seventeenth century the Russian empire had secured control of the Amur region with settlements, *iasak* payments, and fortresses. Realizing that the Russians were moving in, the Qing used coercion to back up unjustified territorial claims, which Russia was too weak to resist. Facing the threat of Qing troops to annihilate the Russian delegation, Golovin was forced to cede territory on the left bank of the Amur and the right bank of the Argun that belonged to Russia in the period from 1640 to the 1680s. Nerchinsk inflicted damage on Russia by cutting off her "natural" access along the Amur River to the Pacific Coast and the Far East. Trade with China did not compensate for these losses. Only in the mid-nineteenth century, with the treaty of Aigun of 1858, were the Russians able to demand renegotiation of boundaries, and the Manchus forced to concede re-measurement of the region. The treaties of Aigun and Peking completed the Russian project of demarcating the boundaries, giving her access to the Pacific. It is false to call this "penetration of China" or "seizure of its territory," since China had never really controlled these territories in the first place.[55]

The Nerchinsk and later treaties, of course, played an important role in the Sino-Soviet dispute after the 1960s, with China demanding renegotiation of the "unequal" treaties of 1858, while Russia refused even in principle any territorial concessions. When Vladimir Putin and Jiang Zemin signed the Sino-Russian friendship treaty in July of 2001, China praised the treaty as the first recent treaty negotiated on a basis of equal relations. Even though the border dispute was not finally settled, once again the threat of a third power, this time the United States, drove the two powers to embrace each other. But the historians' divergent views have not changed.

This dispute can still yield insights on how empires become nations, and how borderlands turn into borders. Russians and Chinese disagree on who gained and who lost at Nerchinsk, but their narratives share many common elements. The divergent views of Nerchinsk illustrate three of the primary tropes of nationalist narratives: victimization, teleology, and the invention of traditions. They also show the inadequacy of nationalist history in encompassing the multiple actors and perspectives involved in any major conflict. They view the gain or loss of territory as a zero-sum game, in which the territorial gains of one's own nation are the justified recovery of lands that always belonged to one people, while one's adversary's acquisitions are the ill-gotten gains of aggression. Both the Russians and the Chinese who criticize the Nerchinsk treaty see themselves as the victims of military force. This victim's perspective does not allow for seeing border negotiations as the turning of unclear claims on both sides into fixed boundaries, nor does it see anyone losing from the outcome except one's own nation. The highly moralistic language that speaks of theft and coercive gain cannot recognize the justice of competing claims.

The teleological assumption sees the nation as the inevitable outcome of a long-term historical process. Russian writers, as noted above, presume that the "natural" course of Russian development required expansion to the Pacific Coast across Siberia and the development of its commercial potential. Nerchinsk, for the critics, blocked this inexorable development, but the 1858 treaties affirmed it. For Chinese writers, the peoples of Mongolia and Manchuria were destined to become parts of the Chinese nation; therefore, their decision to join the Qing against Russian "aggression" reinforced the unity of nationalities within the multi-national state. Both views erase the contingencies of local time and place that determined fluctuating loyalties on this frontier, and they refuse to consider whether different outcomes were possible. Certainly, an autonomous Mongolian state, or one protected by a Russian alliance, was conceivable in the seventeenth and eighteenth centuries, but the dominant narratives rule out this possibility. If we substitute mutual negotiation for victimization, contingency for teleology, and respect for local variation for invented traditions, we gain a clearer view of the interactions on this contested frontier before the two empires froze the border in place.

Narratives of "discent" occur not only within one nationalist tradition, but between different nations. Two nations with a common border can each tell a separate story of how the border came to be defined, based on opposing interpretations. Their stories may be reinforced in such media as textbooks and films for a mass audience. Each nation may find the current border unjust and portray itself as a victim of the other's "aggression," but the logic of the two narratives is the same. It rests on an assumption that only two adversaries struggle over a territory, and one party's gain is another party's loss. This highly melodramatic, limited version of a complex historical process conceals the multiple actors at play in any frontier situation, but it serves the interests of the victors, who have succeeded in abolishing the "middle ground" between them.[56]

Yet the nationalists are not totally wrong. Defined borders are one crucial element of the *habitus* of a nation. In nationalist myth, a territory with a sharp line around it contains a well-defined people with an essential right to exclusive possession of their land. Borders, however, are not a product of a primeval God-given charter, but an outcome of particular historical circumstances. Nationalist myths try to conceal the often arbitrary negotiations that produced a country's borders under doctrines of "natural frontiers" determined by geographical markers, like mountain ridges or rivers, but it is important to examine the particular political configurations that created these territorial definitions. Many of the modern borders of Eurasia were the product of a global process of the seventeenth century that led to the drawing of lines across vast continental spaces, as contending empires and states came into contact with each other. Conventional European history a little too neatly defines the year 1648, the signing of the Peace of Westphalia, as the origin of concepts of absolute sovereignty that underlie the modern law of nations.[57] In fact, treaties defining borders were created not only in Western Europe, but also between the Russians, Qing, Ottomans, Hapsburg, and Safavid empires in the same century. Westphalia was just one small part of a general Eurasian process.[58] After Nerchinsk, the Qing empire had for the first time placed a territorial limit to its span of control and locked in place the peoples on its side of the border. It had laid down one of the primary building blocks for creating a nation—the concept of fixed borders, defended by treaties, boundary markers, and garrison towns—without espousing anything resembling a modern nationalist ideology.

Mary Wright and William Kirby have pointed to the considerable success of Chinese diplomats in asserting sovereignty over the national territory in the twentieth century.[59] They rested their claims on the enforcement of treaty clauses by standards of international law recognized by Western nations. Their seventeenth-century predecessors had done much of the groundwork for them.

Microcosmic Nationality: Networks and Native Places

Economic integration also defines profoundly the *habitus* of a nation, since the peoples of a national community must feel that they are connected to each other. If most of their economic exchanges are with each other, they have a shared interest in preserving the integrity of their economic space and in protecting it against intrusion by outsiders. Like borders, economic networks also draw lines between insiders and outsiders: those entitled to trust receive special consideration. Everyone can trade with strangers, too, but on a different basis, using shorter-term contracts and often higher prices and lower levels of commitment to further exchange. In the interests of stabilizing long-term economic commitments, Chinese merchants, like many others, established networks across the empire linking those who originated from the same home town (*guxiang*). As they moved out from their commercial bases to the frontiers, they constructed guild halls (*huiguan* or *Landsmannschaften*) to provide bases of support for fellow merchants doing business in these remote areas. The powerful expansive force of Chinese mercantile capital depended heavily on the quasi-familial connections created by these institutions. Imahori Seiji (1914–92), when he travelled through Inner Mongolia in the 1940s, found that *huiguan* had penetrated deeply into the smallest market towns, supporting networks of trade whose tentacles reached from remote Mongolia to the major cities of the coast. Merchants had begun to penetrate Mongolia in the seventeenth century, shortly after the Manchu conquest, and established guild halls, with regulations carved on steles, in the early eighteenth century. Later, in Malaya, he found the same organizations performing the same functions.[60]

Chinese merchants had extended their networks both within the territorial boundaries of the empire and well beyond them. These community organizations bound together a huge economic space comprising Inner Asia, China proper, and the overseas communities of Southeast Asia and, later, across the Pacific. None of the merchant networks had an explicitly nationalistic function; their participants saw them as a means of promoting the economic and social solidarity of only their own *guxiang* community. Yet they provided a model of an institution with a global reach that could turn into a powerful source of integration in the nationalist age.

One example, the Ningbo *huiguan* riot of 1874, shows how these apparently "local" organizations could support nationalistic goals.[61] The Ningbo *huiguan* had large landholdings within the French concession of Shanghai. French proposals to build new roads that intersected in one of the *huiguan* cemeteries aroused anger among the members. Crowds formed in the street while negotiations were underway between the French and the *huiguan* directors. After police shot and killed a Chinese man, a riot broke out, ending in seven Chinese dead, twenty wounded, and the destruction of forty foreign homes and three Chinese buildings.[62] A second riot occurred in 1897. Scholars have debated the nationalist content of the rioters' goals, but as Bryna Goodman argues, the most important point is that the *huiguan* organization itself served as the focal point and structure for generating anti-foreign protest. "Whether or not the riots were informed by a developing sense of Chinese national sovereignty, it is significant that native place associations played a crucial role in the first antiforeign disturbances. . . . Both riots were essentially affairs of the Ningbo community, which mobilized to defend sacred burial ground. As such, it would be problematic to assert that they were an expression of nationalism. . . . Nonetheless, public opinion, as articulated in the Shanghai newspaper *Shenbao*, constructed a different meaning for the 1898 riot. Editorials described the riot in universalistic terms, as an assertion of Chinese sovereignty."[63] Native place organizations continued to play a vital role in the creation of new associations mobilized around anti-foreign nationalism in the early twentieth century.

As Imahori discovered, the northwest and southeast frontiers of the Chinese realm were a revealing place to examine the development of these institutions. Merchant capital had arrived relatively recently in both regions, and the *huiguan* had preserved stelae that recorded the penetration of Chinese into both areas since the seventeenth century. Imahori believed that *huiguan*, along with temples and lineage halls, were the fundamental collective building blocks (*kyōdōtai*) that held Chinese society together. By following Imahori's pioneering path, as several Japanese scholars have recently done, we can continue to track the imperial roots of the modern nation-state.

To summarize these thoughts on approaches to Chinese nationalism: we should look beyond intellectuals' doctrines to social practice; investigate alternative definitions of nationality; and examine frontier regions where conflicts over the meaning of nationalist practice are most apparent. In this way, we can root nationalism in a serious examination of historical processes within and beyond China.

Notes

Introduction: The Teleology of the Nation-State

Herbert A. Giles, *The Civilization of China* (London: Williams and Norgate, 1911), opening paragraph.

1. Joshua A. Fogel, *The Literature of Travel in the Japanese Rediscovery of China, 1862–1945* (Stanford, Calif.: Stanford University Press, 1996), 46–61.
2. Laurence Oliphant, *Narrative of the Early of Elgin's Mission to China and Japan, 1857–1859* (Edinburgh: William Blackwood and Sons, 1859), 1: 269.
3. Hibino Teruhiro, "Zeiyūroku" (A record of warts and lumps), in *Bunkyū ninen Shanhai nikki* (Shanghai diaries from 1862) (Ōsaka: Zenkoku shobō, 1946).
4. Thomas D. Conlan, trans., *In Little Need of Divine Intervention: Takezaki Suenaga's Scrolls of the Mongol Invasions of Japan* (Ithaca, N.Y.: Cornell University Press, 2001).
5. Mine Kiyoshi, "Senchū nichiroku" (Daily account on board), reprint in *Bakumatsu Meiji Chūgoku kenbunroku shūsei* (Collection of travel accounts of China from the late Edo and Meiji periods) (Tokyo: Yumani shobō, 1997), 11: 11–23; and Mine Kiyoshi, "Shinkoku Shanhai kenbunroku" (Travel account of Shanghai in China), reprint in *Bakumatsu Meiji Chūgoku kenbunroku shūsei*, 11: 24–35; Haruna Akira, "Mine Kiyoshi no Shanhai keiken: 'Senchū nichiroku' to 'Shinkoku Shanhai kenbunroku'" (Mine Kiyoshi's experiences in Shanghai: The "Daily account on board" and the "Travel account of Shanghai in China"), *Chōfu Nihon bunka* 8 (1998): 27–100.
6. *The Iwakura Embassy, 1871–1873: A True Account of the Ambassador Extraordinary and Plenipotentiary's Journey of Observation Through the United States of America and Europe*, comp. Kume Kunitake, ed. Graham Healey and Chushichi Tsuzuki, 5 vols. (Chiba: Japan Documents; Princeton, N.J.: Princeton University Press, 2002).
7. Eugen Joseph Weber, *Peasants into Frenchmen: The Modernization of Rural France, 1870–1914* (Stanford, Calif.: Stanford University Press, 1976).

Chapter 1. The Emergence of Aesthetic Japan

This chapter is part of a larger project with the working title, "Bonds of Civility: Aesthetic Networks and the Political Origins of Japanese Culture." Due to limitations of space, I cannot discuss in depth here the development and transformation of the Tokugawa aesthetic networks, Tokugawa popular publishing, or the impact of particular state-market relationships on the rise of civility codes.

1. Regarding my sociological view of categorical identities, see Eiko Ikegami, "Sociological Theory of Publics: Culture and Identity as Emergent Properties in Networks," *Social Research* 67, 4 (Winter 2000): 989–1029. On the process of bringing a socially embedded sense of self into proximity with a more subjective sense of self, see Eiko Ikegami, "Epilogue," *The Taming of the Samurai: Honorific Individualism and the Making of Modern Japan* (Cambridge, Mass.: Harvard University Press, 1995).

2. The role of China as Japan's "significant other" was quickly replaced by that of the West after the Meiji Restoration.

3. The Chinese characters here romanized as "Nippon" can be pronounced either "Nippon" or "Nihon," historically. There is a complicated history of debate about the pronunciation of this name, but I am using "Nippon" in this paper as it was more often used by the early Japanese themselves in communications with outsiders.

4. Yoshida Takashi, *Nippon no tanjō* (Tokyo: Iwanami shoten, 1997).

5. Yoshida Takashi, "'Shiki' Shinshikō hongi to 'tennō' gō," *Nihon rekishi* 643 (2001); Amino Yoshihiko, *Nihon to wa nani ka* (Tokyo: Kōdansha, 2000).

6. Yoshida Takashi, *Nippon no tanjō*.

7. To be sure, the geographical boundaries of Japan also changed over the years. Ancient and medieval Japanese did not consider Hokkaidō and Okinawa as parts of "Nippon," and northern Tōhoku was regarded as peripheral.

8. Amino Yoshihiko, "Sōron," in Amino Yoshihiko, ed., *Iwanami kōza: Tennō to ōken o kangaeru*, vol. 1, *Jinrui shakai no naka no tennō to ōken* (Tokyo: Iwanami shoten, 2002). Certainly, one can cite the long continuity of the imperial line as an important factor in the durability of Nippon as the country's name, given that it had originally been a dynastic name. On the other hand, in the medieval and early modern eras, Japan was governed primarily by samurai rulers (shoguns) at the top of a feudally decentralized control system, with the emperor confined to a minimal political role. Thus, the long-term existence of the Japanese monarchy is only a partial explanation of this phenomenon.

9. To be sure, "beauty" in the Japanese tradition differs in some important ways from the Western notion. The two major differences, as I see it, are (1) the strict mathematical (or geometric) component of the classical Western ideal; and (2) the Western dualistic separation of form and matter. One should be wary of imposing such a European sense of the term on the Tokugawa case.

10. This advertisement appeared frequently in popular magazines and newspapers in Japan during 2001. A letter to the editor published in a major Japanese newspaper remarked that the advertisement reminded the writer of the Japanese tradition of the beautiful in manners. The advertising campaign included a male as well as a female version of the ad in order to avoid female-only stereotypes of gracious manners.

11. Of course, I am presenting a somewhat simplified account of the highly debated issues involved in the ritual symbolism of the ancient imperial system. It is difficult to summarize all of the disputed points in a single sentence. See

Ōwa Iwao, *Yūjo to tennō* (Tokyo: Hakusuisha, 1993), for an introduction to this issue.

12. "Kanajō," in *Kokinshū*, ed. and annot. Kyūsojin Hitaku, *Kokin wakashū* (Tokyo: Kōdansha, 1979), 1: 14, 15.

13. Kuroda Toshio, "Chūsei no mibunsei to hisen kannen," in *Nihon chūsei no kokka to shūkyō* (Tokyo: Iwanami shoten, 1975), 365–68. The character *ku* in *kuji* is an alternative pronunciation of the character *kō* (or *ōyake*); Sakurai Yoshirō, "Geinō shi e no shiza," in *Chūsei Nihon no ōken, shūkyō, geinō* (Kyoto: Jinbun shoin, 1988), p. 203; Kuroda Toshio, "Chūsei no mibunsei to hisen kannen," in *Nihon chūsei no kokka to shūkyō*.

14. This is a subject that requires further study in order to understand the cultural emergence of Japan. The scope of this paper, however, does not permit more extensive discussion of this subject.

15. Tetsuo Najita, *The Intellectual Foundations of Modern Japanese Politics* (Chicago: University of Chicago Press, 1974), 148.

16. Concerning the comparative evaluation of Japan's early modern state formation, see Eiko Ikegami, *The Taming of the Samurai*.

17. *Gotōke reijo*, no. 3.

18. In one of the shogunate's most famous legal cases, the episode of the forty-seven *rōnin*, one of the critical reasons the avengers were sentenced to die by *seppuku* (disembowelment by their own hands) was that they committed the crime of forming a party (*totō*). Even though the murder of the lord who had killed their master was considered an honorable act of revenge, the shogunate took it extremely seriously that these vassal samurai formed a private alliance to achieve their end.

19. Moriya Takeshi, *Kinsei geinō shi no kenkyū* (Tokyo: Kōbundō, 1985), 65–67.

20. Ihara Saikaku, *Nihon eidaigura*, reprinted in Isoji Asō and Fuji Akio, eds., *Taiyaku Saikaku zenshū* (Tokyo: Meiji shoin, 1975), 12:19. Kichizō and Sansuke were names with lowly associations; they were common given names among peasants, servants, or less prosperous merchants.

21. Nishikawa Joken, *Chōnin bukuro*, reprinted in *Kinsei chōnin shisō: Nihon shisō taikei* 59, ed. Nakamura Yukihiko (Tokyo: Iwanami shoten, 1975), 98.

22. According to Miyata Masanobu's study, one of the earliest examples of the no-author-name system occurs in *Nakōdo guchi* (1709), in the records of the monthly sessions of a master poet named Baika. Miyata, *Zappai shi no kenkyū, fugō bungei shi josetsu* (Kyoto: Akao shōbundō, 1972).

23. *Mukashi mukashi monogatari*, attributed to Niimi Masaasa. He was said to be eighty-one years old in 1732. Reprinted in *Nihon shomin seikatsu shiryō shūsei* (Tokyo: San'ichi shobō, 1969), 8: 397.

24. On naming and art organizations, see Nishiyama Matsunosuke, *Iemoto no kenkyū* (1959; Tokyo: Yoshikawa kōbunkan, 1982). On *haikai* poetry and naming, see Tanaka Yūko, *Edo no sōzōryoku* (Tokyo: Chikuma shobō, 1990).

25. One of the earliest surviving records of a publishing house comes from the shop of Nakamura Chōbei in 1608, five years after Tokogawa Ieyasu assumed the title of shogun. Another publisher has been identified by a colophon dated 1609, which reads *Honya Shinpachi*—literally, "Shinpachi's bookstore." Nakano Mitsutoshi, *Edo no hanpon, shoshigaku dangi* (Tokyo: Iwanami shoten, 1995), 34–35.

26. At the time of the Meiji Restoration in the nineteenth century, there were about six hundred public baths in the city of Edo.

27. *Genroku taiheiki*, reprinted in *Edo sōsho* (Tokyo: Edōsōsho kankōkai, n.d.).

28. The term can be spelled with two different sets of Chinese ideograms.

29. For tourists who required more specific geographical information, "travel books" were published from the mid-seventeenth century onward. Early publications in this genre included *Kyō warawa* (1658), *Edo meishoki* (1662), *Kyō suzume* (1665), *Edo suzume* (1677), *Edo kanoko* (1687), and *Nihon kokka manyōshū* (1697). Tourist guides of this sort were useful not only for actual travelers, but also supplied enjoyable reading for "armchair travelers" who wanted a taste of the liveliness and sophistication of a large city like Edo without traveling there in person. The traditions of ancient Japanese *waka* poetry also helped to make the *meishoki* popular reading. *Waka* poetry made frequent references to *uta makura*, or place names that became associated in readers' minds with the strong emotional and aesthetic impact of the poetry itself. By reading the Tokugawa "travelers' guides," poetry lovers could gain a clearer sense of what the celebrated locations actually looked like. "Travel books" were even found on the bookshelves of literate farmers and other rural readers. On the history of woodblock "travelers' maps" (*dōchūzu*), see Yamashita Kazumasa, *Edo jidai kochizu o meguru* (Tokyo: NTT shuppan, 1996).

30. For example, Ihara Saikaku's *Nihon eidaigura* (1688).

31. Waseda University Archive.

32. The Dutch traders did not want to tell the Japanese the truth about the relative geographical size of their homeland. They also emphasized the Christian identity of their competitors for trade—the Spanish and Portuguese who had come to Japan earlier than the Dutch. Christianity was officially prohibited by the shogunate.

33. Kaibara Ekken, "Sanrai guketsu." See also *Daishorei shū—Ogasawara ryū reihō densho*, ed. annot. Shimada Isao and Higuchi Motomi (Tokyo: Heibonsha, 1990). Ise Sadatake, *Teijō zakii* (1843; Tokyo: Heibonsha, 1985) which featured similar instructions. Inoue Tadao and Ishige Naomichi, eds., *Shokuji sahō no shisō* (Tokyo: Domesu shuppan, 1990)

34. This reluctance to displace the emperor as the ultimate repository of aesthetic standards should not be taken to imply that the Tokugawa shoguns and daimyos had no interest in enhancing their authority through cultural activities and self-cultivation. Although Kyoto remained the center of imperial high culture, several other court societies emerged, the court at the shogun's residence in Edo castle being the most prominent. To a lesser degree, the courts that grew up around the great daimyo houses in the provincial castle towns also became centers of cultural activity. In addition to supporting the arts, the Tokugawa rulers attempted to establish the authority of their court by setting up rules for ritual propriety. The shoguns employed a number of performing artists, painters, and scholars to decorate their court as well as to mingle socially with the courtiers who enjoyed these arts. Although the Tokugawa shoguns were generally less concerned with using their political power to define the authenticity or significance of artistic projects, the artists who enjoyed the shogunate's patronage increased their prestige tremendously. When the provincial daimyos began to cultivate these arts, their vassal samurai copied their masters' cultural preferences for the same reason.

35. Regarding emergent properties, see Eiko Ikegami, "A Sociological Theory of Publics: Identity and Culture as Emergent Property in Networks," *Social Research* 67, 4 (Winter 2000): 989–1029.

36. Franklin F. Mendels, "Proto-Industrialization: The First Phase of the Industrialization Process," *Journal of Economic History* 12, 1 (1972): 241; Peter Kriedte, Hans Medick, and Jürgen Schlumbohm, *Industrialization Before Industrialization*, trans. Beate Schempp (Cambridge: Cambridge University Press, 1981).

37. Richard Tilly and Charles Tilly, "Agenda for European Economic History in the 1970's," *Journal of Economic History* 31 (1970): 185.

38. Saitō Osamu, *Puroto kōgyōka no jidai* (Tokyo: Nihon hyōronsha, 1985); Osamu Saitō, "The Rural Economy: Commercial Agriculture, By-Employment, and Wage Work," in Marius Jansen and Gilbert Rozman, eds., *Japan in Transition* (Princeton, N.J.: Princeton University Press, 1986); Saitō Osamu, *Shōke no sekai, Uradana no sekai: Edo to Ōsaka no hikaku toshi shi* (Tokyo: Riburopōto, 1987).

39. Natsume Sōseki,"Civilization of Modern-day Japan," in *Kokoro and Selected Essays*, trans. Edwin McClellan and Jay Rubin (London: Madison Books, 1992), 272.

40. Ōishi Shinzaburō, *Edo jidai* (Tokyo: Chūō kōronsha, 1977), 66.

Chapter 2. The North(west)ern Peoples and the "Chinese" State

I would like to thank Jao Tsung-i, E. Bruce Brooks and A. Taeko Brooks, David Keightley, Guangda Zhang, Lynn Struve, Axel Schuessler, Elling Eide, Michael Witzel, Peter Golden, Ludo Rocher, Wolfang Behr, Edward Shaughnessy, David Prager Branner, David Nivison, David Pankenier, Roderick MacFarquhar, Stuart Schram, Avery Goldstein, Wei Tang, Thomas Gold, Mary Erbaugh, James Millward, Lothar von Falkenhausen, John Major, Wai-yee Li, Y. W. Ma, John Day, Paul Goldin, Denis Mair, Jia Si, and Taishan Yu for their generous help in the preparation of this paper. Bruce Brooks answered countless questions about texts of the Spring and Autumn period and the Warring States period. I am particularly indebted to Peter Golden for expert guidance in Turkological matters. David Keightley offered numerous useful references and insightful comments after reading an early draft. I am especially appreciative of the bibliographical and other references given to me by Guangda Zhang. The evolutionary biologists Friedrich Rösing, Maciej Henneberg, Brian Hemphill, and Kenneth A. R. Kennedy assisted me in devising neutral, accurate terminology for the description of human physical features. Finally, I am grateful to Chung-mo Kwok and Sanping Chen for their translations of the Hu Sanxing and Zhu Xi quotations which serve as epigraphs to two sections. Despite all of the generous assistance afforded me during the writing of this paper, I alone am responsible for the information presented and conclusions reached in it.

1. In this essay, "north(west)ern" is intended as an umbrella term that simultaneously signifies "northern," "northwestern," and "western." When written as "northwestern," reference is roughly to the following areas: northern Shaanxi, western Mongolia (including western Inner Mongolia), Ningxia, all of Gansu except its southeasternmost portion, all of Qinghai (Kokonor) except its southwesternmost portion, and Eastern Central Asia (Xinjiang). The usage of "northwest" in this large-scale view of the EEAH is different from that on the map (see p. 63) where it signifies one much smaller sector out of thirty.

In the earliest period, the directionality of septentrional influence upon the EAH was from the northwest, but with clear links far to the west. With the passage of time, the directionality of influence shifted gradually from the northwest to the north and even, at times, to the northeast.

2. All contemporary political entities mentioned in this paper as geographical locations of events and peoples in pre-modern times should be understood as silently prefaced by the expression "what is now." For example, "in Yunnan" = "in what is now Yunnan," "in Mongolia" = "in what is now Mongolia," and so forth.

3. Susan Naquin, *Peking: Temples and City Life, 1400–1900* (Berkeley: University of California Press, 2000), xxxiii, n. 27.

4. The concept of a "Great Wall" is, of course, itself highly problematic. See Arthur Waldron, *The Great Wall of China: From History to Myth* (Cambridge: Cambridge University Press, 1990). Despite (indeed, because of) its manifest liabilities, I use the term here purely as a rough indicator of geographic location.

5. The concept of a steppe gradient was inspired by William McNeill's perceptive *The Rise of the West: A History of the Human Community* (Chicago: University of Chicago Press, 1968; 1991), and its distillation in his *A World History* (New York: Oxford University Press, 1967, 1971).

6. Documentation for this movement will be provided below (see note 65).

7. It would be very easy to assemble an impressive list of continuities of culture in the EAH that persisted through many dynasties, beginning with the Shang: ancestor worship, rituals, administrative and bureaucratic terminology and practices, calendrical usages, morphosyllabic script, and so on. Limited cultural continuity, however, does not equate to political and ethnic identity. What is more, serious questions have been raised about the extent to which China is actually socially, ethnically, culturally, and linguistically unified. See, for example, W. J. F. Jenner, *The Tyranny of History: The Roots of China's Crisis* (London: Allen Lane, Penguin, 1992).

8. In recent years, unconventional explanations for the continuity of the Chinese politico-cultural system have been advanced. For example, Jin Guantao and Liu Qingfeng have proposed that it was the hyperstable system of the civil service examinations and the literati who took them that sustained the Chinese state across the rise and fall of dynasties. See Jin Guantao and Liu Qingfeng, *Xingsheng yu weiji* (Prosperity and crisis) (Changsha: Hunan renmin chubanshe, 1984). Yet the literati were brutally diminished at the very establishment of the bureaucratic Qin empire (221–209 B.C.E.) and were frequently ignored or decimated by rude militarists and crude eunuchs who wielded supreme authority at various times. Whatever its strengths may have been in preceding centuries, the entire literati ethos collapsed at the end of the Manchu Qing Dynasty (1644–1911), and any vestigial power the literati may have wielded was further eroded during the third quarter of the twentieth century when fierce struggles were carried out against their intellectual heirs by Communist zealots. Consequently, a cybernetic explanation premised on the overarching essentiality of Confucian scholars is an insufficient explanation for the existence of the modern Chinese nation-state.

David Keightley, perhaps most eloquently in *The Ancestral Landscape: Time, Space, and Community in Late Shang China (ca. 1200–1045 B.C.)* , China Research Monograph 53 (Berkeley: Center for Chinese Studies, Institute of East Asian Studies, University of California, 2000), has proposed that the defining features of the Chinese state have been determined by climate and topography. Geographical constraints have admittedly played a key role in shaping agricultural practices, social norms, and cultural preferences. Their importance elsewhere in the world, however, has not ensured the continuity of polities, nor is it a guarantee of the unilineal, millennial evolution of the modern Chinese nation-state.

9. E. Bruce Brooks and A. Taeko Brooks, *The Original Analects: Sayings of Confucius and His Successors* (New York: Columbia University Press, 1998).

10. See www.umass.edu/wsp and follow the link to "Antiquity Frenzy."

11. Yu Taishan, *Gu zu xin kao* (A new study of ancient peoples) (Beijing: Zhonghua shuju, 2000); English version: *A Hypothesis About the Source of the Sai Tribes*, Sino-Platonic Papers 106 (Philadelphia: Department of Asian and Middle Eastern Studies, University of Pennsylvania, 2000).

12. Paul Barber and Elizabeth Barber, *The Myth Principle* (Princeton, N.J.: Princeton University Press, forthcoming), demonstrate how many myths can be scientifically and historically explicated, but they by no means assert that myths should be taken at face value.

13. An Zhimin, "Shilun Zhongguo de zaoqi tongqi" (A tentative discussion on China's early copper/bronze implements), *Kaogu* (Archeology) 12 (1993): 1110–19; Andrew Sherratt, "The Trans-Eurasian Exchange: The Prehistory of Chinese Relations with the West," in Victor H. Mair, ed., *Contact and Exchange in the Ancient World* (Honolulu: University of Hawai'i Press, forthcoming).

14. Anne Birrell, *Chinese Mythology: An Introduction* (Baltimore: Johns Hopkins University Press, 1993); Mark Edward Lewis, *Sanctioned Violence in Early China* (Albany: State University of New York Press, 1990); Tsung-tung Chang, *Indo-European Vocabulary in Old Chinese: A New Thesis on the Emergence of Chinese Language and Civilization in the Late Neolithic Age*, Sino-Platonic Papers 7 (Philadelphia: Department of Asian and Middle Eastern Studies, University of Pennsylvania, 1988); Keith Quincy, *Hmong: History of a People* (Cheney: Eastern Washington University Press, 1988, 1995).

15. Our word "China" derives from Qin (Old Sinitic reconstruction **dz'įĕn*), the name of an originally agro-pastoralist people from the northwesternmost part of the EAH who were noted for their ability to raise horses. After 770 B.C.E., central Shaanxi—the ancient cradle of the Zhou kingdom—became the territory of the Qin. The earliest references to this name outside of China are in Sanskrit texts (transcribed as *āna*) that may be assigned pre-C.E. dates. While there is some dispute over exactly when the name reached India, it is understandable that outsiders would refer to the EAH by the name of the dynasty (Qin/*āna*/China) that first united it as a centralized empire and expanded it to an EEAH of unprecedented size. Berthold Laufer, "The Name China," *T'oung Pao* 13 (1912): 719–26. In a word, we may say that the First Emperor of Qin truly created "China." See Paul Pelliot, *Notes on Marco Polo* (Paris: Imprimerie Nationale, Librairie Adrien-Maisonneuve, 1959–63), vol. 1, no. 155: 264–78; Paul Pelliot, "Encore à propos du nom de 'Chine,'" *T'oung Pao* 14 (1913): 427–28; Paul Pelliot, "L'Origine du nom de 'Chine,'" *T'oung Pao* 13 (1912): 727–42.

When the graph used to write Qin appears on the Zhou oracle bones and early bronze inscriptions, it is with the meaning of some kind of cereal that was used to produce a drink. See Axel Schuessler, *A Dictionary of Early Zhou Chinese* (Honolulu: University of Hawai'i Press, 1987), 487b. This meaning is reaffirmed by the visual form of the graph which shows two men threshing grain with a large pestle. It is curious that the Sanskrit transcription of Qin (*āna*) also signifies a cereal grain, *Panicum miliaceum* (panicled millet, common millet, or Indian millet—called *ji* in Modern Standard Mandarin, MSM). See Monier Monier-Williams, *A Sanskrit-English Dictionary Etymologically and Philologically Arranged with Special Reference to Cognate Indo-European Languages* (Oxford: Clarendon Press, 1899), 399b. Be that as it may, the name Qin worked its way into Sinitic once again during the Middle Ages as a back-transcription of the Sanskrit transcription in the form Zhina. This term was popular among Buddhists of the EAH right up until the early decades of the twentieth century, and probably would have remained current even today had it not been for its becoming tarnished in the mouths of the Japanese occupiers during World War II. The Japanese pronounced as Shina the same two graphs that in MSM are pronounced Zhina. "Shina," in fact, was *the* word for China in Japanese, but it has now been virtually outlawed. Occasionally, however, one still comes upon Zhina in the writings of modern Chinese authors, some of whom use it with evident pride and historical consciousness.

Although it was relatively short, the northwestern state of Qin was so closely identified with the unification and expansion of the empire that other nations continued to refer to the people of the EAH as Qinren ("men of Qin") long after the dynasty had collapsed. Sima Qian—even though he lived and wrote during the Western Han period—uses this term in contrast with the inhabitants of Kangju (later called Samarkand) in his *Records of the Scribe-Historian*. However, when Ban Gu, writing about a century and a half later during the Eastern Han period, copied the same passage into his *History of the Han*, he silently changed Qinren to Hanren ("men of Han"). See *China in Central Asia: The Early Stage, 125 B.C.–A.D. 23: An Annotated Translation of Chapters 61 and 96 of the History of the Former Han Dynasty*, trans. A. F. P. Hulsewé, Sinica Leidensia, Institutum Sinologicum Lugduno Batavum 14 (Leiden: E.J. Brill, 1979), 232, n.898, see also 169, n.546. Furthermore, the term *Qinyu* ("Qin language") continued to be used to signify Sinitic ("Chinese") in some Buddhist texts and elsewhere still in the Six Dynasties. That is to say, though lasting little more than a decade, the northwestern dynasty of the Qin was so epochally determinative that the very language of the EAH came to be called "Qin speech." The Qin dynasty was similarly transformative for the script, for axle widths, weights and measures, laws, and many other facets of government and daily life. It is no wonder, then, that many peoples, all the way to the other end of Eurasia, referred to the EAH long after by derivatives of the name Qin (Greek Sinai, Latin Sinae, Arabic Sin) and why most of the world still today refers to the current nation-state of the EAH as "China," not *Zhongguo* ("Central Country"). It is particularly revealing, in light of the argument to be presented below, that many of those peoples who did not refer to the major polity of the EAH as "China" (or a variant thereof) have traditionally called it by a name derived from the ethnonym of another northwestern group, e.g., Tabgatch (or Tawghach, the rulers of the Northern Wei, 386–534) among Turkic speakers and Kitai (from Khitan, rulers of the Liao dynasty, 907–1125) among Slavic speakers (cf. Cathay in English).

16. Toward the end of the Qing (Manchu) Dynasty, a few individuals, such as the statesman Lin Zexu (1785–1850), occasionally mentioned the term *zhongguo*, but not as the name of a specific state. Rather, *zhongguo* during this period would appear to have been used for its old historical resonances.

17. The name Xia itself should give all cautious investigators cause for reflection. So far, it has not been confidently identified on the oracle bones and occurs only late in bronze inscriptions. A few (mostly small, usually relatively short-lived, and as often as not founded by non-Sinitic peoples) states much later in history adopted Xia for their names (e.g., 407, Xiongnu; 618, peasant rebellion; 1032, Tangut).

18. The sequence of Western or Former Han and Eastern or Later Han is not an exception to this pattern, since the short Xin period which separated them is considered to be an interregnum.

19. For example, the Ming is generally considered to be a purely Sinitic dynasty. Yet the ethnic origins of the founder himself, Taizu (Zhu Yuanzhang [1328–98], who reigned as the Hongwu emperor from 1368 until his death), are sufficiently dubious to warrant caution. Zhu Yuanzhang was a poor peasant who became a mendicant after having been orphaned at age sixteen. Thus, the records of his youth remain rather hazy. Nonetheless, *The Mongolian Chronicle Altan Tobči*, trans. Charles Bawden (Wiesbaden: Otto Harrassowitz, 1955), 63–64 declares that he was "the son named Jüü of an old man of the Jurčens." I am in-

debted to H. T. Toh for supplying this and other supporting information from his book manuscript entitled "Materials for a Genealogy of the Niohuru Clan (with introductory remarks on Manchu onomastics)," xxi–xxii. Supposedly, Taizu's second son and his most illustrious successor, Chengzu (Zhu Di [1360–1424], who reigned as the Yongle emperor from 1402 until his death), was—like his putative father—of imposing stature. But both his paternity and his maternity have been called into question. His "legal" mother was the influential Empress Ma (a Muslim), but his real mother was most likely a secondary consort of Korean origin, and his biological father is alleged to have been the Mongolian paramour of this Korean consort. Be that as it may, Zhu Di was nicknamed "the emperor on horseback" for cultivating Mongolian ways, and he was surrounded by non-Sinitic counselors and confidants. The importance of the roles played by Muslims, Northeast Asians, and Inner Asians as officials (including at least one provincial governor), naval personnel (including the renowned admiral Zheng He [1371–1433] and many of his most important subordinates), craftsmen, technicians, and the like during the early Ming period can hardly be overestimated.

For the non-Sinitic heritage of the Sui and Tang founders, and the particularly close relationship of the latter with Turkic steppe leaders, see Woodbridge Bingham, *The Founding of the T'ang Dynasty: The Fall of Sui and Rise of T'ang. A Preliminary Survey* (Baltimore: Waverly, 1941), 4–5, 75, 95, 122–23. For the northern background of the Sui and Tang rulers, see also Peter A. Boodberg, "Marginalia to the Histories of the Northern Dynasties," *Harvard Journal of Asiatic Studies* 4, 3–4 (December 1939): 253–70, 282–83; and the first chapter of Chen Yinke, *Tangdai zhengzhi shi shulun gao* (Draft account of the political history of the Tang dynasty) (Beijing: Sanlian, 1956). Sanping Chen, in his brilliantly argued studies on the ethnic identity of the Tang imperial house, shows that—despite their manifestly northern background—the rulers of this quintessentially "Chinese" dynasty were complicit (but ultimately unsuccessful) in efforts to pass themselves off as "Han." See Sanping Chen, "A-gan Revisited: The Tuoba's Cultural and Political Heritage," *Journal of Asian History* 30, 1 (1996): 46–78; and Sanping Chen, "Succession Struggle and the Ethnic Identity of the Tang Imperial House," *Journal of the Royal Asiatic Society* 6, 1 (April 1996): 379–405. Li Yuan, who founded the Tang Dynasty and ruled as Gaozu (r. 618–26), like Wendi (founder of the Sui, r. 581–604), came from a northern aristocratic family with a long tradition of government service. He was the grandson of Li Hu who had helped to found the strongly Särbi Northern Zhou Dynasty. Numerous tomb figurines vividly depict the presence of north(west)ern peoples in the Tang capital of Chang'an. As north(west)erners themselves, the Tang rulers and their families were accustomed to frequent travel, and the ox-cart often formed the centerpiece of figurine processions placed in early Tang tombs. The extent of north(west)ern kinship felt by members of the Tang royal family can be seen in the behavior of the heir apparent of the second Tang emperor, Taizong (r. 626–49), who "became obsessed by his Tartar ancestry and adopted Turkic habits. Wearing Turkish clothes, he spoke only Turkish and lived in a felt tent, stealing sheep and cooking them in nomad fashion over a camp fire." See Ann Paludan, *Chronicle of the Chinese Emperors: The Reign-by-Reign Record of the Rulers of Imperial China* (London and New York: Thames and Hudson, 1998), 88–89, 92–93; and Jane Gaston Mahler, *The Westerners among the figurines of the Tang dynasty of China*, Serie orientale Roma 20 (Rome: Istituto Italiano per il Medio ed Estremo Oriente, 1959).

20. See Victor H. Mair, "Was There a Xia Dynasty?" (forthcoming).

21. Albert Herrmann, *An historical atlas of China*, ed. Norton Ginsburg (Chicago: Aldine, 1966), prefatory essay by Paul Wheatley, new edition based on Albert Herrmann, *Historical and Commercial Atlas of China* (Cambridge, Mass.: Harvard-Yenching Institute, 1935); Tan Qixiang, *Zhongguo lishi ditu ji* (Historical atlas of China), 8 vols. (Hong Kong: Joint Publishing, 1991–92); Michael Loewe and Edward L. Shaughnessy, eds., *The Cambridge History of Ancient China: From the Origins of Civilization to 221 B.C.* (Cambridge: Cambridge University Press, 1999); Nicola Di Cosmo, *Ancient China and Its Enemies: The Rise of Nomadic Power in East Asian History* (Cambridge: Cambridge University Press, 2002); and *The Cambridge History of China.* The locational data for the Shang period are drawn from David Keightley, "The Late Shang State: When, Where, and What?" in Keightley, ed., *The Origins of Chinese Civilization* (Berkeley and Los Angeles: University of California Press, 1983), 526–48. Locational data for the other ruling houses are extracted chiefly from the standard histories, but are supplemented and refined through reference to archeological and other written sources.

22. See E. G. Pulleyblank, "The Chinese and Their Neighbors in Prehistoric and Early Historic Times," in Keightley, ed., *The Origins of Chinese Civilization*, 413, substituting "Sinitic" for "Chinese" and "Zhou" for "Chou."

23. Cf. Jessica Rawson's recent argument that the Zhou were not Chinese, but were foreign ("Western Zhou Material Culture"): "Was Western Zhou Material Culture 'Chinese' and How, If at All, Did It Contribute to the 'Chineseness' of Later Chinese Culture?", paper presented to the symposium, "What Made Chinese Civilization 'Chinese'?", University of Washington, Seattle (February 26–28, 1999).

24. See their "Shangdai Yinxu renlei yihai de jianding yu yanjiu" (Evaluation and research on human remains from Yinxu of the Shang period), in Song Wenxun, Li Yiyuan, and Zhang Guangzhi, eds., *Shi Zhangru yuanshi baisui zhu shou lunwen ji—kaogu, lishi, wenhua* (Studies in celebration of the hundredth birthday of academician Shi Zhangru—archeology, history, culture) (Taibei: Nantian, 2002), 190, 204.

25. David Keightley, ed., *The Origins of Chinese Civilization*, 551–52, emphasis added.

26. David R. Knechtges, trans., annot., and intro., *Wen xuan, or Selections of Refined Literature*, vol. one, *Rhapsodies on Metropolises and Capitals* (Princeton, N.J.: Princeton University Press, 1982), 241, emphasis added. Originally edited by Xiao Tong (501–31).

27. David R. Knechtges, *Wen xuan*, 240 with slight modifications.

28. James Legge, trans., *The Shoo King, or The Book of Historical Documents.* Vol. III (in 2 parts) of *The Chinese Classics* (Hong Kong and London: Oxford University Press, 1865), 220–23, with slight modifications and added explanations and emphasis.

29. David Anthony, personal communication, October 21, 2001.

30. *Encyclopaedia Britannica*, 15th ed. (Chicago: Encyclopaedia Britannica, 1988), 11: 785a.

31. Thomas Allsen, *The Royal Hunt in Eurasia*, in preparation.

32. In actuality, the Manchus—certainly by the time of the Qing Dynasty—were not true nomads of the steppes. Rather, they—and their Tungusic ancestors for the previous millennium—were hunters, herders, and agriculturalists. Nonetheless, the Manchus—perhaps partly carrying on the imperial heritage of the Mongols—maintained the tradition of the mobile royal camp as a symbol of the martial virility of their ruler and his bannermen-warriors. The large-scale

hunting expeditions in which they regularly engaged would also have served to prevent Manchu aristocrats from becoming effete and militarily ineffective. See Nicholas K. Menzies, *Forest and Land Management in Imperial China* (New York: St. Martin's, 1994), 55–64; Mark C. Elliott, *The Manchu Way: The Eight Banners and Ethnic Identity in Late Imperial China* (Stanford, Calif.: Stanford University Press, 2001), 182–87 and passim.

33. Li Liu, "Settlement Patterns, Chiefdom Variability, and the Development of Early States in North China," *Journal of Anthropological Archaeology* 15 (1996): 237–88, argues that—during the third millennium B.C.E.—the Longshan Culture of the Central Plains was the crucial matrix in which the first states of the EAH evolved out of earlier Neolithic societies. She asserts that these early states "emerged from a system of competing chiefdoms, which was characterized by intensive intergroup conflict and frequent shifting of political centers." These archeological findings would seem to be in harmony with those of the present investigation.

34. David Keightley, ed., *The Origins of Chinese Civilization*, 552, emphasis added.

35. The total inventory of decipherable graphs among the oracle bone inscriptions indicates that the scribes who incised the divinations were aware of other media (the famous case of the characters for *ce* ["wooden (?) tablets/strips strung together"] and *dian* ["canonical work (composed of such strips)"], for example). It is also evident from the inscriptions themselves that the scribes were sometimes relying on workbooks; see David N. Keightley, "The Diviners' Notebooks: Shang Oracle-Bone Inscriptions as Secondary Sources," in *Actes du Colloque International Commémorant le Centenaire de la Découverte des Inscriptions sur Os et Carapaces; Proceedings of the International Symposium in Commemoration of the Centennial of Oracle-Bone Inscriptions Discovery* (Paris: Éditions Langages Croisés, 2001), 11–25. However, none of this indirect evidence for other possible categories of texts during the Shang contravenes the distinct impression gained from tens of thousands of extant inscriptions that the primary function of writing during the Shang was for the purpose of recording divinations.

I view plastromancy as a very early Sinitic adaptation of scapulimancy, which has a greater spatial and temporal distribution worldwide. Given the need to find a large, hard, flat, bony surface for writing comparable to the scapulae of cattle—which are so plentiful among herding peoples—it is not surprising that the early non-herding peoples of the EAH would have turned to turtle plastrons for the purpose.

36. The relationship of the Eurasian parallels to the system of divination in the *Yi jing* (Book of change) is an intriguing topic concerning which I have been collecting materials for more than two decades. See J. P. Mallory and Victor H. Mair, *The Tarim Mummies: Ancient China and the Mystery of the Earliest Peoples from the West* (London: Thames and Hudson, 2000), 155.

37. Huang Zhongye offers compelling textual and archeological evidence that the Shang had northern roots. See "Cong kaogu faxian kan Shang wenhua qiyuan yu woguo beifang" (An archaeological research proved that the Shang dynasty culture originated in the north part of China), *Beifang wenwu* (Northern Cultural Relics) 1 (cum. 21) (1990): 14–19. See also Jin Jingfang, "Shang wenhua qiyuan yu woguo beifang shuo" (A hypothesis that Shang culture arose in the north of China), in Zhu Dongrun, ed., *Zhonghua wenshi luncong* (Papers on Chinese literature and history), 7 (Shanghai: Shanghai guji chubanshe, 1978), 65–70.

38. Peng Ke and Zhu Yanshi, "New Research on the Origin of Cowries Used in Ancient China," *Sino-Platonic Papers* 68 (May 1995): i, 26.

39. Robert Bagley, "Shang Archaeology," in Loewe and Shaughnessy, eds., *Cambridge History of Ancient China*, 194–202.

40. Victor Mair, "The Horse in Late Prehistoric China: Wresting Culture and Control from the 'Barbarians,'" in Marsha Levine, Colin Renfrew, and Katie Boyle, eds., *Prehistoric Steppe Adaptation and the Horse*, McDonald Institute Monographs (Cambridge: McDonald Institute for Archaeological Research, Cambridge University, 2003).

41. Wang Haicheng, "Zhongguo mache de qiyuan" (The origins of Chinese chariots), *Ou-Ya xuekan* (Eurasian Studies) 3 (2002): 3–75.

42. Anthony J. Barbieri-Low, *Wheeled Vehicles in the Chinese Bronze Age (c. 2000–741 B.C.)*, Sino-Platonic Papers 99 (Philadelphia: Department of Asian and Middle Eastern Studies, University of Pennsylvania, 2000), i–v, 1–98, 10 color plates; Edward L. Shaughnessy, "Historical Perspectives on the Introduction of the Chariot into China," *Harvard Journal of Asiatic Studies* 48, 1 (1988): 189–237.

43. For *Shi ji*, Kaiming ed., scroll 8, p. 33c; Burton Watson, trans., *Records of the Grand Historian* (Hong Kong: Renditions; New York: Columbia University Press, 1993), 1: 51. For the *Han shu*, Kaiming ed., scroll 1A, p. 291d; Homer H. Dubs, trans. and annot., with the collaboration of P'an Lo-chi and Jen T'ai, *The History of the Former Han Dynasty* (Baltimore: Waverly, 1938), 1: 29.

44. Alfred Forke, trans. and annot., *Lun-hêng. Part I: Philosophical Essays of Wang Ch'ung*, supplementary volume to the *Mitteilungen des Seminars für Orientalische Sprachen, Jahrgang XIV* (1907; New York: Paragon, 1962), 1: 305.

45. *Shi ji*, scroll 28; Burton Watson, trans., *Records of the Grand Historian*, 1: 9.

46. Long after I had written the above paragraph, Michael Carr called to my attention the following web site on the number 72, which gives many additional instances of its Eurasian applications: http://pages.globetrotter.net/sdesr/nu72.htm.

47. *Hou Han shu* (History of the Later Han), Kaiming ed., scroll 1A, p. 647a.

48. *Shi ji*, Kaiming ed., scroll 8, p. 33c; Jenny F. So, "Bronze Weapons, Harness and Personal Ornaments: Signs of Qin's Contacts with the Northwest," *Orientations* 26, 10 (November 1995): 36–43.

49. A. F. P. Hulsewé, *Remnants of Ch'in Law. An annotated translation of the Ch'in legal and administrative rules of the 3rd century B.C. discovered in Yün-meng Prefecture, Hu-pei Province, in 1975*, Sinica Leidensia, XVII (Leiden: E.J. Brill, 1985), 15–16.

50. Hulsewé, *Remnants of Ch'in Law*, 103, 105 (twice), 115, 116, 118, 123, 127, 130 (twice), 141 (three times), 142, 149, 150, 151, 153 (five times), 154 (twice), 155, 156, 157, 159 (twice), 161 (twice), 163, 164, 171, 174, 176 (four times).

51. Szuma Chien, *Selections from Records of the Historian*, trans. Yang Hsien-yi and Gladys Yang (Peking: Foreign Languages Press, 1979), p. 156.

52. It does not concern us here whether the Jie themselves were Xiongnu or whether they were merely part of the Xiongnu confederation. What matters are their manifest physical characteristics.

53. Otto J. Maenchen-Helfen, *The World of the Huns: Studies in Their History and Culture* (Berkeley and Los Angeles: University of California Press, 1973), 372.

54. *Jin shu* (History of the Jin), Kaiming ed., scroll 107, p. 1363c.

55. Chen Chien-wen, "Yuezhi de mingcheng, zushu yiji Handai xichui de heise ren wenti" (On the question of the name and race of the Yuezhi and the dark-skinned people of the Western Regions during the Han dynasty), *Guoji jiandu xuehui huikan* (Bulletin of the International Institute for Studies on Documents of Bamboo and Wooden Strips) 1 (1993): 111–43; Chen Chien-wen, "Further Studies on the Racial, Cultural, and Ethnic Affinities of the Yuezhi," in Victor H. Mair, ed., *The Bronze Age and Early Iron Age Peoples of Eastern Central Asia*

(Washington, D.C.: Institute for the Study of Man, with University of Pennsylvania Museum Publications, 1998), 2:769, 773, 777, 778.

56. Mallory and Mair, *The Tarim Mummies*, 204.

57. *Brewer's Dictionary of Phrase & Fable* (New York: HarperCollins, 1999), 105a.

58. For a careful, illuminating study of the Xi Hu ("Western Hu / Bearded [Ones]"), see Wang Guowei, *Wang Guantang xiansheng quanji* (Complete works of Wang Guowei) (Taibei: Wenhua chuban gongsi, 1968), 2: 588–602.

59. As a Peace Corps volunteer from 1965–67, my gigantic nose, sunken blue eyes, pale complexion, blond hair, hirsute calves and forearms, and great height elicited endless wonder (and even occasionally outright fear among small children) when I visited remote towns inhabited by Tibeto-Burman speakers—and I usually was not even sporting a full beard!

60. Sample quotations are available in Wang Guowei, *Wang Guantang xiansheng quanji*, 2: 588–602.

61. See, for example, Han Kangxin, *Sichou zhi lu gudai jumin zhongzu renleixue yanjiu* (Racial anthropological studies on the ancient inhabitants of the Silk Road), Sichou zhi lu yanjiu congshu (Silk Road Studies Series) 3 (Ürümchi: Xinjiang renmin chubanshe, 1993); Mallory and Mair, *The Tarim Mummies*.

62. The long-standing difference of opinion over Sinicization is well summarized in the articles of Ho Ping-ti, "In Defense of Sinicization: A Rebuttal of Evelyn Rawski's 'Reenvisioning the Qing,'" *Journal of Asian Studies* 57, 1 (February 1998): 123–55, and Evelyn S. Rawski, "Reenvisioning the Qing: The Signification of the Qing Period in Chinese History," *Journal of Asian Studies* 55, 4 (November 1996): 829–50, with Ho being staunchly in favor of it and Rawski raising stiff challenges against it. I stand the Sinicization question on its head by proposing the concept of Tabgatchization. See Victor Mair, Review of James O. Caswell, *Written and Unwritten: A New History of the Buddhist Caves at Yungang, Harvard Journal of Asiatic Studies* 52, 1 (June 1992): 358–60; and Scott Pearce, "A Survey of Recent Research in Western Languages on the History of Early Medieval China," *Early Medieval China* 1 (1994): 138–39. Considering, for example, that Beijing was a Mongol city constructed by architects and craftsmen brought from across the breadth of Eurasia, and that one of the most characteristic features of the traditional city, the *hutong* (Mongol *quduq/qudun*, "well [in an alley]"), was bequeathed by the Mongols, we would also be justified in speaking of Mongolization. Likewise, since the distinctive late imperial female dress (the *qipao*) of the EAH and the traditional male hairstyle (the queue) were both derived from the Manchus, it would not be unreasonable to speak of Manchuization.

63. The historical linguist David Branner views the changes in lexicon, grammar, and phonology between early and medieval Sinitic to have been so massive and fundamental that, for purposes of formal classification, they should be considered as two different types of language. See David Prager Branner, *Problems in Comparative Chinese Dialectology: The Classification of Miin and Hakka*, Trends in Linguistics. Studies and Monographs 123 (Berlin: Mouton de Gruyter, 2000), 160–66. This transition occurred rougly during the period 100–600 C.E., when north(west)ern peoples were particularly active in the EAH. Other scholars who have attributed significant linguistic impact upon Sinitic to north(west)ern peoples are Mantarō Hashimoto, Charles N. Li, Jiang Lansheng, Tsu-Lin Mei, and Jerry Norman.

64. Victor Mair, "Old Sinitic *$*m^y ag$, Old Persian *maguš*, and English 'Magician'," *Early China* 15 (1990): 27–47.

65. Průšek presents considerable evidence that the rise of Chinese civilization was completely unrelated to Turkic peoples (similarly for Tungusic and Mongo-

lian peoples). See Jaroslav Průšek, *Chinese Statelets and the Northern Barbarians in the Period 1400–300 B.C.* (Dordrecht—Holland: D. Reidel, 1971). This sensibly leaves the stockbreeding, chariot-wielding, horseriding Indo-Europeans as the main players on the steppes during the first two millennia BCE. See Tzehuey Chiou-Peng, "Western Yunnan and Its Steppe Affinities," in Mair, ed., *The Bronze Age and Early Iron Age Peoples*, 280–304; Roberto Ciarla, "A Long Debated Question: Pastoralism in South-Western China. A Different Approach," in Bruno Genito, ed., *The Archaeology of the Steppes: Methods and Strategies*, Istituto Universitario Orientale, Dipartimento di Studi Asiatici, Series Minor 44 (Naples: Istituto Italiano per il Medio ed Estremo Oriente, 1994), 73–85; Marcello Orioli, "Pastoralism and Nomadism in South-West China: A Brief Survey of the Archaeological Evidence," in Bruno Genito, ed., *The Archaeology of the Steppes*, 87–108; and Zhang Zengqi, "Again on the Influence and Diffusion of the Scythian Culture in the Yunnan Bronze Age," in Genito, ed., *The Archaeology of the Steppes*, 667–99.

66. Owen Lattimore, *Inner Asian Frontiers of China*, American Geographical Society, Research Series 21 (New York: American Geographical Society, 1940); Yü Ying-shih, *Trade and Expansion in Han China: A Study in the Structure of Sino-Barbarian Economic Relations* (Berkeley: University of California Press, 1967); Claudius C. Müller, "Die Herausbildung der Gegensätze: Chinesen und Barbaren in der frühen Zeit (I. Jahrtausend v. Chr. bis 220 n. Chr.)," in Wolfgang Bauer, ed., *China und die Fremden: 3000 Jahre Auseinandersetzung in Krieg und Frieden* (Munich: C.H. Beck, 1980), 43–76; Helwig Schmidt-Glintzer, "Ausdehnung der Welt und innerer Zerfall (3. bis 8. Jahrhundert)," in Wolfgang Bauer, ed., *China und die Fremden*, 77–113; Klaus Tietze, "Vom ostasiastischen Grossreich zur mongolischen Provinz (7. bis 14. Jahrhundert)," in Wolfgang Bauer, ed., *China und die Fremden*, 114–60; S. A. M. Adshead, *China in World History* (New York: St. Martin's, 1988); Thomas J. Barfield, *The Perilous Frontier: Nomadic Empires and China* (Cambridge, Mass.: Basil Blackwell, 1989); Sechin Jagchid and Van Jay Symons, *Peace, War, and Trade along the Great Wall: Nomadic-Chinese Interaction through Two Millennia* (Bloomington: Indiana University Press, 1989); Jenny F. So and Emma C. Bunker, *Traders and Raiders on China's Northern Frontier* (Seattle: Arthur M. Sackler Gallery, Smithsonian Institution, in association with the University of Washington Press, 1995); Nicola Di Cosmo, "The Northern Frontier in Pre-Imperial China," in Loewe and Shaughnessy, eds., *The Cambridge History of Ancient China*, 885–966.

67. Tikhvinsky states that in 1577 the Manchus numbered no more than 100,000. S. L. Tikhvinsky, ed., *Manzhou Rule in China*, trans. David Skvirsky (Moscow: Progress Publishers, 1983), 8. Even after Nurhaci's conquest of neighboring tribes, their union consisted of no more than 400,000 to 500,000 people. In the following year, the Ming Dynasty census gave 63,599,541. L. Carrington Goodrich, *A Short History of the Chinese People* (New York: Harper, 1959), 202, n.17. In the second decade of the seventeenth century, Nurhaci had just 60,000–70,000 men in arms (personal communication, Lynn Struve). It is astonishing that so few men could control so many. The numbers were even more disproportionate when the Mongols conquered nearly the whole of Asia and much of Europe four centuries earlier. At the time of Chinggis Khan's rise to power, the total number of adult males fit for military service was no more than 50,000–100,000. In 1206, the size of the Mongol army has been estimated at over 100,000. Nearly every adult male was drafted into the central military apparatus, and men from other tribes were brought in as well. See Nicola Di Cosmo, "State

Formation and Periodization in Inner Asian History," *Journal of World History* 10, 1 (1999): 17.

68. Peter Alford Andrews, *Felt Tents and Pavilions: The Nomadic Tradition and Its Interaction with Princely Tentage*, 2 vols. (London: Melisende, 1999).

69. Karl A. Wittfogel and Fêng Chia-shêng, with the assistance of John De Francis, Esther S. Goldfrank, Lea Kisselgoff, and Karl H. Menges, *History of Chinese Society. Liao (907–1125)* (Philadelphia: American Philosophical Society, 1949), 508–9; *Hanyu da cidian* (Great dictionary of the Chinese language) (Shanghai: Hanyu da cidian chubanshe, 1988–94), 5: 295a.

70. Gerhard Doerfer, *Türkische und mongolische Elemente im Neupersischen.* Band II: *Türkische Elemente im Neupersischen* alif *bis* tä (Wiesbaden: Franz Steiner, 1965), no. 452, 32–39.

71. Clauson speculates on a possible connection to *ortu:* (*orto:*), meaning "middle, center," the chief's camp being the defining, though shifting, center. Gerard Clauson, *An Etymological Dictionary of Pre-Thirteenth-Century Turkish* (Oxford: Clarendon, 1972), 203b–204a. However, one cannot help but notice a resemblance to Old English *ord*, Germanic *ort* ("place"), which are probably ultimately derived from Indo-European **ud-dho* < *dhē-* ("put, place").

72. Douglas Q. Adams, *A Dictionary of Tocharian B* (Amsterdam: Rodopi, 1999), 196, transcribes this word as *kercci*. He indicates that the etymology is uncertain, but that it may possibly be related to √*gher* ("to grasp, enclose"), whose suffixed zero-grade form would be **ghr̥-dh-*. Cf. English "yard," from Old Norse *gardhr* ("enclosure, garden, yard") and "garden," from Old North French *gart* ("garden").

73. I suspect that an even more well-known Turkic term, *yurt* (*yurd?*) ("circular, domed portable tent"), which has been taken up into English via Russian, may also be distantly cognate with *ordu*. Even though it became a common Turkic word later on, during the early period it was actually quite rare. Early occurrences mean "an abandoned camping-site," and in the medieval period *yurt* simply comes to mean "dwelling-place, abode," without any sense of abandonment. In all modern Turkic languages *yurt* (and its close cognates) means "residence, abode, dwelling; a particular type of felt tent; a community; a country; one's own country, i.e., fatherland." See Clauson, *An Etymological Dictionary of Pre-Thirteenth-Century Turkish*, 958ab. Considering the enormous number of Turkic words that were adopted into Mongolian, it is curious that *yurt* did not stick. Instead, the equivalent Mongolian word is *ger* ("yurt, house, dwelling, domicile"; cf. the discussion of √*gher* in note 72). Ferdinand D. Lessing, with Mattai Haltod, John Gombojab Hangin, and Serge Kassatkin, comps., *Mongolian-English Dictionary* (Berkeley and Los Angeles: University of California Press, 1960), 377b.

74. Martti Räsänen, *Versuch eines etymologischen Wörterbuchs der Türksprachen*, Lexica Societatis Fenno-Ugricae 17, 1 (Helsinki: Suomalais-Ugrilainen Seura, 1969), 364b.

75. Clauson, *An Etymological Dictionary of Pre-Thirteenth-Century Turkish*, 203ab. This name occurs in the famous dictionary of Kashgari and in Yusuf Khass Hajib's Qarakhanid mirror for princes entitled *Qutadghu Bilig*, both written in the eleventh century CE.

76. Lessing et al., comps., *Mongolian-English Dictionary*, 617a.

77. Ibid., 617b.

78. Although much of the Ordos is now covered by sand, the vegetation of the region during the Northern Wei period (386–534 C.E.) was still quite lush, and as late as the Qing period there were forests in the northern, eastern, and southern parts. The sandification process has accelerated with more intensive agri-

cultural practices and increased settlement from the south. See Jiang Hong, *The Ordos Plateau of China: An endangered environment* (Tokyo: United Nations University Press, 1999), 15ff.

79. See the provincial maps (especially the topographical and historical maps) in Guojia wenwuju (State Bureau of Cultural Relics), ed., *Zhongguo wenwu dituji: Shaanxi fence* (Atlas of Chinese cultural relics: Shaanxi volumes), 2 vols. (Xi'an: Xi'an ditu chubanshe, 1998).

80. More detailed studies on the ethnic background of the ruling houses of all dynasties would undoubtedly reveal that many of the so-called ethnic Han ruling houses had significant admixtures of non-Sinitic ancestry. Similar investigations of the major military figures and statesmen who helped to establish and maintain the successive dynasties are also suggested. The extraordinary martial prowess of the northern peoples, which evoked both grudging admiration and outright terror on the part of the Sinitic peoples, was a common theme in Chinese literature and folklore.

81. Glen Dudbridge, "China's Vernacular Cultures," Inaugural Lecture delivered before the University of Oxford on June 1, 1995 (Oxford: Clarendon Press, 1995).

82. Du Ruofu, Yida Yuan, Juliana Hwang, Joanna Mountain, and L. Luca-Cavalli-Sforza, *Chinese Surnames and the Genetic Differences between North and South China,* Journal of Chinese Linguistics, Monograph Series 5 (Berkeley: Journal of Chinese Linguistics, 1992).

83. One of the northern opponents of the Shang most frequently mentioned on the oracle bones were the Gui Fang. The Gui Fang were not polar opposites of the Shang, but rather bore many similarities to them. Contrary to written accounts of the Gui Fang as pure nomads, archeological and climatological evidence suggests that the Gui Fang were agro-pastoralists who not only had extensive herds, but who also were engaged in agriculture. Tang Xiaofeng, "Gui Fang: Yin-Zhou shidai beifang de nong-mu hunhe zuqun" (Gui Fang: A herder husbandry group of people in the northern Shanxi and Shaanxi region during the Shang-Zhou period)," *Zhongguo lishi dili luncong* (Collected Papers on Chinese Historical Geography) 2 (cum. 55) (2000): 15–24. The same holds for many of the other contemporaries of the Shang to the north, northwest, and west.

84. As a senior in high school, I designed an experiment for desalinating water in which amebas were used to absorb salt ions from a solution. (The experiment won first prize in the Ohio State Science Fair.) The situation is analogous to the preponderant influx of steppic elements into the EAH in comparison with negligible outward reflux.

85. Thomas Höllmann, "Das Reich ohne Horizont: Berührungen mit dem Fremden jenseits und disseits der Meere (14. bis 19. Jahrundert)," in Bauer, ed., *China und die Fremden,* 161–96; Tilman Spengler, "Modernität und Fremdbestimmung: Chinas Auseinandersetzung mit dem 'Westen' und der eigenen Vergangenheit (19. und 20. Jahrhundert)," in Bauer, ed., *China und die Fremden,* 197–238.

86. For a general account of this epic withdrawal, see Dick Wilson, *The Long March, 1935: The Epic of Chinese Communism's Survival* (London: Hamish Hamilton, 1971).

87. The numbers vary widely depending upon how one counts the Communist forces and their supporters.

88. Mary S. Erbaugh, "The Secret History of the Hakkas: The Chinese Revolution as a Hakka Enterprise," *China Quarterly* 132 (1992): 937–68, discusses the

key role of Hakka speakers in the Long March. The Hakkas, however, did not have a significant enclave in the far northwest, so their involvement in the Long March can not explain how and why the Communist forces sought refuge in Yan'an—unless the Hakka component of Mao's inner circle was responding to a profound atavistic urge. As attested by linguistics, genetics, history, and legend, the ancestors of the Hakka (Modern Standard Mandarin *kejia* or "guest people") hailed from the north.

89. As a sort of postscript, we may note that the model of the interrelationship between the settled and nomadic (or semi-nomadic) peoples presented in this paper may be applied elsewhere in Eurasia (e.g., northern Mesopotamia, western Anatolia, the northwest part of South Asia). For India see especially the comments of Michael Witzel (in addition to a personal communication of March 25, 2002), "Early Sanskritization: Origins and Development of the Kuru State," *Electronic Journal of Vedic Studies* 1–4 (1995): 1–26, posted at the following URL: http://users.primushost.com/~india/ejvs/ejvs0104/ejvs0104article.pdf; and Jason Neelis, "Ancient Frontiers of Northwestern India: The 'Heartland of the Aryas' (*Aryavarta*) and the Borderlands of the 'Northern Route' (*Uttarapatha*)," lecture delivered at the University of Pennsylvania, Department of Asian and Middle Eastern Studies, March 8, 2002, concerning the peripatetic nature of the kings in the post-Vedic period. There are numerous conspicuous parallels between northwest India in the post-Vedic period and the northwest of the EAH during the roughly contemporaneous Shang period: struggles for superiority among contesting clans of warriors coming from the northwest; the introduction of advanced bronze weaponry; dominance over local populations by aristocrats possessing horse-drawn chariots; reliance on divination; the development of a fossilized hieratic language divorced from the vernacular; and the like. Note that the central territory of the Kurus, namely Kurukṣetra (the nucleus of Āryāvarta; also resonant for the Kurus were the northern reaches known as Uttarāpatha), was likewise called the Middle Country (Madhyadeśa) at the same time and for the same purposes as this notion developed in EAH. See N. N. Bhattacharyya, *Encyclopaedia of Ancient Indian Culture* (New Delhi: Manohar, 1998), 42a, 217b. It would appear that the mechanics of the interaction between the steppe and the sown, between the settled, "civilized" populations of the south and the nomadic, "barbarian" tribes of the north, were similar across the breadth of Eurasia. Wherever such interactions occurred, they require reexamination and reassessment. The Eurasian ecumene may prove to be a far more complex sphere of political, military, ethnic, and cultural engagement than is currently recognized.

Chapter 3. State-Making in Global Context: Japan in a World of Nation-States

1. R. R. Palmer, *A History of the Modern World* (New York: Knopf, 1952), 563.

2. Robert Neelly Bellah, *Tokugawa Religion: The Values of Pre-industrial Japan* (Glencoe, Ill.: Free Press, 1957).

3. Takashi Fujitani, *Splendid Monarchy: Power and Pageantry in Modern Japan* (Berkeley: University of California Press, 1996).

4. Stephen Vlastos, ed., *Mirror of Modernity: Invented Traditions of Modern Japan* (Berkeley: University of California Press, 1998).

5. John W. Meyer et al., "World Society and the Nation-State," *American Journal of Sociology* 103, 1 (1997): 145.

6. John W. Meyer, "The Changing Cultural Content of the Nation-State: A

World Society Perspective," in George Steinmetz, ed., *State/Culture: State-Formation after the Cultural Turn* (Ithaca, N.Y.: Cornell University Press, 1999), 123–28.

7. John W. Meyer, John Boli, and George M. Thomas, "Ontology and Rationalization in the Western Cultural Account," in George M. Thomas, ed., *Institutional Structure: Constituting State, Society, and the Individual* (Newbury Park, Calif.: Sage Publications, 1987), 155.

8. For an imaginative discussion of this issue, see Alexis Dudden Eastwood, "International Terms: Japan's Engagement in Colonial Control," Ph.D. dissertation, University of Chicago, 1998, esp. 1–85, 139–41; and Prasenjit Duara, *Rescuing History from the Nation: Questioning Narratives of Modern China* (Chicago: University of Chicago Press, 1995), 22–23.

9. John Boli and George M. Thomas, eds., *Constructing World Culture: International Nongovernmental Organizations Since 1875* (Stanford, Calif.: Stanford University Press, 1999), 3–4.

10. *Nihon keiryō kyōkai*, ed., *Keiryō hyakunen shi* (Tokyo: Nihon keiryō kyōkai, 1978), 6.

11. Ibid., 6–7.

12. Ibid., 7–11.

13. Ibid., 10–11.

14. Ibid., 11–18.

15. Ibid., 79.

16. See Pierre Bourdieu, *Practical Reason: On the Theory of Action* (Stanford, Calif.: Stanford University Press, 1998).

17. See Peter Frost, *The Bakumatsu Currency Crisis* (Cambridge, Mass.: East Asian Research Center, Harvard University, 1970).

18. Ibid., 15.

19. Matsukata Masayoshi, *Report on the Adoption of the Gold Standard in Japan* (1899; New York: Arno Press, 1979), 5.

20. Ibid.

21. Nakamura Masanori, Ishii Kanji, and Kasuga Yutaka, eds., *Keizai kōsō* (Tokyo: Iwanami shoten, 1988), Nihon kindai shisō taikei series 8: 6–13.

22. This essay is also known as *Tonarigusa*, translated variously as "Neighboring Grasses" and "Essays on a Neighboring Land." See Winston Davis, *The Moral and Political Naturalism of Baron Katō Hiroyuki* (Berkeley: Institute of East Asian Studies, University of California, Berkeley, 1996); and Bob Tadashi Wakabayashi, "Katō Hiroyuki and Confucian Natural Rights, 1861–1870," *Harvard Journal of Asiatic Studies* 44, 2 (1984): 469–92. I rely here on the annotated text in Emura Eiichi, ed., *Nihon kindai shisō taikei*, vol. 9: *Kenpō kōsō* (Tokyo: Iwanami shoten, 1989), 2–25.

23. Wakabayashi argues that the more substantive meaning of "harmony" (*jinwa*) is "popular unity and integration." See Wakabayashi, "Katō Hiroyuki and Confucian Natural Rights, 1861–1870," 471–72.

24. Emura Eiichi, ed., *Kenpō kōsō*, 24.

25. Marius B. Jansen, *Sakamoto Ryōma and the Meiji Restoration* (Princeton, N.J.: Princeton University Press, 1861), 294–311.

26. Emura Eiichi, ed., *Kenpō kōsō*, pp. 32–33.

27. Emura Eiichi, ed., *Kenpō kōsō*, p. 23.

28. Saigō Takamori zenshū henshū iinkai, ed., *Saigō Takamori zenshū* (Tokyo: Yamato shobō, 1976–80), 1: 31–33. Hereafter, *STZ.*

29. See Mark Ravina, *Land and Lordship in Early Modern Japan* (Stanford, Calif.: Stanford University Press, 1999).

30. *STZ*, 2: 233–36.

31. Ibid., 3: 78–79. A variant copy of Saigō's opinion paper makes the same point in different language. Rather than the odd term *Seido*, Saigō explicitly referred to Asia. Clearly Saigō meant to contrast the "West" and the "world." See Yui Masaomi and Obinata Sumio, eds., *Kanryōsei keisatsu* (Tokyo: Iwanami shoten, 1990), Nihon kindai shisō taikei series, vol. 3, 39–40.

32. Shibusawa Eiichi and Nihon shiseki kyōkai, eds., *Tokugawa Yoshinobu kō den shiryō hen* (1917; Tokyo: Tōkyō daigaku shuppankai, 1975), 3: 183–84. There is an approximate translation in Walter Wallace McLaren, ed., *Japanese Government Documents* (1914; Washington, D.C.: University Publications of America, 1979), 1: 1–2.

33. Yoshida Takashi, *Taikei Nihon no rekishi 3: Kodai kokka no ayumi* (Tokyo: Shōgakkan, 1988), 147–50; Tsepon W. D. Shakabpa, *Tibet: A Political HIstory* (New York: Potala Publications, 1967), 25–30.

34. Christopher I. Beckwith, *The Tibetan Empire in Central Asia: A History of the Struggle for Great Power among Tibetans, Turks, Arabs, and Chinese During the Middle Ages* (Princeton, N.J.: Princeton University Press, 1987), 3–36.

35. Warren W. Smith, *Tibetan Nation: A History of Tibetan Nationalism and Sino-Tibetan Relations* (Boulder, Colo.: Westview Press, 1996), 59–65.

Chapter 4. When Did China Become China? Thoughts on the Twentieth Century

1. Most recently, see Richard S. Horowitz, "Central Power and State Making: The Zongli Yamen and Self-Strengthening in China, 1860–1880," Ph.D. dissertation, Harvard University, 1998.

2. Hosea Ballou Morse, *The International Relations of the Chinese Empire*, 3 vols. (London: Longmans, Green, 1910–18).

3. See Alexander Woodside, *Vietnam and the Chinese Model: A Comparative Study of Nguyen and Ch'ing Civil Government in the First Half of the Nineteenth Century* (Cambridge, Mass.: Harvard University Press, 1971).

4. Rana Mitter, *The Manchurian Myth* (Berkeley: University of California Press, 2000), 14.

5. Cited in John Fitzgerald, *Awakening China: Politics, Culture, and Class in the Nationalist Revolution* (Stanford, Calif.: Stanford University Press, 1996), 117.

6. Ibid., 366n.

7. See John De Francis, *Nationalism and Language Reform in China* (Princeton, N.J.: Princeton University Press, 1950), ch. 4.

8. See Frank Dikötter, *The Discourse of Race in Modern China* (Stanford, Calif.: Stanford University Press, 1992).

9. Cited in Fitzgerald, *Awakening China*, 183.

10. For the People's Republic, the distinction between Chinese *gongmin* and *Huaqiao* was drawn decisively during the ethnic riots in Indonesia in the 1960s, when Beijing insisted that Indoncsian Chinese were all, first and foremost, Indonesian citizens. Meanwhile, Taiwan and Hong Kong mobilized (semi-officially) to aid Indonesians of Chinese descent.

11. See Julia C. Strauss, *Strong Institutions in Weak Polities: State Building in Republican China, 1927–1949* (Oxford: Oxford University Press, 1998), 152–80.

12. See Shi Zhe, *Zai lishi juren shenbian* (Beijing: Zhongyang wenxian chubanshe, 1991), 408.

13. William C. Kirby, "The Nationalist Regime and the Chinese Party-State,

1928–1958," in Merle Goldman and Andrew Gordon, eds., *Historical Perspectives on Contemporary East Asia* (Cambridge, Mass.: Harvard University Press, 2000), 211–37.

14. In this regard it is worth noting the linguistic flexibility on the part of would-be unifiers such as Deng Xiaoping (1904–97) and Chen Jiqian, who apparently were prepared to change the name and flag of the People's Republic of China if needed to promote a "greater Chinese" unity with Taiwan.

15. See Wen-hsin Yeh, ed., *Becoming Chinese: Passages to Modernity and Beyond* (Berkeley: University of California Press, 2000).

Chapter 5. Civilization and Enlightenment: Markers of Identity in Nineteenth-Century Japan

1. I examine this issue at greater length in "Territoriality and Collective Identity in Tokugawa Japan," *Dædalus* 127, 3 (Summer 1998): 105–32.

2. See the examples presented in Kitagawa Morisada, *Morisada mankō*, ed. Asakura Haruhiko and Kashikawa Shūichi, 5 vols. (1853; Tokyo: Tōkyōdō shoten, 1992), 2: 15–28.

3. Bob Tadashi Wakabayashi, *Anti-Foreignism and Western Learning in Early-Modern Japan* (Cambridge, Mass.: Council on East Asian Studies, Harvard University, 1986), 26, 27. Tsukamoto Manabu, *Kinsei saikō: Chihō no shiten kara* (Tokyo: Nihon editaa sukūru shuppanbu, 1986), 76–83, makes essentially the same point.

4. Wakabayashi, *Anti-Foreignism and Western Learning*, 18, 28.

5. Ibid., 28–29.

6. Tsukamoto Manabu, *Kinsei saikō*, 75–105, esp. 83–89.

7. Ibid., 87, citing Terajima Ryōan, *Wakan sansai zue* (1712).

8. Ibid., 83–89.

9. Kikuchi Isao, *Bakuhansei to Ezochi* (Tokyo: Yūzankaku, 1984), 158–60.

10. I examine these issues in more depth in "Ainu Ethnicity and the Boundaries of the Early Modern Japanese State," *Past and Present* 142 (February 1994): 69–93.

11. Hasegawa Noboru, *Bakuto to jiyū minken* (Tokyo: Chūō kōronsha, 1977), 53–84.

12. See Philip A. Kuhn, *Soulstealers: The Chinese Sorcery Scare of 1768* (Cambridge, Mass.: Harvard University Press, 1990); Kikuchi Isao, "Kinsei ni okeru Ezo-kan to 'Nihon fūzoku,'" in Hokkaidō-tōhoku shi kenkyūkai, ed., *Kita kara no Nihon shi*, 2 vols. (Tokyo: Sanseidō, 1988–90), 2: 216–21.

13. Oku Takenori, *Bunmei kaika to minshū: Kindai Nihon seishinshi no danshō* (Tokyo: Shinhyōron, 1993), 5–44, 159–90.

14. Douglas R. Howland, *Translating the West: Language and Political Reason in Nineteenth-Century Japan* (Honolulu: University of Hawai'i Press, 2002), 38–45; quotation on 43.

15. See Narita Ryūichi, "Teito Tōkyō," in *Iwanami kōza Nihon tsūshi* (Tokyo: Iwanami shoten, 1994), 16: 175–214.

16. Two of Fukuzawa's representative works have been translated into English: Fukuzawa Yukichi, *An Encouragement of Learning*, trans. David A. Dilworth and Umeyo Hirano (Tokyo: Sophia University Press, 1969), and Fukuzawa Yukichi, *Outline of a Theory of Civilization*, trans. David A. Dilworth and G. Cameron Hurst (Tokyo: Sophia University Press, 1973). Studies of Fukuzawa's thought in English include Carmen Blacker, *The Japanese Enlightenment: A Study of the Writings*

of Fukuzawa Yukichi (Cambridge: Cambridge University Press, 1964), and Albert M. Craig, "Fukuzawa Yukichi: The Philosophical Foundations of Meiji Nationalism," in Robert E. Ward, ed., *Political Development in Modern Japan* (Princeton, N.J.: Princeton University Press, 1968), 99–148. For selections from the journal of the Meiji Six Society, see William R. Braisted, trans., *Meiroku Zasshi: Journal of the Japanese Enlightenment* (Cambridge, Mass.: Harvard University Press, 1976). Douglas Howland, *Translating the West*, 15–18, briefly surveys the literature on the intellectual movement for civilization and enlightenment.

17. On Western thought and its popularity among rural elites, see Irokawa Daikichi, *The Culture of the Meiji Period*, trans. ed. Marius B. Jansen (Princeton, N.J.: Princeton University Press, 1985), and Roger Bowen, *Rebellion and Democracy in Meiji Japan* (Berkeley: University of California Press, 1980). See also the epic historical novel by Shimazaki Tōson, *Before the Dawn*, trans. William E. Naff (Honolulu: University of Hawaii Press, 1987).

18. Douglas Howland's *Translating the West* is the most recent and most intellectually sophisticated contribution to this literature.

19. Throughout his autobiography, Fukuzawa emphasizes how innovative his ideas and outlook were. See Fukuzawa Yukichi, *The Autobiography of Fukuzawa Yukichi*, trans. Eiichi Kiyooka (Tokyo: Hokuseido, 1948).

20. For an explicit statement of this sentiment, see Katō Sukekazu, "Bunmei kaika" (1873–74), in Yoshino Sakuzō, ed., *Meiji bunka zenshū: Bunmei kaika hen* (Tokyo: Nihon hyōronsha, 1929), 5.

21. Yoshino Sakuzō, ed., *Meiji bunka zenshū: Bunmei kaika hen*, 171.

22. For an explicit statement of this sentiment, see Hagiwara Otohiko, "Tōkyō kaika hanjōshi" (1874), in Meiji bunka kenkyūkai, ed., *Meiji bunka zenshū: Fūzoku hen* (1928; Tokyo: Nihon hyōron shinsha, 1955), 236.

23. Katō Kōzō, "Hinin eta gohaishi no gi" (1869/4), in Harada Tomohiko and Uesugi Satoru, eds., *"Kaihōrei" no seiritsu* (Tokyo: San'ichi shobō, 1984), Kindai burakushi shiryō shūsei series, vol. 1, 12.

24. Oku Takenori, *Bunmei kaika to minshū*, 164.

25. The ordinances and explanatory notes can be found in Ogi Shinzō, Kumakura Isao, and Ueno Chizuko, eds., *Fūzoku, sei* (Tokyo: Iwanami shoten, 1990), Nihon kindai shisō taikei series, vol. 23, 3–29; see also the illustrations relating to customs culled from pictorial guides to the ordinances on 30–39.

26. *Fūzoku, sei*, 20.

27. "Joshi no danpatsu sanbi," *Chiba shinbun shūroku* (1871/11); "Joshi no danpatsu wa miru ni shinobizu," *Shinbun zasshi* (March 1872); "Fujoshi no kami wa jūrai dōri," *Shinbun zasshi* (April 1872). All are reprinted in Meiji nyūsu jiten hensan iinkai, ed., *Meiji nyūsu jiten* (Tokyo: Mainichi komyunikeishonsu shuppanbu, 1983), 1: 273.

28. Sharon L. Sievers, *Flowers in Salt: The Beginnings of Feminist Consciousness in Modern Japan* (Stanford, Calif.: Stanford University Press, 1983), 14–15.

29. Oku Takenori, *Bunmei kaika to minshū*, pp. 16–17.

30. Ibid., pp. 18–20.

31. Murano Tokusaburō, "Yōshiki fujin sokuhatsuhō" (1885), in Meiji bunka kenkyūkai, ed., *Meiji bunka zenshū: Fūzoku hen*, 425–34. See also Watanabe Kanae, "Sokuhatsu annai" (1887), excerpted in *Fūzoku, sei*, 306–19; Watanabe was central to the founding of the association.

32. "Chiba machi narabi ni Samugawa Nobuto ryōson e futatsu" (1874/8/12), in Chiba-ken shi hensan shingikai, ed., *Chiba-ken shiryō: Kindai hen: Meiji shoki 3* (Chiba: Chiba ken, 1970), 249–50.

33. Oku Takenori, *Bunmei kaika to minshū*, 12–13.

34. Ibid., 11 (1876 statistics); *Fūzoku, sei*, 27 (1877 and 1878).

35. Edward S. Morse, *Japan Day by Day*, 2 vols. (Tokyo: Kobunsha, 1936), 1: 89, 97–100.

36. Oka Sankei, "Kinseki kurabe" (1874), in Meiji bunka kenkyūkai, ed., *Meiji bunka zenshū: Fūzoku hen*, 157.

37. In Tsukamoto Manabu's phrase, *inaka wa 'i'-naka* (the countryside [*inaka*] is in the midst [*naka*] of barbarism [*i*]): *Kinsei saikō*, 90–97.

38. See Narita Ryūichi, "Teito Tōkyō."

39. The first poorhouse in post-Restoration Tokyo, established in Takanawa in 1869, was designed to accommodate unregistered transients, *nohinin* (unregistered beggars), and *gōmune* (a group of street performers)—all commoners who nonetheless came under the authority of the outcaste *hinin* headmen Kuruma Zenshichi and Matsuemon. Facilities set up in 1872 and after—by which time the outcast authority structure had been abolished—took in vagrants of all sorts. See "Takanawa kyūikusho kyūmindomo tōbun toriatsukai an" (1869/9/27), in Hirota Masaki, ed., *Sabetsu no shosō* (Tokyo: Iwanami shoten, 1990), Nihon kindai shisō taikei series, vol. 22, 289–91, and the discussion in Hirota Masaki, "Nihon kindai shakai no sabetsu kōzō," in *Sabetsu no shosō*, 485.

40. These comments are cited in Matsushita Shirō, *Kinsei Amami no shihai to shakai* (Tokyo: Daiichi shobō, 1983), 6 (Sasamori) and 9–12 (Saigō).

41. See David L. Howell, "The Meiji State and the Logic of Ainu 'Protection,'" in Helen Hardacre, ed., *New Directions in the Study of Meiji Japan* (Leiden: E.J. Brill, 1997), 612–34.

42. Stephen Vlastos, "Opposition Movements in Early Meiji," in Marius B. Jansen, ed., *The Cambridge History of Japan*, vol. 5, *The Nineteenth Century* (New York: Cambridge University Press, 1989), 391–93.

43. Katō Yūichi, *Bunmei kaika*, as cited in Hirota Masaki, "Nihon kindai shakai no sabetsu kōzō," 490–1; Oka Sankei, "Kinseki kurabe," 167.

44. See Imanishi Hajime, *Kindai Nihon no sabetsu to sei bunka* (Tokyo: Yūzankaku, 1998), 185.

45. "Kaika dondonbushi" (1871), in *Yomeru nenpyō: Nihonshi*, rev. ed. (Tokyo: Jiyū kokuminsha, 1995), 827.

46. Oku Takenori, *Bunmei kaika to minshū*, 16–17.

47. "Tōkyō no jūmin daibubun wa danpatsu," *Nagoya shinbun* (March 1873), and "Chikuhatsusha ni wa zekin no ken mo," *Shinbun zasshi* (August 1873), both in *Meiji nyūsu jiten*, 273–74.

48. Edward Morse, *Japan Day by Day*, 2: 36.

49. Oka Sankei, "Kinseki kurabe," 167–68.

50. "Sesshū Watanabe mura etadomo shorui" (1867/5), in Masaki, ed., *Sabetsu no shosō*, 71–72.

51. *Shinbun zasshi* (January 1872), in *Meiji nyūsu jiten*, 540.

52. The following discussion is based on Oku Takenori, *Bunmei kaika to minshū*, 86–99, and Hirota Masaki, "Nihon kindai shakai no sabetsu kōzō," 494–99. For an examination of the nation-building project that focuses on a variety of modern media, see Li Takanori, *Hyōshō kūkan no kindai: Meiji "Nihon" no media hensei* (Tokyo: Shin'yōsha, 1996).

53. *Tōkyō akebono shinbun* (August 23, 1879), as cited in Hirota Masaki, "Nihon kindai shakai no sabetsu kōzō," 495.

54. Oku Takenori, *Bunmei kaika to minshū*, 109.

55. Kyōto buraku shi kenkyūjo, ed., *Kyōto no burakushi*, 10 vols. (Kyoto: Kyōto buraku shi kenkyūjo, 1984–95), 6: 48–50.

56. On the centrality of moral suasion (*kyōka*) to the project of creating modernity in Japan, see Sheldon Garon, *Molding Japanese Minds: The State in Everyday Life* (Princeton, N.J.: Princeton University Press, 1997).

57. For a sampling of the large early Meiji literature on the poor's responsibility for their own unfortunate situation, see Hirota Masaki, "Nihon kindai shakai no sabetsu kōzō," 481–89, and Yamamuro Shin'ichi, "Meiji kokka no seido to rinen," in *Iwanami kōza Nihon tsūshi* (Tokyo: Iwanami shoten, 1994), 17: 126–27.

Chapter 6. Nationality and Difference in China: The Post-Imperial Dilemma

1. Joseph R. Levenson, *Confucian China and Its Modern Fate*, 3 vols. (Berkeley: University of California Press, 1965).

2. Pamela Kyle Crossley, *A Translucent Mirror: History and Identity in Qing Imperial Ideology* (Berkeley: University of California Press, 1999).

3. Mary Clabaugh Wright, *The Last Stand of Chinese Conservatism: The T'ung-chih Restoration, 1862–1874* (Stanford, Calif.: Stanford University Press, 1962).

4. Liang Ch'i-ch'ao (Liang Qichao), *History of Chinese Political Thought During the Early Tsin Period*, trans. L. T. Chen (New York: Harcourt, Brace, 1930), 157, with romanizations changed to pinyin.

5. The text of the 1931 resolution on minority nationalities at Ruijin is reprinted in Zhang Zhiyi, *The Party and the National Question*, trans. George Moseley (Cambridge, Mass.: MIT Press, 1966), 163–67, from Bela Kun, ed., *Fundamental Laws of the Chinese Soviet Republic* (New York: International Publishers, 1934). A historical perspective on this period with respect to the policy of autonomous regions is also rendered in Li Honglie, "Lüetan minzu quyu zizhi de lizhi, zhengce he shixian," *Minzu yanjiu* 2 (1983): 1–7. Li Weihan, who was the head of the United Front Work Department from the Yan'an period until 1965, when he was dismissed on grounds of "capitulationism," returned to the public scene with the publication of *Xizang minzu jiefang de daolu* in 1981. The January 1981 issue of *Minzu yanjiu* applauded his accumulated theoretical insights into the social and economic advancement of minority nationalities. The period of Li's early work with the CCP coincided with the work of Fei Xiaotong among the Yao, and both men's early contributions are framed by the Party's dependence upon the local people of the border regions where the revolution was first consolidated.

6. The criteria for identifying minority nationalities were later given various academic expressions, among them a series of articles, the lead authored by Fan Wenlan, in *Han minzu xingcheng wenti taolun ji* (Beijing: Sanlian shudian, 1957). Fan and G. Efimov also collaborated with Yang Zeyi in an essay that laid out the major formula as follows: common language, common territory, common economic life, common "psychological elements" (*gongtong xinli suzhi*) as manifested in a common culture. See "Guanyu Han minzu xingcheng wenti de yixie yijian," in *Han minzu xingcheng wenti*, 85.

7. Thomas Heberer, *China and Its National Minorities: Autonomy or Assimilation* (Armonk, N.Y.: M.E. Sharpe, 1989), 24–25.

Chapter 7. Cultivating Non-National Historical Understandings in Local History

1. For reasons I will explain below, I think that the dynamics of regional history as produced in versus outside Japan need to be studied and considered. In this paper I treat only Western-produced scholarship.

2. Philip Brown, *Central Authority and Local Autonomy in the Formation of Early Modern Japan* (Stanford, Calif.: Stanford University Press, 1993); David Howell, *Capitalism from Within: Economy, Society, and the State in a Japanese Fishery* (Berkeley: University of California Press, 1995); Karen Wigen, *The Making of a Japanese Periphery, 1750–1920* (Berkeley: University of California Press, 1995); James Baxter, *The Meiji Unification Through the Lens of Ishikawa Prefecture* (Cambridge, Mass.: Harvard University Press, 1994); Arne Kalland, *Fishing Villages in Tokugawa Japan* (Honolulu: University of Hawai'i Press, 1995); Edward Pratt, *Japan's Protoindustrial Elite: The Economic Foundations of the Gōnō* (Cambridge, Mass.: Harvard University Press, 1999); Mark Ravina, *Land and Lordship in Early Modern Japan* (Stanford, Calif.: Stanford University Press, 1999); Luke S. Roberts, *Mercantilism in a Japanese Domain: The Merchant Origins of Economic Nationalism in 18th-Century Tosa* (Cambridge: Cambridge University Press, 1998).

3. Marius Jansen, *Sakamoto Ryōma and the Meiji Restoration* (Princeton, N.J.: Princeton University Press, 1961); Albert Craig, *Chōshū in the Meiji Restoration* (Cambridge, Mass.: Harvard University Press, 1961).

4. John Hall, *Government and Local Power in Japan 500 to 1700: A Study Based on Bizen Province* (Princeton, N.J.: Princeton University Press, 1966), vii.

5. Philip Brown, "Local History's Challenges to National Narratives," *Early Modern Japan: An Interdisciplinary Journal* 7, 2 (November 2000): 38–48. This issue has a number of very interesting articles, by Jonathan Dresner, Edward Pratt, John Van Sant, Brian Platt, and Sarah Thal, dealing with the role of local history within the nation, but with regard to the current essay the observation I would make is the same as that for Brown's summary article so I will not deal with them here.

6. Benedict Anderson, *Imagined Communities: Reflections on the Origin and Spread of Nationalism*, rev. ed. (London: Verso, 1991), 194–97; Prasenjit Duara, *Rescuing History from the Nation: Questioning Narratives of Modern China* (Chicago: University of Chicago Press, 1995). See also sources cited in Applegate below. For Japan, see Margaret Mehl, *History and the State in Nineteenth-Century Japan* (New York: St. Martin's Press, 1998).

7. Celia Applegate, "A Europe of Regions: Reflections on the Historiography of Sub-National Places in Modern Times," *American Historical Review* 104, 4 (October 1999): 1160.

8. Michael O'Brien, "On Observing the Quicksand," *American Historical Review* 104, 4 (October 1999): 1202, 1203.

9. Ibid., 1206–7.

10. The best interpretation of this in English can be found in Ravina, *Land and Lordship in Early Modern Japan*. See also Mizubayashi Takeshi, *Hōkensei no saihen to Nihonteki shakai no kakuritsu, kinsei* (Tokyo: Yamakawa Shuppan, 1987), esp. 177–89, 272–316.

11. Conrad Totman, "Ethnicity in the Meiji Restoration," *Monumenta Nipponica* 37, 3 (Autumn 1982): 269–87, introduces the notion of bi-level ethnicity in order to come to terms with the multiple identities nationally conceived.

12. Originally entitled "Ojikki," it was begun in 1801 and completed in 1843. Now available in the series Shinchō zohō kokushi taikei: *Tokugawa jikki*, vols. 38–47 (Tokyo: Yoshikawa kōbunkan, 1964–66).

13. Ruth West and Willis Mason West, *The Story of Our Country* (Boston: Allyn and Bacon, 1935); Henry Davenport, *Our Great Country* (Philadelphia: Cooperative Publishing Co. 1902).

14. Harold Bolitho, *Treasures Among Men: The Fudai Daimyo in Tokugawa Japan* (New Haven, Conn.: Yale University Press, 1974), 170, 191.

15. Note the discussion in Herman Ooms, *Tokugawa Ideology: Early Constructs* (Princeton, N.J.: Princeton University Press, 1985), 4–6, 287–88.

16. Takayanagi Mitsutoshi et al., eds., *Kansei chōshū shokafu*, 26 vols. (Tokyo: Zoku gunsho ruiju kansei kai, 1964–67).

17. The manuscript copy is I used is held in the Gest Library of Princeton University. This work is also known as *Otoke nenpyō* and *Okuni nendai ki*. It can be found printed in *Tosa no kuni gunshō ruiju* (Kōchi: Kōchi kenritsu toshokan, 1999), 2: 313–94.

18. This was common practice in the day. See George Elison (Jurgis Elisonas), "Hideyoshi: the Bountiful Minister," in George Elison and Bardwell Smith, eds., *Warlords, Artists, and Commoners: Japan in the Sixteenth Century* (Honolulu: University of Hawai'i Press, 1981), 236–38.

19. Currently unavailable in print. Copy held in Kōchi University Library, Kōchi, Japan.

20. The best of these is the *Nanroshi* compiled by the merchant Mutō Yoshikazu. It begins with histories of counties and villages and later moves to the histories of the various dynasties which ruled Tosa. See Akizawa Shigeru, Yorimitsu Kanji, et al., eds., *Nanroshi*, 10 vols. (Kōchi: Kōchi kenritsu toshokan, 1990–99).

21. Sekita Komakichi, "*Hanshi naihen* ni tsuite," *Tosa shidan* 46 (March 1934): 64–69.

22. Luke Roberts, "Tosa to ishin—'kokka' no sōshitsu to 'chihō' no tanjō," *Nenpō kindai Nihon kenkyū* 20 (Tokyo: Yamakawa shuppan, 1997).

23. Watanabe Hiroshi, *Higashi Ajia no ōken to shisō* (Tokyo: Tokyo University Press, 1997). The most relevant portion is in his preface which I have translated in "About Some Japanese Historical Terms," *Sino Japanese Studies* 10, 2 (April 1998): 32–42.

24. Fujita Satoru, *Bakumatsu no tennō* (Tokyo: Kōdansha, 1994). The word *tennō* itself was used in the Edo period but it only applied to emperors who died before Juntoku (d. 1241). I do not know the direct origin of the abandoment of the *tennō* title, but it likely had to do with the Shōkyū Rebellion of 1221 in which Juntoku was forced to abdicate and which established Kamakura warrior authority over Kyoto.

25. The modern word in Japanese for government, *seifu*, was relatively uncommon in the Edo period but when used was used both within domainal discursive spaces and in Tokugawa discursive space.

26. Not all terms. *Tenka* for example was never applied to a domain as far as I have seen. However terms which later play a role in Japanese nationalism all apply to the domainal country rather than to Japan. Japan was politically unified most strongly by the Tokugawa, but not unified mainly along national state lines (Such notions of Japan existed but played weakly in politics.) Rather, it was primarily unified by household allegiances and duties.

27. Mark Ravina's study of Tokushima relations with the Tokugawa is an excellent example of the possibilities opened up by a less nationalized approach to understanding. *Land and Lordship*, 154–93.

28. This word comes in the modern period to be used to translate "feudal." The translation has a certain usefulness, but *hōken* came with its own ideological

baggage. See Ozawa Eichi, "Bakuhanseika ni okeru hōken/gunken ron josetsu," *Tōkyō gakugei daigaku kiyō, dai san bumon, shakaigaku* 24 (1972): 111–29.

Chapter 8. Where Do Incorrect Political Ideas Come From? Writing the History of the Qing Empire and the Chinese Nation

1. Diana Lary, "The Tomb of the King of Nanyue—The Contemporary Agenda of History: Scholarship and Identity," *Modern China* 22, 1 (January 1996): 3–27; Tim Oakes, "Land of Living Fossils: Reproducing Ancient and Modern China in Guizhou Localities," paper presented at workshop, "Locating China: Space, Place, and Popular Culture," Zhejiang University, Hangzhou, 2001; Ralph Litzinger, "The Greening of Postsocialism: NGOs and Global Environmentalism in Yunnan," paper presented at workshop, "Locating China: Space, Place, and Popular Culture," Zhejiang University, Hangzhou, 2001.

2. Gary G. Hamilton, Chang Wei-an, and Lai Chi-kong, "The Influence of Commercial Organization on Commodity Production of Cotton Textiles in 19th and 20th Century China," in Giovanni Arrighi and Mark Selden, eds., *The Rise of East Asia: 500, 150, and 50 year Perspectives* (Berkeley: University of California Press, forthcoming); Mayfair Meihui Yang, *Gifts, Favors, and Banquets: The Art of Social Relations in China* (Ithaca, N.Y.: Cornell University Press, 1994); and see Morton H. Fried, *The Fabric of Chinese Society* (New York: Praeger, 1953).

3. Stuart R. Schram, *The Political Thought of Mao Tse-tung* (New York: Praeger, 1969): 261.

4. Edward Friedman, Paul G. Pickowicz, and Mark Selden, *Chinese Village, Socialist State* (New Haven, Conn.: Yale University Press, 1991), 224.

5. Audrey Donnithorne, "China's Cellular Economy: Some Economic Trends since the Cultural Revolution," *China Quarterly* 52 (1972): 605–19.

6. Prasenjit Duara, "Knowledge and Power in the Discourse of Modernity: The Campaigns Against Popular Religion in Early Twentieth-Century China," *Journal of Asian Studies* 50, 1 (1991): 67–83.

7. On the concept of "everyday life," see, for example, Henri Lefebvre, *Everyday Life in the Modern World* (New York: Harper Torchbooks, 1971); and Thomas C. Holt, "Marking: Race, Race-Making, and the Writing of History," *American Historical Review* 100, 1 (1995): 1–20.

8. James C. Scott, *Seeing like a State: How Certain Schemes to Improve the Human Condition Have Failed* (New Haven, Conn.: Yale University Press, 1998).

9. Philip A. Kuhn, *Les origines de l'état chinois moderne*, intro. Pierre-Etienne Will (Paris: A. Colin, 1999), 30; English translation: *Origins of the Modern Chinese State* (Stanford, Calif.: Stanford University Press, 2002). See also Lucian Pye, *The Mandarin and the Cadre: China's Political Cultures* (Ann Arbor, Mich.: Center for Chinese Studies, 1988).

10. Kuhn, *Les origines*, 153.

11. Timothy Brook, *The Confusions of Pleasure: Commerce and Culture in Ming China* (Berkeley: University of California Press, 1998).

12. Kuhn, *Les origines*, 123–54.

13. Peter C. Perdue, *China Marches West: The Qing Conquest of Central Eurasia* (Cambridge, Mass.: Harvard University Press, forthcoming).

14. See David Anthony Bello, *Opium and the Limits of Empire: The Opium Problem in the Chinese Interior, 1729–1850* (Cambridge, Mass.: Asia Center, Harvard University, forthcoming).

15. Peter C. Perdue, "Identifying China's Northwest: For Nation and Empire,"

paper presented at the workshop, "Locating China: Space, Place, and Popular Culture," Zhejiang University, Hangzhou, 2001.

16. Prasenjit Duara, "Historicizing National Identity, or Who Imagines What and When," in Eley and Suny, eds., *Becoming National*, 151–78.

17. Liah Greenfeld, *Nationalism: Five Roads to Modernity* (Cambridge, Mass.: Harvard University Press, 1992); Eric J. Hobsbawm, *Nations and Nationalism Since 1780* (Cambridge: Cambridge University Press, 1990); Benedict Anderson, *Imagined Communities: Reflections on the Origins and Spread of Nationalism*, rev. ed. (London: Verso, 1991).

18. Ernest Gellner, *Nations and Nationalism* (Ithaca, N.Y.: Cornell University Press, 1983).

19. For this critique of Gellner, see R. Bin Wong, "Two Kinds of Nation, What Kind of State?" in Timothy Brook and Andre Schmid, eds., *Nation Work: Asian Elites and National Identities* (Ann Arbor: University of Michigan Press, 2000), 117.

20. Ernst Renan, "What Is a Nation," in Eley and Suny, eds., *Becoming National*, 45.

21. Hue-tam Ho Tai, "Remembered Realms: Pierre Nora and French National Memory," *American Historical Review* 106, 3 (2001): 918.

22. Benjamin I. Schwartz, "Themes in Intellectual History: May Fourth and After," in John K. Fairbank, ed., *Cambridge History of China*, vol. 12, *Republican China 1912–1949, Part 1* (Cambridge: Cambridge University Press, 1983), 416.

23. Eric Hobsbawm, and Terence Ranger, *The Invention of Tradition* (Cambridge: Cambridge University Press, 1983).

24. Tom Nairn, "Scotland and Europe," in Eley and Suny, eds., *Becoming National*, 91.

25. Olivier Roy, *The New Central Asia: The Creation of Nations* (New York: NYU Press, 2000), xiv.

26. Pierre Bourdieu, *In Other Words: Essays Towards a Reflexive Sociology* (Stanford, Calif.: Stanford University Press, 1990), 190; Pierre Bourdieu, *Esquisse d'une théorie de la pratique* (Paris: Éditions du Seuil, 2000).

27. Hobsbawm, *Nations and Nationalism Since 1780*, 66.

28. David A. Bell, "Recent Works on Early Modern French National Identity," *Journal of Modern History* 68, 1 (1996): 84–113.

29. Peter C. Perdue, "The Qing Empire in Eurasian Time and Space: Lessons from the Galdan Campaigns," in Lynn A. Struve, ed., *The Qing Formation in World-Historical Time* (Cambridge, Mass.: Harvard University Asia Center, 2004).

30. Peter C. Perdue, "Boundaries, Maps, and Movement: The Chinese, Russian, and Mongolian Empires in Early Modern Eurasia," *International History Review* 20, 2 (June 1998): 263–86.

31. James A. Millward, "Coming onto the Map: The Qing Conquest of Xinjiang," *Late Imperial China* 20, 2 (1999): 61–98.

32. Laura Hostetler, "Qing Connections to the Early Modern World: Ethnography and Cartography in Eighteenth-Century China," *Modern Asian Studies* 34 (2000): 623–62; Laura Hostetler, *Qing Colonial Enterprise: Ethnography and Cartography in Early Modern China* (Chicago: University of Chicago Press, 2001); Emma Jinhua Teng, "Travel Writing and Colonial Collecting: Chinese Travel Accounts of Taiwan," Ph.D. dissertation, Harvard University, 1997.

33. Benedict Anderson, *Imagined Communities*, 163–85.

34. Peter C. Perdue, "A Frontier View of Chineseness," in Arrighi and Selden, eds., *The Rise of East Asia*.

35. Lucian Pye, "How China's Nationalism Was Shanghaied," *Australian Journal of Chinese Affairs* 1 (1993), pp. 107–34.

36. Zhang Binglin, "Letter Opposing Kang Youwei's Views on Revolution," in Wm. Theodore de Bary, ed., *Sources of the Chinese Tradition* (New York: Columbia University Press, 2000), 312–13.

37. Zhang Binglin, "Shehui Tongquan shangdui," *Minbao* 12 (1907): 18; Michael Gasster, *Chinese Intellectuals and the Revolution of 1911* (Seattle: University of Washington Press, 1969), 206; Onogawa Hidemi, "Shō Heirin no hai-Man shisō," in Onogawa Hidemi, *Shinmatsu seiji shisō kenkyū* (Tokyo: Misuzu shobō, 1969).

38. Onogawa Hidemi, "Shō Heirin no hai-Man shisō," 287.

39. Edward J. Rhoads, *Manchus and Han: Ethnic Relations and Political Power in Late Qing and Early Republican China, 1861–1928* (Seattle: University of Washington Press, 2000), 3.

40. Shimada Kenji, *Pioneer of the Chinese Revolution: Zhang Binglin and Confucianism*, trans. Joshua A. Fogel (Stanford, Calif.: Stanford University Press, 1990), 105.

41. John Fitzgerald, *Awakening China: Politics, Culture, and Class in the Nationalist Revolution* (Stanford, Calif.: Stanford University Press, 1996), 122; see also Pamela Kyle Crossley, *A Translucent Mirror: History and Identity in Qing Imperial Ideology* (Berkeley: University of California Press, 1999), 345, 351.

42. Zhang Binglin, "Shehui Tongquan shangdui," *Minbao* 12 (1907): 17.

43. "The range of monographs situating nationalism in a strong and sophisticated context of social history as we have come to know it since the 1970s is still surprisingly small, and all the smaller in European history than in the analysis of non-Western societies, where the approach has been far more innovative." See Eley and Suny, eds., *Becoming National*, 18.

44. Tom Nairn, "Scotland and Europe," in Eley and Suny, eds., *Becoming National*, 82.

45. The following section is taken from my manuscript on the Qing conquest of Central Eurasia. See Perdue, *China Marches West.*

46. The best modern study of Nerchinsk is Yoshida Kin'ichi, *Roshia no Tōhō shinshutsu to Neruchinsuku jōyaku* (Tokyo: Kindai Chūgoku kenkyū sentaa, 1984). Note that the standard account in English by Mark Mancall was written before the publication of many important Russian archival documents, including Golovin's official report. Mark Mancall, *Russia and China: Their Diplomatic Relations to 1728* (Cambridge, Mass.: Harvard University Press, 1971), 153–62. See also Gaston Cahen, *Histoire des relations de la Russie avec la Chine sous Pierre le Grand (1689–1730)* (Paris: F. Alcan, 1912); trans. and ed. W. Sheldon Ridge, *Some Early Russo-Chinese Relations* (Shanghai: National Review Office 1914; Bangor, Me.: University Prints and Reprints, n.d.), E12–14, F43–47; Arthur W. Hummel, ed., *Eminent Chinese of the Ch'ing Period* (Washington, D.C.: U.S. Government Printing Office, 1943), 442–43, 630, 663–66, 794; Yanagisawa Akira, "Garudan no Haruha shinkō [1688] kō no Haruha shokō to Roshia," in *Shinchō to Higashi Ajia: Kanda Nobuo sensei koki kinen ronshū*, ed. Kanda Nobuo sensei koki kinen ronshū hensan iinkai (Tokyo: Yamakawa shuppansha, 1992), 179–96.

47. Peter C. Perdue, "Boundaries, Maps, and Movement," *International History Review* 20, 2 (June 1998): 263–86.

48. N. F. Demidova and V. S. Miasnikov, eds., *Russko-kitaiskie otnosheniia v XVII veke: Materialy i dokumenty* (Moscow: Nauka, 1969–72), 2: 514.

49. Demidova and Miasnikov, eds., *Russko-kitaiskie otnosheniia*, 2: 516.

50. Mancall believes the Jesuit pretext that "the Mongolian translators on each side were so poor that the negotiations reverted to Latin immediately," but Cahen demonstrates by referring to Golovin's report that the Russians were ca-

pable of communicating with the Manchus, but prevented from doing so by Jesuit interference. Mark Mancall, *Russia and China*, 156; Gaston Cahen, *Histoire des relations de la Russie avec la Chine*, 47; Demidova and Miasnikov, eds., *Russko-kitaiskie otnosheniia*, 2: 514, 516, 521, 523, 528, 544.

51. James Mann, *About Face: The History of America's Relationship with China* (New York: Vintage, 1998).

52. Demidova and Miasnikov, eds., *Russko-kitaiskie otnosheniia*, 2: 5–54; Yoshida Kin'ichi, *Roshia no Tōhō shinshutsu*, 345ff.

53. Dai Yi, *Jianming Qing shi* (Beijing: Renmin chubanshe, 1984), vol. 2.; "The Asian Language: Nerchinsk," *Asiaweek* (October 31, 1997).

54. *Great Soviet Encyclopedia* (New York: Macmillan, 1978), 17: 463.

55. Demidova and Miasnikov, eds., *Russko-kitaiskie otnosheniia*, 2: 53–54.

56. Richard White, *The Middle Ground: Indians, Empires, and Republics in the Great Lakes Region, 1650–1815* (Cambridge: Cambridge University Press, 1991).

57. Derek Croxton, "The Peace of Westphalia of 1648 and the Origins of Sovereignty," *International History Review* 21, 3 (1999): 569–91.

58. Michel Foucher, *L'invention des frontières* (Paris: Fondation pour les études de défense nationale, 1986).

59. Mary C. Wright, "Introduction: The Rising Tide of Change," in Mary C. Wright, ed., *China in Revolution* (New Haven, Conn.: Yale University Press, 1968); William Kirby, "The Internationalization of China: Foreign Relations at Home and Abroad," *China Quarterly* 150 (1997): 433–58.

60. Imahori Seiji, *Malaya no Kakyō shakai* (Tokyo: Ajia keizai kenkyūjo, 1972); Imahori Seiji, *Chūgoku hōken shakai no kōzō: sono rekishi to kakumei zenya no genjitsu* (Tokyo: Nihon gakujutsu shinkōkai, 1978); M. Sanjdorj, *Manchu Chinese Colonial Rule in Northern Mongolia*, trans. Urgunge Onon (New York: St. Martin's Press, 1980).

61. Bryna Goodman, "The Locality as Microcosm of the Nation? Native Place Networks and Early Urban Nationalism in China," *Modern China* 21, 4 (1995): 387–419; Bryna Goodman, *Native Place, City, and Nation: Regional Networks and Identities in Shanghai, 1853–1937* (Berkeley: University of California Press, 1995).

62. Bryna Goodman, "The Locality as Microcosm of the Nation?" *Modern China* 21, 4 (1995): 392.

63. Ibid., 391, 393.

Contributors

Pamela Kyle Crossley (Ph.D., Yale) is Professor of History at Dartmouth College. She has written *Orphan Warriors: Three Manchu Generations and the End of the Qing World*, *The Manchus*, and *A Translucent Mirror: History and Identity in Qing Ideology*. Her ongoing research concerns comparative ruling ideologies in early modern Eurasia, the history of coercive social institutions in China, and the comparative history of horsemanship in Eurasia, 500–1500 C.E.

Joshua A. Fogel (Ph.D., Columbia) is Professor of History and East Asian Languages and Cultural Studies at the University of California, Santa Barbara. In recent years he has written *The Literature of Travel in the Japanese Rediscovery of China (1862–1945)*, edited and contributed to *Sagacious Monks and Bloodthirsty Warriors: Chinese Views of Japan in the Ming–Qing Period*, and translated Yosano Akiko's *Travels in Manchuria and Mongolia*. He is currently exploring the first Japanese missions to China in the modern era, in the 1860s, and the emergence of a Japanese expatriate community in Shanghai from that time until the end of the nineteenth century.

David L. Howell (Ph.D., Princeton) is Professor of Japanese History at Princeton University. He is the author of *Capitalism from Within: Economy, Society, and the State in a Japanese Fishery* and *Geographies of Identity in Nineteenth-Century Japan*. He is presently working on a study of violence, social disorder, and intellectual ferment in the hinterland of Edo (later, Tokyo) in the nineteenth century.

Eiko Ikegami (Ph.D., Harvard) is Professor of Sociology at New School University. The author of *The Taming of the Samurai: Honorific Individualism and the Making of Modern Japan*, she is currently working on a book tentatively entitled *Bonds of Civility: Aesthetic Networks and the Political Origins of Japanese Culture*, closely related to her essay in this volume.

William C. Kirby (Ph.D., Harvard) is Geisinger Professor of History and Dean of the Faculty of Arts and Sciences at Harvard University. His work examines China's economic and political development in an international context. His most recent publications include two edited volumes: *State and Economy in Republican China: A Handbook for Scholars* and *Realms of Freedom in Modern China.*

Victor Mair (Ph.D., Harvard) is Professor of Asian and Middle Eastern Studies at the University of Pennsylvania. He is the author of *Tun-huang Popular Narratives, Painting and Performance,* and numerous other works on Buddhist popular literature. He is also interested in the cultural exchange between the peoples of East Asia and their neighbors to the west, and has lately been involved in various lexicographical projects.

Peter C. Perdue (Ph.D., Harvard) is T. T. and Wei Fong Chao Professor of Asian Civilizations and Professor of History at Massachusetts Institute of Technology. He has written *Exhausting the Earth: State and Peasant in Hunan, 1500–1850 A.D.* His current interests focus on environmental change, ethnicity, and the relationship between long-term economic change and military conquest in the Chinese and Russian empires. His forthcoming book, *China Marches West: The Qing Conquest of Central Eurasia, 1600–1800,* combines these perspectives into an integrated account of the Chinese and Russia conquest of Siberia and Central Eurasia in the seventeenth and eighteenth centuries.

Mark Ravina (Ph.D., Stanford) is Associate Professor of History and Director of the East Asian Studies Program at Emory University. His first book, *Land and Lordship in Early Modern Japan,* appeared in Japanese translation in 2004. He recently published *The Last Samurai: The Life and Battle of Saigō Takamori,* a biography of Saigō. His current research focuses on the Meiji Restoration and on globalization as a historical process.

Luke S. Roberts (Ph.D., Princeton) is Associate Professor of History at the University of California at Santa Barbara. He has published *Mercantilism in a Japanese Domain* and coauthored with Sharon Takeda *Japanese Fishermen's Coats from Awaji Island.* He is currently writing the biography of a samurai from Tosa domain and researching political language use in Japan of the Tokugawa era.

Index